WITH SPRING COMES HOPE

A Collection of Words on Motherhood and Beyond by Jade Anna Hughes

ISBN: 1544764545

ISBN-13: 978-1544764542

www.jadeannahughes.com

Contents

Introduction

I've always been a writer; from as far back as I can remember. It's never been easy for me to state my opinion with my spoken voice, but writing out my thoughts and feelings has always been my way of processing life. I have piles and piles of journals and folders full of papers going back into my early years, round letters turning into spidery, barely legible script, and I will continue to write, both on paper and on my laptop, until my dying day. Writing IS life to me, my life would never be complete without it. From primary school crushes, through childhood loss, teenage angst and the deepest depth of depression, into happiness and travel and everything in between, my life is a string of memories jotted down on paper and hard drives. I promised myself that one day I would conjure up the courage to get it all out there into the world, and share my words with others.

It started with a blog, From the Inside, which has existed in some shape or form since 2003, on the eve of my departure to the Middle East. Over the years I have posted short stories, tales from my childhood, rants on the world, anxious moments, and ultimately more and more of my life as it unrolled. Every post gave me the confidence to dig deeper, to let the fear go, until recently I realized that it was time to actually do that book thing that I have dreamed of since I was a child. From the Inside has never been a niche blog, and it never will be, I will always post whatever comes to mind at any given moment. I have a couple of half-written manuscripts that will never see the light of day in the form they are now, but instead of dwelling upon the idea of a novel, I will instead be publishing several collections of work spanning over several decades. This first collection has been the easiest to compile as it details my journey into motherhood, starting in 2013. It was hard to find a cut-off point because this journey is only in its early stages for me, but now seems like the right time. On my third, and last, pregnancy, I am at my calmest and most productive right now, and I feel that once tiny little baby arrives my focus will shift to the next period of my life. And while there will be many more words to come on that part, they will most likely fit perfectly into another collection of work. One day I will write that novel, but in the meantime collections of essays, stories and poems will see the light of day.

With Spring Comes Hope is a journey of change, challenges, hope and LOVE. This love can never be described correctly due to its power and omnipresence, but everyone knows what I am talking about. May you all be blessed with this love and pass it along so that our next generations can keep its flame alight and healthy. And may I never forget how powerful this love has made me, even in the face of many an adversity.

There is No I in Me Anymore

By the time you are reading this you probably already know (if you are very close to me), have an inkling something has changed, or really just don't know and are going to be super surprised. In any case, it's all been a little surreal for myself over the past eight weeks... Yup. There is no I in Me anymore, there is an Us. Me and It, It being a little munchkin that is eventually going to grow into a He or a She and eventually be born in late March/early April of 2014.

Everything seems surreal and exciting and scary at the same time. There was that moment I had that dream where I took a home pregnancy test and the test appeared to be positive with a due date marked in the screen... Which lead me to run out to Walgreens as soon as I woke up in the morning to buy a real one, and then sat around staring at the packet for hours until I finally dared to do it. The two lines appeared almost automatically, and at that moment I decided there was no way I was going to be able to keep a child and I needed whatever it was inside of me removed as soon as possible. Needless to say, by the next morning, on my way to Planned Parenthood for a "proper" test, I had already changed my mind dramatically and was hoping that the home test wasn't a fake positive... I mean I knew it wasn't. I already knew I was pregnant, there are certain signs that you can't ignore. And yes, it was positive.

That Friday I went around in a haze, lying on the grass in the middle of Washington Square Park, trying to fathom the idea of having a child, and then raising said child. I stopped smoking and drinking that very day, and surprisingly enough it was easy. I mean REALLY easy. No nicotine withdrawal, no crankiness, no nothing. Just the knowledge that there was a little me growing right inside of me. For the next 10 days it still didn't feel real. I told a few people close to me, but that was it, my little munchkin was going to remain a secret until I was ready for the world to know about it.

I don't have health insurance. That was my main concern about actually having a child. Planned Parenthood lost all funding to provide prenatal care, so they just gave me a number for a low-cost women's health clinic in Brooklyn, and I was able to get an appointment for 10 days after I found out I was pregnant. In the meantime I found out I was eligible for Medicaid, so I started working on all the paperwork I needed for that. In the end, the clinic filed for me (they are amazing – and there I was worried that I would have to pay for everything by myself!). I had blood work done, and exams, and went over all different kinds of things with the technician and the nurse and the midwife, and then finally got a referral appointment for an ultrasound at the Brooklyn Hospital for the following week. I am really happy with the people who are following my pregnancy – they made me feel comfortable and a lot less nervous than I was before I got there.

Unless you have already been through this yourself, you can only imagine what it feels like to see your baby inside of you and then to hear the heartbeat... It's mind-blowing. That little blob on the screen, the size of a bean, which is beginning to form into a person is actually part of you and created by you. And that heart beating... Honestly it was only then that it fully became real to me – I now have two hearts beating in my body, and one of them needs to be protected and nurtured and loved at all costs. Every day I wake up and (after the immediate feelings of absolute hunger and thirst, followed by a wave of nausea) I feel blessed that this is happening to me. I remember my 17 year old self writing in my diary and telling my best friends that I wanted a child by the age of 19, and that I would call her Luna. Instead I got a cat and called her Luna, and as the years went by started to wonder if I would ever have a child. Growing up with an amazing mother but with a father figure who disappeared too early and another who wasn't around for too much longer I always promised myself I wouldn't have a child unless I was completely sure the child would have parents who would stay together forever. Well, unless you remain a complete and hopeless romantic with no shred of cynicism in your bones all of your adult life you will certainly realize that this was quite a tall order. And a straight shot to never having children. And I have to say that at the beginning of this year I was really starting to think that maybe I wouldn't have kids, and that, in a way, that was allright (as long as my siblings were going to have them). I could just live in New York City for the rest of my life and live like I have enjoyed living for the past 8 years…

And when have I ever done anything conventionally anyway?! Every time I try to I fail, so I gave up on trying a few years ago and started living life in the way I wanted to. I have never been happier, or more comfortable in my own skin, and everything is just another adventure to embark on… This one probably being the most amazing adventure I will ever jump into head first. And don't get me wrong, little munchkin's father is more than present, and won't be going anywhere (unless I decide to move, because then he will be moving with me, and munchkin). Which brings up the idea of moving… For some silly reason being pregnant kind of changes your perspective on everything. I mean everything. Obviously the idea of moving away from NYC has come to me over the past eight and a half years, but I've never actually really acted upon it. But now I just want to move to California, be nearer my family over there and actually be able to live in a house with a back yard where I can grow my own food, not feel like I am constantly hustling to make ends meet like I do here. I will always love New York, but I don't know if I really want to bring up a child here. I'm most certainly going to have the baby here, but after that, who knows? Within the next 18 months I am pretty sure that I will be making a move over to California. It's always been my dream to live in Santa Cruz, but I think I will probably have to start in Sacramento and then see where life leads me.

But all of that is not for a while yet… In the meantime I am going to enjoy the amazingness that being pregnant is (especially now that the uncomfortable first trimester is over), and be happy.

End of the Second Trimester

It still feels like a dream. Even now, while I am heading into my 27th week, and starting to feel those little kicks on a regular basis. It still feels like a dream, an amazing, wonderful dream; a dream that I am going to be a mother in just a few more months. That we have created this little girl who is growing inside of me and who I am going to love and be responsible for, for the rest of my life and beyond that. How incredible is all of this? And yes, I know that millions and millions of women have done the same thing since the beginning of time, but it's all such a new and wonderful feeling that I can't get enough of it. Every day I wake up knowing that I am carrying the being that I will love more than anything I have ever loved in my life, and that I am responsible for bringing her into this world and making sure she is as healthy and happy as possible. Everything else seems just so ephemeral, but this is real, however much it may feel like a dream.

I feel like I am lucky as I am having a relatively good pregnancy – although I don't really have anything to compare it to, so I am just assuming that it is. I'm still working 55-60 hours a week, maybe a little bit slower and clumsier than before, but I'm still able to do it. Yes, I get aching feet and my ankles sometimes double in size, but it's nothing physically crippling. The back ache that I get on the cold days when I have been standing for too long is definitely annoying and the days when I get the indigestion/backache/feet ache/headache/tummy ache all combined together are the worst, but I'm mainly at the healthiest I've ever been in my life. That might come from the fact that for the past 6 months I have been thinking that one glass of water is the equivalent of a pint of water and I have been trying to down 8 of them a day. I only learnt last week that one glass is the equivalent of 8 fl oz, and therefore half of a small bottle of water. Not feeling as much of a water drinking failure anymore!

I think for me the worst symptom of all is one that I just cannot manage, and one that I have had from the moment I got pregnant: the tears. I literally can cry at the drop of the hat and there is no stopping it whatsoever. Something makes me angry: I burst into tears. Something makes me sad: I burst into tears. Something makes me happy: I burst into tears. That cute little doggie that needs a home? I cry. Don't even get me started on reports of starving children, bombs and civil wars… I don't mind crying, it's a good release and it helps get rid of some pent up emotions. But it's really, really annoying when you are trying to manage a restaurant and the basement starts leaking at 2am when you are about to go home and instead of formulating a plan of action to make sure it doesn't flood the basement all you can do is burst into tears. Or when someone annoys you and you try to explain to them in a decent manner why they are wrong, but all you can do is lock yourself in the bathroom and hope that ice cold water will make the redness in your eyes disappear so that you don't appear to be some kind of pregnant maniac who can't keep her emotions at bay.

Or you just go with it and just hope that being pregnant will give you some kind of VIP pass to be able to cry in public without anyone batting an eyelid. I mean there are much worse things that I could do in public in my condition apparently, things that I may experience once the baby is bigger and heavier…

Talking about being big… One thing that has been bothering me is the weight gain. Actually lets reword that, the weight gain itself isn't really bothering me at all, it's on par with the course and I expected it. It's the talk about weight gain that bothers me. I never expected to be one of those women who only gain a few pounds with a large tummy and stick-like limbs. I know what the other women in my family looked like pregnant, and I also know that they naturally went back to their pre-pregnancy weight afterwards. I also know that doctors recommend a weight gain of 25-35 pounds on average while pregnant. And I also know that they monitor your weight gain every time you go to the doctor and talk to you about it. Yes, I am eating more than I did before I was pregnant. But yes, I was on the low end of what is considered normal for my height and build. Yes, I am eating healthy, with some exceptions, but I naturally crave veggies and healthy carbs and protein. I do eat chocolate and crisps and cheese, but I don't eat more than I did before I was pregnant. I don't drink soda or anything other than water, tea and the occasional fruit juice. And no, I am not going to cut down! I'm enjoying food! Although nowadays I have to start eating smaller portions as I feel like my stomach is beginning to get slightly squished... Actually, as a piece of advice to anyone: don't look at a picture of what your insides look like at the end of the second trimester... Who would have thought that your stomach would start getting squished into your lungs?! Then again where on earth did I think all my organs were going to go?! So yes, I have gained quite a bit of weight, and yes, I will be going over the high end of the recommended average. But I am still on the slim side... Apart from the belly which is growing very, very fast now.

This brings me to the next subject: people and their words. In normal circumstances one would never tell anyone else that they are "huge" or "enormous", would they? So what makes it OK to tell a pregnant woman these things? Weight gain is always going to be a sensitive issue for women, so telling anyone, especially a pregnant woman who is probably hiding her feelings about her weight gain, that she is enormous, is never an acceptable thing to do! Just like the woman who asked me if I was having twins and if I was sure I wasn't... Yes, lady, I am very sure I am having one child. Everyone is different, some people show fast, some don't show for months, in the end the most important part is that we are healthy and doing our best to ensure that our babies are growing correctly and in a healthy manner. And yes, I am going to have fries with that because they are absolutely delicious and I don't feel like restricting myself! I really hope that I was never one of those people who mentioned the words "huge" or "enormous" inadvertently to a pregnant woman in the past, because if I did I apologize profusely!

I have a feeling that these next 3 months are going to fly by, as my movements get slower, time is just going to get faster. There is so much to prepare for, and so many things that I still need to learn and I know that there is not enough time left to do it all. That's all right, I am sure that I will learn as I go, as will Cesar. There is only so much you can prepare for, and the rest is just going to happen anyway. I'm so excited about it all (and I little scared too, I don't think there is anything wrong with admitting that), and wondering if this will still feel like a dream when the belly gets even bigger and the kicks harder. Those little kicks are pretty amazing too, and I am so glad that I am feeling them all the time now – I was getting a little worried that I wasn't feeling enough movement. All I needed was to voice my concerns to the doctor last week and little Munchie decided it was time to step up her movements in the womb. I guess it's true what they say about the baby being able to hear now!

2014 is going to be such an amazing year.

I'm So Happy

I'm so happy.

Despite the fact that it has snowed at least once a week since the beginning of the year, that the pavements are icy and slippery and despite the fact that the wind is bitterly cold. Despite the fact that my belly feels like it's getting heavier by the day and despite the fact that I feel like my bones have expanded and I have become a clumsy woman with a waddle.

I'm so happy.

Every day I wake up and feel excited as well as nervous about the idea that we are one more day nearer the moment that I will give birth to our daughter, and therefore one more day closer to the fact that I am nowhere near ready. Or I don't feel anywhere near ready. Mentally I have always felt ready, but practically I feel that there is so much more to do, so many things to fit into so little time. I know that everything will work out and I am forcing myself to stress out as little as I can about it. Which doesn't make it too hard when I am walking around in such a state of happiness...

After signing the lease and then a lot of back and forth on getting the keys to the new place we finally have our new home in Flushing, Queens. It is fully renovated and cleaned and waiting for us to move in as soon as we can. Our room in Brooklyn now looks in a state of distress, half full with boxes and half full with just stuff. My next steps are to cancel the electricity here and install a new account at the new place, find movers and decide on a day to move that is on the only day Cesar and I have off together, and then set up the new place in the way we want to before the baby arrives. That's the really exciting part as we are really starting from scratch again, new couch, TV, dresser, tables... All furniture that we need to buy at some point in time. Nothing can be rushed though, for three weeks we practically lived like paupers so that we could pay the three months upfront for the apartment. Thankfully we work enough hours in a restaurant that we can eat most meals there, and I wasn't too tired to take the subway home at 2am. The latter is only something I can do while still in Brooklyn as it's only 6 stops away - once we get to Flushing I don't think I will be doing the late nights anymore, so there won't be the anxiety of having to find a cab that doesn't charge you through the roof to take you to Queens...

We are now into the single digits, with 9 more weeks to go. I love how so many of my regular customers at work take a real interest in how the pregnancy is going and love to chat about it and hear updates. I love how everyone at work is excited to see the growth and excited to finally meet the baby. I also love how surreal it still seems to this day. Even after I finally managed to put my registry together another pregnant friend and I were walking around baby stores exclaiming how we still couldn't believe that this was us, deciding on the best type of stroller rather than the cutest new party dress. I am pretty sure that I will always talk about the best party dress to pair with a Doc Marten boot, but nowadays I'm more into what type of sleepwear I want to dress my daughter in when she comes home from the hospital with me.

Cesar and I went for a tour of the Labor and Delivery department of Brooklyn Hospital the other day as that is where I will be having the baby if all goes to plan (and I really hope that it does). It's a lovely hospital (if you can actually say that about hospitals...). Not that I have much experience of hospitals – the last time I was in one for myself was when I was born. My knowledge of hospitals comes from the TV show ER. But I am determined to have my baby in a hospital. I want to have my baby naturally, but I want to be hooked up to monitors and have access to pain medication if I want to, and also be surrounded by people who can help if something goes wrong. Of course I am hoping that the delivery will be as easy and as great as my pregnancy has been – but who can predict that? Walking around the labor and delivery rooms, and then seeing the rooms that you stay in after the baby is born reassured me a lot, and made Cesar feel more nervous. This is all very very real now, even if it still feels surreal! The lady who showed us the rooms asked me if I had a birth plan, to which I just responded "Umm… delivering the baby here?" Should I be writing one of these? Yes I want to breastfeed so I suppose I need to write that down so people know. At the same time I am hoping I am going to be fully conscious so I can voice all of this myself, and I also don't want to set a rigid plan that probably isn't going to work out anyway. I want to be flexible and make sure that whatever happens is the best for me and the baby.

Ah, before I forget, as a gift to ourselves (amidst all of the stress of finding an apartment and really not having any money to spare) we booked a 3D ultrasound in a place in Midtown. It really wasn't too expensive, especially seeing as my Medicaid is covering for everything else and this really was a little extra, just because I wanted to see Munchie again… We went to Goldenview Ultrasound and booked the Silver package. It was a really lovely experience, although I would only recommend it to women whose placenta is not anterior – it's much harder to get a clear picture of your baby if they are hiding behind the placenta all of the time! The technician was lovely and tried all sorts of techniques to get Munchie to move away from the placenta, which she was cuddling like a teddy bear, as well as take her hands away from her eyes. She finally moved in the end and we got to see her lovely little face, her chubby cheeks, her little hands and her big feet! I do have to say though, that seeing your baby that way is a little creepy and they look a little deformed. It's a little scary and quite wonderful at the same time!!

I have been so consumed by all of this, as well as trying to work as much as possible and relax when I can that my writing has totally fallen by the wayside (which is also the most common excuse I always have whenever I start slacking in writing). It will get better… Once I have a little more time. But will I have more time?! Maybe I will be able to get a few sentences in here and there between baby feedings? Maybe I will be so overwhelmed by motherhood that all I will be able to write about is how much I love my daughter? (I kind of already know that is going to happen). We will see. In any case, there are still many stories and reviews and essays to come out of me, enough ideas for more than a lifetime of writing.

In any case, despite the next impending snowstorm and despite the fact that I really wish I didn't have to work for these next couple of months, I am still so happy. I feel like there is so much happiness that is still inside of me, waiting to get out and I can't wait to share it with everyone. Well everyone who deserves it anyway.

Setting Up the New Home

Ah it has all been a bit of a whirlwind these past few weeks, and I have been getting so tired that between work, the commute and trying to make our new apartment into a real home before the baby gets here I haven't had a moment to really write anything down. Although there is a lot to be said... I feel like so much has happened and I need to record it now before I forget due to baby brain, or have even less time on my hands! I know full well that the moment the baby gets here I will hardly have time to sleep let alone anything else.

Between the endless (or what seems to be that way) snowstorms and icy winter days and nights we managed to move a lot of our belongings from the old apartment on Troutman St in Brooklyn to the new place in Flushing at the beginning of February. Our moving truck man got stuck in the slushy snow pile outside the building, and tried to put Joey Ramone the howling cat in the back with the furniture, but we made it to our new home without breakages or damages. And what a home! It's big, airy, bright and so quiet. I slept so well the first night and woke up to the sounds of birds singing, not to the sounds of the endless construction on the streets of Bushwick. There were still quite a few of my belongings left in the old place, but my mum and wonderful best friend went to pick it all up for me last week so I didn't have to deal with it. I just don't know if I could have faced any more moving at that point.

Setting up home has been so much fun, apart from the fact that every time we save some money, we end up spending it on very important things... Necessary things of course, but the money part is beginning to worry me, as we have four weeks left until the baby gets here... I know deep down everything will be fine, but I am taking 2 months off, and am not used to not making my own money and not being financially independent! All for a very, very good cause though, as I will be busy looking after our little Munchie and giving her the best start in life that we can give her. Buying a new couch was the most fun part, turning up at Bob's Furniture and walking around trying all types of different couches, and looking at sectionals as we have the space for one. We ended up going for a lovely coffee colored one with large pillows and enough room for us to both lie down on it and watch TV on our brand new 42 inch HDTV... Which we ended up getting at a super discount price because someone had messed up on the pricing at Best Buy... There are still boxes and boxes that need to be emptied or put away, but there is no real rush with this. I've been doing one or two a night, and trying to imagine how I would like our home to look like when it is all done. I feel like we are finally really making a home for our family, a place that is ours and no one else's!

I'm still working 40 hours a week, and Cesar is still at his 60 plus hours, and it's been a little strange for us both as I am now working day times and he is still working the usual night time hours. We are going to have to make real efforts to spend enough time together on this schedule as I spent a lot of the first week feeling a bit thrown off and missing him, even though we live together and work on the same premises. I know he did too. Thankfully we both have Wednesdays off together still and these have become even more important than before. We have been trying to explore our new neighborhood (we already have found "our" deli and "our" diner), looking for places to eat and shop and hang out. It's been a little difficult with the weather that has limited my movements a lot (on top of the fact that I get tired fast when I am walking now, as Munchie is really growing fast). I love how multicultural the neighborhood is, how there is a church that has service in 5 different languages on Sundays, that it feels like it's still NYC, but a little quieter and more relaxed than where I lived in Brooklyn before. Then again, I wasn't too happy when I had to get the shuttle bus instead of the subway last week and people kept pushing me, despite the fact that I have a very obvious baby bump. I'm sorry to anyone who got my elbow in their face, but being pushed and squashed makes me do those types of things!

I don't really want to get started on the whole getting up and giving your seat to a disabled, elderly or pregnant person on the subway, but I do want to mention it. I was brought up in countries where this was a normal thing to do. You don't look up, look at a person and look down again, without getting up from your seat. Yes, maybe I chose to be pregnant and ride the subway, but standing up for long periods of time in a crowded subway at this point in my pregnancy actually makes me feel light-headed and faint, and easily able to lose my balance. In any case, it's always other women who give me their seat, never has a man offered his seat, not even when I am standing right above them. I'm not the type to ask for a seat, nor am I going to glare at you angrily to make you feel bad, but people need to be a little more aware. It's quite sad really! The best moment for me was the time I asked a woman to move her bag so I could sit down and was looked at as if I were some kind of cockroach trying to crawl into her personal space. Of course I didn't feel bad!

My amazing mother came out for a week to help us with everything and to participate in the baby shower that my lovely best friend threw for me. It was really perfect, as I really don't like being the centre of attention, but she made it into a lovely tea party at the Kings' Carriage House where people I love joined me to celebrate the impending arrival of my little girl. Everyone has been so generous and it is really helping us get ready for having a baby in our home. I have the best people in my life, and I hope I am the same type of friend to them as they are to me. Mum took some wonderful photos of the afternoon that display how lovely (and pink) it really was.

So this is it really... Four weeks left (give or take a few depending on when she decides it's time to come out), and I am hovering between stages of feeling elated and intensely nervous. Not about the actual birth which still feels like something surreal that is going to happen but that I have no idea how, but more about afterwards. Am I going to be able to breastfeed easily? Is everything going to be OK? Will I be a good mother?!? Will my baby be happy and healthy?

In the meantime I shall continue to feel content and to breathe through all the mini moments of panic, and just know that everything WILL be OK. Both Cesar and I are happy and healthy and prepared to do anything to make sure our child is happy and healthy too. And I really really really can't wait to finally meet her outside of the womb, and talk to her little face and tell her how she spent the last month inside me kicking my ribs and making me laugh.

This continues to be the most amazing journey of my life.

38 Weeks and Still Growing

It's hard to accept the fact that you are allowed to be tired, that you are allowed to actually not really do anything all day except for watch that TV series that everyone has been telling you to watch for the past year. It's hard for me, because most of the times in my life when I feel this tired it's entirely my fault (out partying, up all night writing, stress-related insomnia), so I am so used to pushing myself through it that I feel guilty just letting go and just being tired.

Yesterday I woke up at 3am and couldn't get back to sleep again for a lot of different reasons. I had to be up at 6am anyway due to an early doctor's appointment. So I waddled my 38 week pregnant belly to the subway and went to the clinic in Fort Greene to get everything checked up. I guess I am now the one nearest her due date so everyone is very excited for me (they actually were all a lot more excited than I was, it took me enough energy to muster the courage to keep my eyes open during the appointment). I could give birth any day! I waddled back to the subway in the gorgeous sunshine, trying not to burst into tears until I got home.

And then I did what I have never done before, I asked my boss if she had anything important for me to do, because if not I was just going to rest. And guess what?! She told me to rest! Yes, Jade... There IS a reason you are working from home now, and this is because you are supposed to be resting! So for 10 minutes I tried to work, but numbers and words kept flying in front of my face and I couldn't do anything correctly so I grabbed a cup of tea and went to the couch. Where I stayed until just after 8pm. And from the couch I graduated to the bed, and fell asleep, sleeping about 12 hours of interrupted sleep until this morning. You can't be too demanding – there is no way on earth I can sleep more than 2 or 3 hours without having to get up. Bathroom trips, water drinking breaks and of course, a cheesecake eating break at 3am when Cesar got home. I still feel tired today, but more able to function. I think this is the new golden rule… No fighting the fatigue or the sleep: naps and bed whenever my body wants it.

So now the waiting game has begun. Any day now little Munchie could decide that she wants this to be her birthday and she will start making that journey towards daylight. While I would like her to wait until her due date of April 1st, I have now accepted the fact that she might want to come early, or that she might want to come late too. And that's absolutely fine. I think I am ready to cope. Everything is pretty much ready (apart from all of her little baby clothes need to go to the laundry and I don't know why we are procrastinating about that); she has a bed and a bouncy chair thing and blankets and clothes for every occasion and diapers and wipes and even heart-shaped sunglasses to match her mummy. She also has a hopefully endless supply of food that my body will provide for her (the alternative is not an option right now, so I really, really hope everything will work properly). And, so important, she has so much love waiting for her here, all that love that we hope we have projected into my womb over the past 9 months, and much, much more. So many people are waiting for her arrival and to finally meet her. Not the least her parents of course!

To be honest I think I have had a wonderful pregnancy, and I have been very lucky that up until a few weeks ago I really didn't feel uncomfortable or too heavy. I'm not super huge, my weight gain stabilized in the third trimester (so much that I have actually lost a few pounds even though Munchie has gained quite a few); I've had a few aches and pains but nothing major. My feet only started swelling this week, after I started to work from home (so now I need to go for little walks every few hours so as not to sit at the table all day without really moving). I just recently had to develop an elaborate roll to get out of bed and that can only be done in at least 3 steps, and I don't remember what it was like to jump out of bed in a spritely manner! Actually, I don't remember what "normal" feels like anymore. What actually WAS "normal"?? To be honest I don't really think

I care, because that "normal" has gone, and will be replaced by another "normal", one that I am more than ready to embrace. My main issue other than not being able to walk fast anymore (and I mean SLOW), is a burning pain I began to feel last month at the top of my belly on one side, that has now graduated towards the other side too. I realized that it's basically from the skin stretching so much, but it wasn't until I did some research on the web last night and read people describing it as just like a sunburn, without the redness (and without the sun, because that big golden orb has been on another planet for the past 3 months). Aloe Vera! Luckily I always have a big bottle of aloe in the cupboard as I spend enough time on the beach in the summer, and it really helps relive the soreness! Better than any other lotion that I have already tried. Who would have known that all you really need (outside of a good doctor or midwife) is a large bottle of aloe, a large bottle of Tums, a comfy body pillow and a healthy diet to get through these 9 (I mean 10) months? And yes, my iron level is STILL normal, even though I was anemic as a teen and I am a vegetarian. I guess I did something right by listening to my body.

And I will continue listening to my body after Munchie is born. I'm not too worried about losing the extra weight immediately – it will happen naturally. My body has never been one to put on weight too fast, and if I make sure I get enough exercise I will be fine. I'm honestly looking forward to evening runs in Flushing, and using them to discover new places to go and new parks to take Munchie to in the summer.

Oh summer... I am looking forward to you. Showing my little daughter all of the things that I love about life: sunsets on the beach, waves, walking barefoot in the sand, listening to The Cure while dancing in the living room (not just for summer of course), and reading on a warm park bench under the trees... So much to be excited about! In the meantime I will continue to wait at home, not feel guilty about resting anymore, and watch as our cat follows me everywhere I go, just so that he knows that I am OK. Maybe the next chapter will be one with newborn news, or maybe it won't – now that I am at home I have a little more time and energy to devote to catching up on writing. I say "a little" because a lot of that energy is put into making sure I am happy with how our apartment is set up. And catching up on TV shows. And thinking about making food, and then ordering salads from the delicious diner down the street.

The Waiting Game

So it's been the waiting game for the past 5 days now... Will she arrive suddenly, or will she take her own, sweet time making an entrance into this world, basically when she feels ready for it? I wonder what it feels like to be all squished up in there, with so little room to move nowadays. How can that be comfortable? Doesn't she want to stretch her arms and legs out and open those eyes and see daylight?

For 9+ months you go every day hoping you won't see any signs of labor, no early contractions, no cramps, no waters breaking; and then you hit your due date and all you want to see is all of those combined so that you know that things have started and that you are finally going to be able to cuddle your child within a matter of hours or days. April 1st passed by and although I've been having Braxton Hicks, or "practice" contractions for a while, I have not had any signs of labor at all. So I was scheduled for a non-stress test at the hospital and everything looked fine. I got to see my daughter make kissy faces on the sonogram and was sent home with another appointment for the Friday morning (unless I gave birth before). The clinic where I have been going for prenatal visits and the hospital are in Fort Greene. It was annoying enough when I had to get there from Bushwick, but now that it takes me ages to walk (waddle) anywhere AND we live in Flushing I literally have to leave with a 2 hour window, just in case.

So on Friday I was overjoyed when I started feeling what seemed to be contractions at 5am. Regular contractions that weren't unbearable but were definitely not painless. And even though I moved around, drank water, walked, ate something, they still didn't go away. I had my last doctor's visit where they scheduled me to be induced (on Tuesday), but there I was hoping that I wouldn't have to wait until then because labor

22

had started. Off to the hospital we went (poor Cesar hadn't slept a wink as he had worked late, but came with me anyway just in case I had to stay in the hospital) – another non-stress test, another sonogram, both revealing that I was having contractions (so at least I wasn't making that up). The sonogram technician said that everything looked fine, but if I wanted to go home without worrying I would need to come back in a few hours I should go to Labor & Delivery to get checked. An hour later and I was sent packing from the hospital (in the nicest way possible) with the advice to "walk a lot" and hopefully I would give birth before I was to be induced.

So back home we went, hoping that it would be hours and not days… No such luck, it's now Sunday, I still have those contractions on and off, but no other signs, no intense pain or anything else… Obviously my daughter is quite happy being shy and stubborn and just waiting for HER time. I'm not really worried about it; I just want to finally hold her in my arms after all this time!! And there was I, worried earlier on in my pregnancy that she would decide to make a rapid entrance, waters breaking dramatically on the subway, ambulances and all that. I think it will just end up with me being induced on Tuesday and her arriving peacefully in the hospital the next day. So let's see what happens! Apparently I was just the same with my mum, not in any rush whatsoever!

There is one thing that I never really thought about before I got pregnant, and that is that the only time I have been in a hospital as a patient was when I was born. And even then, it was a tiny maternity ward in a tiny hospital. I have absolutely no idea what a patient is supposed to do when they go to hospital, what they need to bring, how they are supposed to act and what on earth the order of all the different doctor roles are. For someone who loves hospital shows I am absolutely clueless about the seniority in interns, residents, attendings, doctors etc etc. All I can say after Friday's visit in L&D Triage is that the nurses are always the nicest and kindest people, and I will be more than happy to just have nurses deliver my baby – especially if they are gentler than the residents! If everything goes according to plan then I won't need a doctor anyway –

just a midwife and nurses. Fingers crossed! And then hopefully that will yet again be my last visit to a hospital until I have another child.

So in the meantime, I have been pottering around at home, putting butterfly decals up, watching more series on Hulu and Netflix (I've now learned all I could from Call The Midwife on Netflix) and rested (even though I still feel exhausted). Mum got here last night which is wonderful, and I know that even if Munchie doesn't feel like coming out just yet, she will have to by Tuesday or Wednesday at the latest. It's pretty amazing to me that between me, my siblings, and now my daughter, we were (will be) all born between the last days of March and the first days of May. Spring babies! And all late too!

Luna Marlena's Birth Story

Years and years ago, when I was a mere teenager I told myself that one day I would have a daughter and would call her Luna. In the years that followed I did not have a daughter, but did acquire a tiny little cat that I called Luna and who stayed with me for many years until she passed away from old age. And then I got pregnant and at 21 weeks we found out I was expecting a little girl. Cesar must have read a blog post that I had written one day in which I mentioned the above story, and told me that we should name our daughter Luna. Marlena (pronounced Mar-lay-na), is a nod towards Marlene Dietrich, my favorite actress and an inspiration. I love names that end in "a". And we obviously chose right because her name fits her perfectly, although she has also kept the nickname of Munchie as it has followed her out of the womb and into our arms...

Luna Marlena was born on April 9th 2014, 8 days after her due date. Even though a premature birth was always something that I had worried about in the back of my mind all throughout the pregnancy, I had a gut feeling that she would not be in a rush to get out and would probably make it right up until they scheduled to induce me. Her due date of April 1st came and went and I was scheduled to be induced on April 8th. I had mixed feelings about being induced, and really wanted her to come naturally, but it was hospital policy to not let anyone go for longer than 41 weeks. And when I got to 41 weeks I was ready to give birth! I had some false labor contractions three days before, but nothing else, and when I woke up on April 8th at 6am I knew that she would finally be born within the next 40 hours as I was going to be induced that morning. Of course it all wasn't going to be THAT simple, as my waters broke just before I got into the shower... Hence the fact that there was no time to take a photo of me at 41 weeks as everything became a little more urgent at that point! Seeing as I had been having what I thought were Braxton Hicks contractions all weekend (based on what the doctor had said on the Friday at the hospital after my baby stress test), I had no idea if labor was going to be long or short now that my waters had broken. We got stuck in traffic and it took us 90 minutes to get from Flushing to Fort Greene. I remained somewhat calm – to be honest I was more worried about making a mess in the cab and being late for the 8am appointment than being in pain (I am British after all). Thankfully little Munchie decided she was in no real hurry to make an appearance, so I got settled in at the hospital and checked out by the doctor on duty.

The idea at that point was to wait and see if the contractions I was having were getting stronger or not before giving me any type of induction medication. I had a birth plan, but it really wasn't set in stone – I was only intent on making sure I had the option for an epidural if I felt like it, but that I had the choice to not have any pain medication if I didn't, that I could breastfeed exclusively without having to worry about anyone feeding my daughter formula if I had to have a c-section, and lastly, that I would only have a c-section of absolutely necessary. To be honest I had no idea what to expect so wasn't going to put any demands on myself or on my child. Through-out my pregnancy I had always hovered between being worried about everything and just listening to my body and knowing that everything would be OK if I were healthy and happy. I was right. While pregnancy was all too real, especially when I started really showing, the actual idea of child birth was totally surreal. You mean a baby was going to come out of me? I know it's been done a million times before, but not to me. So it was basically a "let's see what happens when it happens" part of my life, and as soon as my waters broke I was excited, scared and actually composed. I had been waiting so long to meet my daughter and it was finally time (and the acid reflux towards the end of my pregnancy was driving me insane).

Unfortunately, even though I was having contractions they weren't really doing anything and my cervix was literally still closed a few hours after I was admitted. Due to the fact that I had lost all of the amniotic fluid that morning I wasn't allowed to leave the hospital bed (not even to go to the toilet which became really annoying. Why would I, extremely healthy person, need to use a bedpan?! UGH). The doctors decided to give me Pitocin to speed up the contractions and make them more affective as well as antibiotics to ensure that there was no risk of infection to the baby. Three hours later and I was only 1cm in and the contractions were getting a lot stronger. I was also exhausted and hungry (make that starving, all I had managed to eat that morning was a small bowl of cereal). They won't let you eat or drink anything just in case you have to be rushed into surgery – even when you plead with them. I wasn't even allowed to suck on boiled sweets. Only ice chips... By 3pm or so all I wanted to do was get some sleep and not have to use a bedpan so I decided to go for the epidural (and I am really glad I did for this birth, I think I may opt out with the next one though, more on that later). The anesthesiologist was lovely and took her time putting the epidural in to ensure that it worked, and I understood why they asked you to do it sooner rather than later – it takes about 30 minutes to do and you need to remain super still, which is quite impossible when you are having contractions every 5 minutes. By 4 pm my lower body was completely numb and although I could feel the pressure of the contractions, the pain completely disappeared. As did any ability to move my legs – I needed to ask Cesar and my mum to help me move if I needed to change positions. It was around this point that I realized even more than I ever had before the depths of my love for both Cesar and my mother – there was no one else that I would have been comfortable with having there all the way through, and at the same time couldn't imagine doing it without them there. I knew at that point that this is where you realize there is no room for modesty in childbirth and that you don't really care anyway – for someone who hates people even hearing me pee it still shocks me today how I just didn't care what I looked like during labor – all that mattered was that I was able to give birth to a healthy and happy little girl and that my boyfriend was there to witness and live through the whole thing.

My first nurse was lovely – she came to check on us every hour on the dot, was really friendly and answered all of my questions. As the baby was still faring well and had a healthy heartbeat they just continued to give me

Pitocin, antibiotics and check on progress every 4 hours. I managed to doze off a little, as did my mum and Cesar in their uncomfortable chairs. My lovely, wonderful best friend came to visit and smuggled hard candy into the room so that I could try to alleviate the heartburn I was feeling, but by this point I started to feel really woozy and completely out of it. My day time nurse was replaced by the evening nurse, who wasn't as kind or friendly, and didn't come in nearly as much. I knew that they had monitors at the nurses' station anyway, so I wasn't too worried about anything bad happening... But it would still have been nice to have someone who appeared to actually give a damn! By 7pm I still wasn't even at 2cm and I started to worry that I was never going to be able to give birth naturally. The doctors reassured me that I still had a lot of time, that everything was going OK and that I should relax, so I tried to do just that. Not easy when you have a bunch of wires coming out of your arm and back, no feeling in your lower body and are then told to wear the oxygen mask, even though your acid reflux is so bad you want to vomit. The nurse also started to worry me because she said the oxygen was for the baby – making me immediately think that the baby didn't have enough oxygen! All this sounds just delightful, I know... It wasn't that bad, just very strange for me, seeing as the last time I had been in hospital was for my own birth. I was just very happy that I was in the best hands if anything happened to go wrong, and was honestly not expecting to feel comfortable at all... It all still felt very surreal. Kind of like an out of body experience to be honest!

By 11pm when the doctor came back I was worried that there wouldn't be a change yet again, but I had jumped to 8cm! The doctor seemed pleased, but said he would come back to check up on me around 2am, and told me to sleep. I tried, but I couldn't sleep – not with knowing that my little one would be born at some point that night! The doctor also told me that severe acid reflux is a sign of imminent labor, therefore a good sign, and to not worry about it. I'm sure that if they had let me eat it would have been better though! More dozing... More watching the movies that were playing on the TV (I honestly can't really remember what the movies were, and I couldn't really focus on anything at this point, not on the TV, not on the magazines or the books I had, and definitely not on any type of meaningful conversation). I'm so glad that Cesar and my mum were there, even though they were probably exhausted and bored. It was reassuring that they could be my voice if for any reason I couldn't use mine anymore, and that they were there to hold me when I felt awful and in pain.

Just after 2pm another doctor came in to check me, said that I was ready and told me how to push and then disappeared. At this point I was wide awake and ready – but had no idea if I was supposed to start pushing immediately, or wait for someone to come and assist me... I asked the nurse that question when she came in to change the heartbeat monitor paper and she mumbled that I should be pushing and walked out again. At this point I started getting a little distressed and teary – what, was I supposed to push my baby out by myself?? What was the point of being in hospital?? My mum called the nurse back and she finally transformed herself from zombie into a wonderful human being and stayed with me, helping me to practice my pushing technique. The problem with the epidural is that it's sometimes hard to determine when the contraction starts so you don't always know when to push. You have to really focus, and if this is your first child you have nothing to compare it to. The woman in the room in front of me was obviously having a difficult labor as I could hear people going in and out for ages, and the woman in the room behind me had been howling in pain for hours, so I guessed that the night doctors weren't ready for me to give birth right at that moment as they were busy, hence the fact that nobody actually told me that it was really time (even though I was ready?!).

And then, around 3:15am, doctors and nurses poured into my room and started setting everything up. My bed suddenly became a labor chair, a huge light beamed down on me and three doctors crowded around, getting ready to deliver my daughter. The head doctor gave me a lovely speech on how having an epidural is a great way to control the pushing and therefore helps them to preserve to perineal area, which is always their aim (yeah... well that backfired completely, but no one needs to read about those kind of details) – and then handed the reigns over to the student and the intern. I started to push, and felt so strange doing it, Cesar and my mum holding my arms on each side. I had a feeling I was never going to be able to do it, that the baby would get stuck – even though they kept telling me that the head was right there... Then all of a sudden I heard a short baby cry, and realized that my daughter was already crying while she was still mostly inside me, and in shock pushed her out in one go, head, shoulders and the rest of her body... She was already howling while Cesar cut the umbilical cord and was whisked over to be measured and weighed and tested and cleaned and wrapped up. I was in shock – crying and laughing and not really believing that I had just delivered a baby, my own baby. My eyes still tear up when I think about how amazing that moment was, there is nothing in the world to compare it to. All I wanted was to cuddle my baby for the rest of time, but the doctors spent about 45 minutes fixing what they had to fix (and this is why I am glad I had the epidural), so Cesar got to cuddle her, until one of the nurses said that they needed to take her to the nursery for more tests and to be cleaned properly. Thankfully I got to cuddle her for a few minutes before she was taken away. I was still pretty much in shock at that point – while the whole experience, from losing my waters less than 24 hours before to seeing her little body be pulled from me, still seemed surreal, all of a sudden everything was very, very real. The past 10 months had all culminated into this very moment: the birth of my daughter.

Luna Marlena was born at 4:13am on April 9th, 2014 at the Brooklyn Hospital Center, weighing 7lbs 13oz, and measuring 18 inches, perfectly healthy and with a good strong pair of lungs and a full head of hair – looking like the spitting image of her dad (with my hair, hands and feet). A pure beauty. I was already in love with her from the moment I found out I was pregnant, so there was no exact moment that I felt like I fell in love, it was more like a feeling of not knowing how to express or communicate all the love that I felt once I had given birth to her. I felt completely gobsmacked and overwhelmed, and a little confused too – I didn't know why they were taking so long to fix me and why I couldn't go and join my baby immediately. We were reunited again an hour later in a room in the post partum ward, Luna fast asleep, and me unable to sleep because all I could do was stare at her beautiful little face and hold her tight in my arms. Even today, a little over a month later I still hold her tight and stare at her for hours, still amazed at how Cesar and I created this perfect little human being who already has a strong character and who rules this house like no other.

It's as if all I have done in my life was preparation for the next stage: life with the loves of my life, my daughter and my boyfriend, and maybe one day with another little blessing...

Recovery

About halfway through my pregnancy I started to imagine those two months I would take off work after childbirth, and conjured up images of myself being the perfect home builder-mother type person, keeping the house perfectly clean, laundry done, groceries shopped for and freshly made meals prepared every day, so that Cesar could come home late at night and heat up his dinner. Oh yes, I imagined that the first couple of weeks would be difficult, but after that I would magically snap back into my normal self. Little did I know that instead of being worried about the last months of pregnancy or childbirth I should have been preparing for the recovery.

I learnt that there is no "perfect" way to be a mother. You aren't going to be that woman in the baby food commercial, hair perfectly coiffed, matching outfit and wobbly bits miraculously disappeared. And that's OK – because you ARE perfect, to your child. You are the most important person in your child's life, and that's the most important thing you keep in mind. Motherhood is what you make it, and that's the wonderful part about it all.

Read what you will about pregnancy and childbirth, recovery is often glazed over (or maybe I glazed over it?). I wish books were more honest with how hard it actually is. You know when they say prepare meals and put them in the freezer? DO IT. And not just for a week or two. Make enough for a month. Stock up on tea and coffee and things that don't perish easily. Have take out menus and Seamless on hand because if you often find yourself home alone with your child and you are breastfeeding you may not find the time to prepare a meal. And you get HUNGRY. I forgot what it was actually like to be hungry during those last months of pregnancy, but now my stomach actually rumbles every few hours. Don't worry too much of dishes aren't done immediately and things get a little dusty – because recovery isn't called recovery without reason. **You have to rest**.

I really thought I would be up and about after 2 weeks. After 5 weeks I was still nowhere near the image in my imagination of before. I finally started going out for walks every day. I finally stopped wearing pajama bottoms and started wearing actual clothes. After 7 weeks I felt a LOT better, and started making trips into the city and making it back alive. Going back to work was something that I never want to have to consider again (um are you asking me to actually LEAVE my child with someone else?!! No way.), and we finally had the breastfeeding thing down for the most part (more on that later). There are so many things that I would like to warn other first time mothers to be about that I wish I had known (or acknowledged when people were trying to warn me). Granted, it may be very different for others, but I think I would have been easier on myself if I had known the toll it would take on me.

No one told me during labor that all the Pitocin and antibiotics they pumped into me could delay my milk coming in for a bit longer than average. Or maybe it doesn't affect everyone like that, but all that medicine took a toll on my body, maybe more so because I hardly ever take antibiotics. I mean I don't ever remember taking any at all! The first night in the hospital Luna was crying her eyes out, and I kept thinking she must be hungry, even though I had read that all they need in the first few days was the colostrum you produce until your milk comes in. The night nurse came in to check on us and basically told me that my child was starving and that if I couldn't feed her properly myself then I needed to give her formula. Even when I tried to explain that that was not true and I didn't want to give my child formula she kept pressing the issue. Those close to me know how important it was for me to breastfeed exclusively, but after labor and no sleep for 30 hours, a brand new newborn crying in despair in my arms and someone pushing a solution on me, I gave in. The next morning, after a few hours sleep I felt like myself again and was really angry for not being listened to and decided to not let my arm be twisted again. And yes, the formula did shut her up and comfort her, and yes, we did give her a tenth of a bottle over the first couple of nights she was home, but she really disliked it and just wanted to nurse. And nursing was SO painful. I literally cried in pain and gritted my teeth so that Luna wouldn't feel my stress and pain every time she latched on. The lactation consultant I had seen in the hospital was a complete waste of space (she didn't even come near enough to actually show me how to make sure I was doing it properly). When my milk finally came in 6 days after birth so did the cracked and painful nipples. Breastfeeding is NOT easy, and whoever says it is must have been really lucky. We struggled for at least 3 weeks to get it right, but I am very proud of us both for succeeding and persevering. Oh, and you will not starve your child if your milk isn't there immediately… Before formula existed women could only breastfeed (or hand their child over to a wet nurse), so don't listen to people who think better. Case in point: Luna actually put on weight over the first week after her birth and grew 2 inches, and that was NOT due to the tiny amount of formula we gave her the first few days – it was due to what I was giving her, however painful it was. I even started to get over my fear of breastfeeding in public, and did it in Washington Square Park without a cover (only because there were other mothers doing it and I felt less self-conscious – I used a cover on the subway!). I'm aiming on doing this for a year if possible, even after we start her on solids after 6 months. She's growing so fast, so it's definitely doing her the world of good!

I mentioned the subway just above – apart from walking the only form of transport that I use to get around the city… Luna loves her carrier (although the one we have plays havoc on my back after a while so we are saving up to get an Ergo which will help), but if I am going to be out and about in the city for a while I need to be able to put her down at times, and this has been impossible the last few times I have taken her out in it. And she gets really hot in the carrier… It's a great option for short journeys and if you are going from one location to another but difficult when you are strolling around. She also loves the stroller (and I use it when she refuses to sleep during the day which she does all the time), but the stroller is heavy with the infant seat in it and I can't carry it up and down stairs by myself just yet. So I figured out which stations have elevators and did a trial run the other day. It's doable, a little confusing at times (especially 74th St/Roosevelt Ave), and most people were really helpful and lovely (bar the lady who was in a rush and shouted at me that some people didn't have the luxury of staying home with their kids...). It's all part of living in the city. And part of the reason that I really want away from all the stress. I LOVE this city and I LOVE that it has been my home for the past 9 years, but I am starting to consider a change... But those thoughts are for another time. In the meantime I won't let it stop me from getting out and about, but I will be spending a lot of time out and about nearer home.

There will be people who tell you how to parent your child, but I learnt well over the first couple of weeks that none of that really matters – it's what works for you as parents and your child that is the best. I remember being in the drug store with a friend when Luna started crying while I was paying at the check-out. She literally had time to let out one little wail when a woman behind me said loudly to the rest of the people in the store "somebody needs to give that child a pacifier!" Oh really? I was actually a little shocked and just muttered something about how rude she was and then posted about it on Facebook. A friend left a comment about just ignoring these types of comments gracefully, as I would hear them all of the time, and she was absolutely right. And babies cry, it's normal. It may be irritating to others, but no one is going to be able to keep their child inside until they are two years old, and at the same time, nobody wants to shut their child up just for the sake of others. There is nothing wrong with a child vocalizing what they want – and the only way for a baby to do it is by crying. I have a baby who is very vocal and I am not going to apologize for it! In the end, I am the one who has been blessed with this beautiful child, and Cesar and I are the only ones who will have a say in how she is raised.

And that's the whole point, isn't it? Through-out my pretty wonderful pregnancy and less than wonderful recovery the main point is that we created an amazing little human being who is growing and thriving every day. I already have forgotten the discomfort of the first trimester and the miserable hugeness of the last two weeks of the third trimester, and at nearly 8 weeks post partum I have already completely glazed over the pain of the recovery. To be honest if I hadn't started writing this before I probably wouldn't even have written anything about it. Because it was ALL completely worth it. I look at my daughter's beautiful little peaceful face while she is sleeping and have to restrain myself from kissing her cheeks every 2 seconds. She smiles at me in the morning and laughs when I do silly things to make her giggle. It still blows my mind that Cesar and I were able to create this little person, the most important action we have ever done in our lives. I'm still completely overwhelmed with happiness and I doubt this feeling will ever go away!

I'm Feeding My Baby

So much to write about and not enough time, even though I am at home full time with the baby. This piece is being written with the gentle whirr of the swing in motion and Baby Mozart in the background, what has recently become our go to for nap times. Amazing how that 28 minute DVD actually works, but more on that another time.

I've now been exclusively breastfeeding Luna for nearly 10 weeks, from the moment she was born. Apart from the 5 minute meeting with the lactation consultant on duty at the hospital and a 2 minute discussion with one of the nurses I have done this all alone, with advice from a few friends in California and the unwavering support of my boyfriend. I think the worst weeks are finally over (touch wood, you never know), and we are finally getting the hang of it. I'm still being woken up every 2-3 hours at night but I know at some point that is going to get better. In the meantime I am not working so I can nap at other times to stop myself from going completely insane. Luna has thrived from day 1, despite our latching issues and the pain that that caused me. Granted we probably could have fixed things sooner by consulting another lactation consultant or going to a La Leche League meeting, but I could barely leave the house during the first 4 weeks, and I was insistent that was going to make this work and that it was all going to be fine. And if I say so myself, I have to applaud my stubbornness because my daughter now weighs 13lbs (at 2 months), when she was born at 7 lbs 13 oz. She's healthy, happy and growing very fast, hitting all the milestones and showing alertness and an ability to resist sleeping for as long as she can. I mean, really, what can be better than feeding your child the food that your body is creating for him or her?

Just to preface the following, this is not a post about how everyone should breastfeed or about how it is better than formula feeding. It's up to every parent to choose what works for them and I completely respect that. For myself there really was no choice, I was brought up breastfed and surrounded by people who breastfed their children. My close friends who have children have all breastfed them, so to me it was the most normal thing in the world. Formula was really the second option. Keep in mind that I grew up in Europe, but assumed it would be the same in the US. I was a little bit confused when I started doing my research during pregnancy and most websites and books tell you to write a birth plan and if you plan on breastfeeding to make sure you let everyone know before you deliver. And if you plan on exclusively breastfeeding to make sure the nurses knew so that no one would feed your child except for you. It made me wonder why it was so important to state this, but I thought that it was a "just in case" thing. Then my doctor warned me about how nurses often feed babies formula in the hospital to make sure they sleep in the nursery. OK, warning taken into account. I made sure everyone knew that I was planning on exclusively breastfeeding. Even though one of my friends did try to warn me that it wasn't always possible and to not be disappointed with myself if it wasn't there was no way on earth I was not going to be able to breastfeed. I'm not a Taurus for nothing: we succeed in what we set our minds on doing!!

Fast forward to the delivery room. I was not given the option for skin to skin contact immediately after birth, even though it was in my birth plan. The nurses whisked Luna over to the table to do all the tests. Fine. There were three doctors around me and at least Cesar got to hold Luna until they needed to take her to get cleaned up and for all the other additional tests (I did get a couple of minutes but she was already swaddled up). When she was finally brought into my room a few hours later she was fast asleep. I didn't want to try to feed her until she was awake. Anyway, she had a big Exclusively Breastfed sign on her bassinet and the lactation consultant came in and talked to me for 5 minutes, as I had requested someone come to make sure that I was doing it right. It was later that night that the nurse tried to push me to supplement with formula to make her sleep. Excuse me? She had been nursing all day and all a baby needs for the first few days is the colostrum that we produce! Wait... Is my child REALLY hungry then?!

Wait a minute... I thought that the hospital was meant to promote breastfeeding?? That was one of the main reasons I actually agreed to deliver there! Not push first time mothers to formula feed their babies! Thankfully the hospital pediatrician reassured me that Luna was doing fine and to not give up. And obviously I didn't. While we were going through all of our trials and tribulations of getting used to it (why does it hurt so much when all the books say it shouldn't? Why is it so damn hard?? How will I know if she's getting enough food?) I did a lot of research on the subject (I should obviously have done this before she was born, but I had no idea it was going to be such an issue). Guess what I found out? That more people formula feed their children in the US nowadays. Or at least breastfeed and supplement. And that there is a big movement to bring breastfeeding "back". Wait, WHAT? So it went away?? How on earth did this happen? Children have been breastfed I assume since the dawn of times, and before the time of formula that was all you had! I know that nowadays there are many different sorts of formula and it is probably easier to feed your child that way (again, no judgment, whatever works for you and your child as long as your child is healthy), but for the main percentage of children to be formula fed bewilders me. I had a chat with my doctor at my post partum visit about this, as she congratulated me on still going strong. She mentioned that women didn't get the support they should get and often gave up, starting off with supplementing as they were told that their supply wasn't enough (although all they needed to do was nurse on demand and their supply would increase or decrease as needed), and once they started supplementing would often just give up on the breast feeding. Also, with maternity leaves being so short, many women couldn't face the idea of pumping breast milk multiple times a day so would just go straight to formula. Also it takes dedication to be up every two hours to nurse your child during the first few weeks. And then there was the question of nursing in public.

I've nursed in public from the moment I left the house with Luna. If we are out for more than 2 hours I know that she is going to be hungry. Doctors office waiting room, subway car, mall, restaurant, park, street, even the back room of the bar I used to work in. If Luna is hungry I need to feed her. Sometimes with a cover, sometimes without, whatever is more comfortable. Mainly with, for my own peace of mind, as with many things in life I started out being a little self-conscious, not because I might show some boob in public, but more because I felt like we were already struggling with it and I didn't want people thinking that I sucked at feeding my child. That was in the beginning, now it's all good and I know that we are doing fine. And it's also getting hot now, and summers in NYC are hot and sticky. If Luna gets annoyed because I'm covering her face with a cloth or a light blanket who can blame her. I don't do that when we are at home! But ever since I have been doing it myself I haven't noticed too many other women nursing in public. Even at the park. It's not like I ever looked out for this, as I've said before it was never something I even thought about noticing, "OMG that woman is FEEDING her child in PUBLIC!!!!" But now I do. I don't really mind what people may think, as feeding my child is more important than anyone's thought on whether I should or should not do it in public, with or without a cover. It took a few weeks to get used to doing it though, and I can understand that it could be extremely daunting for people with a little less confidence or stubbornness than myself, as there are times when people stare or look at you strangely. Like the one time on the subway when a woman literally stared at me for the 20 minutes it took me to feed Luna. It was actually making me feel uncomfortable as I had no idea if she was actually sleeping with her eyes open or just openly staring at me, silently judging me. Well, it was that or let Luna scream the subway car down, so we all know what the better option was there.

Anyway, I was planning on writing a post on breastfeeding from day 1, but kept pushing it off, especially after things got much, much easier for me. With hindsight there are a lot of things I would advise to women that I didn't do (sign up for WIC earlier as they have free lactation consultants on duty for anyone who needs help, go to La Leche League meetings before I gave birth etc), but I will definitely do it all again. I think my main concern was that I never felt like I was getting the support that I needed from professionals, even from the moment Luna was born. The lactation consultant spent less than 5 minutes with us and tried to help me by instructing me from afar. Honestly, the text message service the WIC lady had me sign up for has been more helpful than the consultant ever was. The first time we tried the nurse on duty just grabbed Luna's head and latched her on and then left me to it. I requested the consultant come back the next day but she never did. Then there were the nurses who tried to push formula on me to "help the baby sleep", and when I tried to explain that I was breastfeeding lifting their eyebrows and telling me she was hungry… There was the head pediatrician who I saw on the last morning before we were discharged who said she was doing fine and not to listen to people. Then Luna's pediatrician, who I actually really like and who is otherwise really good, telling me that it's OK to supplement a few times a day. But why? And then telling me at Luna's two month visit that it would be fine to add rice cereal to her milk so that she sleeps through the night. I reminded her that I was breastfeeding and made it clear that my daughter would not be eating solids until she was at least 6 months old, and even then I would only slowly be introducing them. Yes, I could take the easy road and fill her up so much that all she can do is sleep, but I honestly think that a few months of waking up every two hours to breastfeed to ensure what I feel is the best nutrition a mother can give a child outweighs the effects of sleep deprivation. I mean I could be napping right now, but I feel so strongly about the subject that I am writing about it instead of catching up on sleep!

I actually haven't spoken about breastfeeding to many of my friends with kids, only a few who have either been a great help to me in persevering, or others who have been there to commiserate as they were going through the same issues as me. And then just last week one of my friends posted an excellent blog article on Facebook that opened my eyes to a lot of things. It wasn't the article per se that opened my eyes, but the sheer amount of comments that were made on it. As I commented on it myself I was subsequently subscribed to all future comments and I couldn't believe some of the things I was actually reading! I know that I should have unsubscribed after a while, because it was making my blood boil, but I found myself addicted to reading all these different opinions, and getting more of a broader view on why women were not so hot about nursing in public.

The article in question was written by Annie Reneau and is called *What's So Hard About Covering Up to Breastfeed in Public?* Annie basically wrote an essay explaining why it may be hard to cover up while breastfeeding and why it shouldn't be such issue. A very informative and realistic article. The hundreds of comments that appeared (and keep getting posted even though the article was initially written in 2013) ranged from the agreeing, the supporting and the thankful, via the I understand but can't agree on this for myself to the outraged and the angry. Some of the latter were so incredulous that they actually would make me laugh if there were only one person thinking that way. Sadly there are apparently many many people who think that women who don't cover up while breastfeeding are creating an uncomfortable environment for everyone around them and should go and hide in a corner until they are done. One person actually said that if one were inept at covering up then one should not be a mother (ever tried latching on a squirming and thrashing kid while simultaneously keeping a cover over you in 80 degree weather?). Or that not covering up was making someone's 14 year old stare because he was seeing boobs and it wasn't healthy. Hmm, if ANYONE is staring at a breastfeeding mother with sexual intent then I think that the problem lays with them, not the nursing mother. Anyway, you can read all of that and make up your own opinion about it all yourself. I'm not going to rehash what has already been said. I just feel that now I understand much more why breastfeeding has become such a debated subject... With the support not always there for first time mothers coupled with the image that women need to be modest when it comes to feeding their child (when paradoxically the media bombards us with boobs all the time),it must be hard to feel comfortable when out and about and you need to sit down and nurse. And that is sad because it's easy to be discouraged and give up. On one of the baby message boards that I am on the topic of nursing in public often comes up and sadly many of the women say that they either bring a bottle of formula with them if they go out, or pump their own milk and bottle feed it to their child to avoid having to nurse. And no, I will never be the type of person who feels comfortable being half naked in public but I will not let anyone make me feel bad for feeding my child when she is hungry. Wherever I may be.

It was really refreshing to go into the WIC offices here in Flushing today and to be congratulated and supported for breastfeeding my child. Those ladies sure know how to make a first time mother feel good! And it makes me happy to know that my daughter is thriving, no matter how hard it was the first month. And it's true what they say – it DOES get easier. And fortunately (or unfortunately?) like with everything else related to pregnancy and childbirth the difficulties become glazed over and rosy and not-so-bad-after-all...

To finish of this rambling essay of personal thoughts I came across some worldwide breastfeeding information on the In Culture Parent website (the whole website has some really cool information if you are raising a multicultural child, and even if you aren't). The statistics are quite shocking... While the World Health Organization recommends exclusively breastfeeding for the first six months of life, only 33% of infants under 3 months are exclusively breastfed in the US. In Peru this percentage is 69%! All sources are listed in the website. It's quite sad really, when you think that many mothers and children miss out on the bonding because there is such a push to promote formula in hospitals and doctors' offices. After seeing these statistics and comparing them to other countries I now understand this movement to "bring breastfeeding back". I guess it had really gone away! And no, I'm not going to become a militant breastfeeding mum, telling everyone what they should do, but I do think there should be more real support to help those who would like to exclusively breastfeed, even for a short while.

The Question of Weight

I keep thinking that I should go out for a run or something. The thought is a nice one, strap on those running shoes and nimbly skip out into the street, run a mile or 5, and come back home feeling energized and refreshed.

Not going to happen!

I mean, logistically it's impossible! I can't just leave Luna at home while I go out (and if I could, a jog wouldn't be top priority – something more along the lines of a pedicure/manicure/haircut/long nap in a cloud would be a more obvious choice). And then physically it would be too – my joints are really painful. I never had a knee ache during my pregnancy, not even in those last days of oh my god I put on 54 pounds and weigh 184 pounds how on earth did that happen craziness. And now my body aches all the time, my knees hurt every time I get up and I know it's due to the extra weight my body has been carrying. I lost 29 of those 54 pounds pretty much right away – but the remaining 25 are still there. Yes, I know, that still makes me very far from fat. But it's still a lot more than I have ever weighed in my life.

I shouldn't have tried my pre-pregnancy jeans on two weeks after I gave birth. It did actually make me cry – for about two minutes until my rational brain kicked my baby brain out of the way- I mean OF COURSE they weren't going to fit (ever again). I was a super slim person wearing super skinny jeans! I had hips before, but now they are obviously larger, and well the belly is not flat (or anywhere near what you would call flat). So, after those two minutes, I told myself it was time to celebrate the body that carried my daughter for 41 weeks and be happy for all of the good things my body does for me. Like not being prone to stretch marks for example. Or for always having an excellent blood pressure and iron

44

levels, even if I have maintained a vegetarian diet for the past 18 years. Like having an amazing immune system. Or for nourishing my daughter completely, so that she is growing and thriving. All the really important things.

I had to remind myself of all of that again when I had the great idea of going to the mall to try on some jeans. I picked a few different pairs up, two or three sizes above my pre-pregnancy size. NEVER EVER do that 5 weeks post partum. You will cry. Cesar just looked at me like I had lost my rational brain and that baby brain had officially taken over. Why on earth did I need to buy jeans if it was nearly summer?! What was I going to gain by buying a pair of jeans that was going to make me cry? Nothing. BUT what DO I like to wear? Dresses. And skirts. Especially maxi dresses and long flowy skirts. Flattering and pretty and many styles that allow easy access to nurse in, with places like Target and Old Navy selling them for decent prices. Oh… And these are dresses I can wear if/when I get pregnant again. Bingo! That solved the clothing problem. No more crying over skinny or not so skinny jeans. And dresses look nice with sandals, which is wonderful as my feet are as slim as they were before I got pregnant. And I kind of like looking at them now I can see them again.

And, you know, I am not really that bothered about the weight. It will come off when it feels ready to, it took 9 months to creep up on me, so it can take the same time to leave. I'm too tired to not eat that slice of red velvet cheesecake deliciousness that Cesar brought home for me the other night. And I'm constantly hungry anyway – if cardio is out of the question right now, dieting is even more so. Maybe one day when Luna is fully on solids and weaned from breast milk (not happening for many months). In the meantime I am just going to eat when I am hungry, and try to get a variety of everything (and yes that includes cake and chips – YUM). Positive thinking! Also, the only people whose opinion on my body I really care about (boyfriend and child) seem to like it just the way it is.

And then I read things about how other women lost the weight "just like that – 60 pounds fell right off me in the space of an hour!" or "I ate a vegetable and ran a mile and I bounced back in no time!" This is where I have to force my rational brain to stay on top of things again. I'm 36 – I don't have that amazing metabolism I had at 25 anymore. That's life. But I can fix the few things that ARE bothering me right at home, the real things that are not just physical: my abdominal muscles that were stretched to their limits, my joints that are finally crying out in pain after carrying a lot more weight than they were used to and my body's entire alignment that feels completely out of whack. So it's going to be sit-ups and yoga and Pilates from now on – all things that I can do in the comfort of my own home while Luna sits happily in her swing listening to Stevie Nicks or Marilyn Manson (her two favorite artists). I will start tomorrow – I promise! Although I do need a yoga mat as a towel isn't going to cut it on these hard wood floors… (Yes, that was an excuse – but a good one as it means I will have to go on a nice walk up and down hills with the stroller to the mall to find one).

And in all honesty I am doing this so that my body doesn't have a hard time if/when we are expecting a second child. Not because I absolutely need to fit back in those skinny jeans again. I want my joints to feel strong again and my body to feel realigned so that it can carry another healthy and happy baby for the full 40 weeks. And this time I will be following my own instincts, with the knowledge of how things work in the hospital here, and will be going all natural in a birthing center. That's why I need to be as healthy as possible. I wouldn't be 100% comfortable with an at-home birth (although I do love the idea of having the midwife who does your pre-natal checks be the same one who delivers your baby) – but the idea of a birthing center ticks all boxes for me. More on that if/when it happens though. In the meantime I am going to work on being as healthy as I can – for myself and for my family. Not for some idea of what I should look like three months after birth. Honestly I don't have the time – my daughter wakes up every three hours at night for a snack, I'm not good at napping during the day (neither is she), I cook and clean and do laundry when I am able to put her down and do some writing and reading when she goes to bed. I'm definitely beginning to get an upper body work-out with all the carrying of a wriggly 13 pound child about though!

So yes, my body has definitely changed, and it's bigger, but in a way it's better… For many, many reasons. Oh and if you ever want to bring me anything, please consider a delicious green smoothie – it's currently the best and easiest way for me to get all my veggies in. And smoothies are yummy.

Something No Parent Wants to Hear

The last thing any parent wants to hear is that there is something wrong with your child, whether it is something small or something scary and big. You go through your pregnancy hoping that everything is OK, sighing with relief at your mid-pregnancy anatomy scan, counting the kicks every day and wondering if you should buy your own Doppler so that you can check the baby's heart every day (not necessary). Labor goes very well and your baby is born into this world happy and as healthy as can be; passes all the newborn tests with flying colors and starts to grow fast, fitting into 3-6 month clothes before her three month birthday. Her first pediatrician visits go by well, no issues. And then there is that one visit.

A few weeks ago I took Luna in to see her doctor as I was worried she had an upset tummy (she didn't, I was just being a real first time mum and worrying about everything). I'm so glad I took her in, because although she was fine tummy-wise, her doctor detected a heart murmur. I have to preface this with saying that our daughter is a little wriggly bum, she hates sitting still, especially when she's being examined by the doctor. This time she had actually fallen asleep in my arms in the waiting room, so the doctor was able to get a good listen to her heart. She did say that most murmurs are nothing, but she referred us to a cardiologist at the hospital just to be sure.

I was a bit shaky when I got home and made the appointment, but I do tend to always look on the bright side of things and was determined not to worry. I also know at least 5 people with heart murmurs that do not affect them in the slightest. Anyway, we had the appointment last Wednesday and were there for 6 hours. Luna's cardiologist happens to work out of the pediatric clinic in the New York Hospital Queens, so there were quite a few people there (next time I must remember to bring snacks – lots of them!). It started off with an EKG (Electrocardiogram), blood pressure tests, and oxygen levels, weighing and measuring. At exactly 13 weeks she weighed in at 13 lbs 12 oz and measured 24 inches – so still growing up and out at a very good rate. The tests took a while because it's hard trying to get a 3 month old to lie still while you attach electrodes to her skin. Once that was all done we had to go back and wait for the doctor to see us for the next steps...

Because there were more! The doctor checked Luna's heart, confirmed she heard the murmur too and sent us back out into the waiting room to wait for the most important test, the Echocardiogram. I was actually surprised that Luna was taking all of these tests so well – she did try to pull the wires off her body during the EKG (I mean, who wouldn't?!), and the blood pressure machine was acting up so I actually had to nurse her so that she would remain calm while the technician redid it several times. I didn't realize what a nightmare we had waiting for us... Basically an echocardiogram is a sonogram of the heart. I have wonderful memories of the sonograms I had during my pregnancy. I do not have wonderful memories of this. It started off OK, and I really didn't think it would take longer than 20 minutes or so. Wrong! Two technicians and two parents and we still couldn't get her to stop wriggling, then squirming and then pulling and then screaming. Luna won't take a pacifier and she's fussy on a normal day, so once she was bored of being held on a table for 10 minutes she made it very clear she wanted off. The technicians managed to get a good portion of the images they needed done, but when the doctor came in after 45 minutes Luna was so upset that she told us to take some time to calm her down and get her to sleep. I did hear her mention the word "PFO" so as soon as we got Luna to sleep started to Google it and immediately wished I hadn't.

30 minutes later we had a sleeping baby in her stroller and back in we went. This time the doctor finished the echo off herself, which took another good 45 minutes, with a lot more crying and wriggling. By this point I was nearly in tears myself, and started getting worried about all the acronyms the doctor was mentioning to her assistant. For all I know

about the heart they could mean anything! Once it was finally over we got Luna dressed and while I was nursing her to calm her down the doctor explained what they had found.

I'm going to preface the following by saying that although it was and still is distressful for us to find this out, we are very happy that this was detected so early and that our daughter is in no kind of danger or pain right now.

Luna's cardiologist explained that they had found a medium sized hole in Luna's heart, between the two atria (the top chambers), with a shunting of blood between the two sections. In more medical terms, Luna has a congenital heart defect called Atrial Septum Defect with Pulmonary Stenosis. The size of the hole leaves it possible for it to get smaller or larger over time. If it doesn't get smaller by school age she will have to have an operation to close the hole. Usually in this day and age most of these types of CHDs can be fixed by inserting a catheter through the groin into the vein, so no need for open heart surgery. Also, there are often no real symptoms apart from the murmur and for this reason ASDs can often go undetected. If there are symptoms as a child then they could be one or more of the following: getting tired easily during exercise, breathing issues, catching pneumonia frequently and slow growth. Luna hasn't had any issues yet, but will of course be monitored. Issues can appear later on, maybe as a teenager, but usually as an adult: higher risk of a stroke, enlarged heart, blood vessel disease, heart attack...

Yes it's bloody scary. And even though we know that she will be monitored very closely with check-ups every 4 months with the cardiologist, and that she is obviously very healthy, it doesn't really make it any easier. We have had a week to digest all of this information now and we have promised ourselves to be positive, not to Google too much apart from reputed sites (per doctor's recommendation) and to talk to people who also have children with CHDs. We are going to make sure that this does not affect Luna's quality of life. I did have to stop myself from wondering if it was my fault in any way, but I really was so healthy during my entire pregnancy, and also stopped smoking immediately when we found out (before 5 weeks). But it's one of those things that can literally happen to anyone, so there is no point in me beating myself up about something that we most likely couldn't have prevented.

And as Cesar says... She's a Castro-Hughes so she was born a fighter! We have both been through enough ups and downs and amazing and horrific things in our lives and are as strong as oxen – she is part of each of us so double that strength and it is our mission to make sure that she mainly experiences ups and amazing, hopefully less of the downs and the horrific.

(It helps me to write all of this down. It's always helped me to write everything down, the easiest way for me to express something that I am having a hard time talking about. I also want to share something that maybe one day will help someone else going through the same thing. Again, no one ever wants to hear that there is something "wrong" with their child, and really there isn't anything "wrong", just something that may need to be fixed down the line. I always will be positive about everything, especially this as there is no reason to fear the worst).

The Evolution of Love

Just One Drink After Work

"You tell me you don't love me over a cup of coffee, And I just have to look away, A million miles between us, Planets crashing to dust, I just let it fade away" – Garbage, Cup of Coffee

Although it was me telling you that this wasn't going to work out, over a pint of Guinness, and you telling me that you just wanted to see me happy, and if that meant me being alone or with another man, then that was what needed to happen. Then we both cried and hugged and decided that we could spend one more night together before it was all over, one more night where we held each other tightly, one more day spent cuddling and laughing before it was time to let go. And yes, it's been a few days, and yes, we see each other at work, but it's still hard. I do miss you, I do miss you holding me tight and telling me you love me and that there is no one else that makes you feel the way I do. But we have to be strong, we have to pull through this, I have to go and figure out what I really want from my life and you need to do the same. Maybe this is just a break and that next week we will be right back where we started again. But what I haven't told you is that I am late, and I need to bite the bullet and take this test, hoping and praying that it is negative.

It first happened months ago. A group of us went to a random bar in the East Village after work, and after multiple beers and shots we ended up kissing in the bar, in front of everyone. You stayed with me that night, and I was adamant it wouldn't happen again. We had obviously been attracted to each other for a while before this happened, we would chat and talk about music and life in general. But the whole Valentine's Day incident started a slow running roller coaster ride that neither of us could stop, especially when it gained momentum and started speeding down hills and climbing back up other ones. There is something to say about feeling lonely and knowing that there will always be someone to answer your calls, at whatever time of day or night (and this works both ways). But were we just lonely or was it more than that at this point?

I didn't want a secret relationship with you, and I didn't want a relationship with someone I worked with. I resisted and told myself I wasn't falling in love, and you just waited patiently, confused about why, but still there. And neither of us seemed to give up; I knew the passion between us was like a fire that couldn't be stomped out just like that. I don't know why I am always trying to run away, but that is the story of my life. Protect myself from anything that may end in sadness.

For the past month or so things have started to change. We have spent a lot of nights together, drinking, hanging out, going on "adventures" to different places, seeing different things. Laughing and having fun, you carrying me home when I was too drunk to walk, me making sure that I got you home when you were too drunk to make sense. You looking after me when my cat passed away, and telling me to not cry anymore because you couldn't stand seeing me so sad. Us hiding away in our favorite secret bar after work, keeping up our secret relationship, although everyone knew something was going on, even if they couldn't actually confirm it. There was something that tied us together, looks, smiles, and a force that neither of us could push away, not right then. But then it all became too much for me. You live life day to day; I need to plan some kind of future for myself. I was getting scared of what I was ultimately feeling and I realized I needed to free us both from this, so that we could move on in different directions, while still remaining friends and excellent work colleagues. But how?

I began to get upset and angry about everything, and you began to try to make me angry and hurt me. And it came to a point where neither of us were happy anymore, and if we didn't sort it out we were both going to end up hating each other, which would make work the worst place on earth for both of us. So as the adults that we sometimes were we decided to talk about it properly, to part ways, to let each other go and to let our hearts fix themselves. I was surprised at how well we both reacted, and how well we have been keeping to our promise since. It helps that I haven't been drinking this week, as it makes it easier to go straight home after work and not give in to the "one drink" which leads to three and then a cab home together and sometimes sex, sometimes not. I want to keep this momentum going, and not fail and fall into your arms again, as I have been doing over the past few months. You deserve so much better than this.

And so the test is positive. How did I get to the age of 35 without this ever happening, and now have to deal with this? And no, I cannot have a child and will not have a child right now. I feel so damn stupid. What on earth was I thinking?? So now I will have to go through another experience I have wanted to avoid for most of my adult life. This isn't really an adventure, more like a nightmare while awake.

"All the lilies bloomed and blossomed, Wilted and they're shivering, I can't stop their withering, Oh, this world is a war" – Hole, Petals

One more cup of (herbal) tea

This time a few months ago I would usually wake up on Monday's with a splitting headache and a nauseous stomach as well as achy legs. Two double shifts followed by Guinness and multiple large shots of whiskey being the culprits. You can stop drinking for years but you never, ever forget what a hangover feels like, do you? That sick feeling that you did this to yourself, so there is no way you can't wallow in it and feel sorry for yourself. You have to get up and walk out that door and function like a normal person at work, and hope that you make it through to the end of the night. Tomorrow will always be another day, a day when you will feel like yourself again. And then it all starts over, like a vicious circle you really don't want to break, because it is way too much fun (until it becomes less fun, but that is an entirely different chapter, or book).

The last time I sat down to write an essay about life in general I had just taken a pregnancy test. A positive pregnancy test. A test so positive that the two lines appeared within a second of me peeing on the tip; telling me that I was under no circumstance not pregnant and that the achy boobs and the fact that literally anything could start tears rolling down my face at any given moment, were not just signs that I was going to have a really bad period, worse than I have ever had before. No, this wasn't just a scare. I was really pregnant. And my first thoughts were "I can't do this – please get this out of me as soon as possible – how can I have a child – I am never going to be able to do this!!!".

Those thoughts lasted about 12 hours.

And now I am nearly 12 weeks pregnant, and my Monday mornings consist of me waking up with achy legs from the two doubles I did over the weekend and a bottomless pit of hunger because if I don't eat every 4 hours or so my body screams at me for MORE. You know that type of hunger when you haven't eaten for a day and your head hurts and you feel like you are going to collapse? Yes, that's how I feel after four hours of not eating. Little fig-sized munchkin definitely has a voracious appetite! Which doesn't bother me in the slightest because all this not drinking and not smoking and not going out is actually leaving me with spare money that I can spend on good food in restaurants. Eating out! FOOD. Everything tastes so much better and my sense of smell is so good that any type of fragrant smell makes me gasp and any type of slight stink makes me want to vomit. I'm so glad my near constant nausea has not lead to any vomiting, because if it had I would literally be stuck with my face in the toilet all day due to all of the strong smells I walk through. Take the subway, for example, at any given time there will always be the following in your car: someone smelling of BO, someone eating something that smells really strongly, someone who poured a bottle of perfume all over themselves and someone who bought a jacket at a secondhand shop and didn't bother to have it dry-cleaned. Thankfully there are also bakeries and flowers and laundries and Lush shops and other places that smell so deliciously delicious that they counter the smell of garbage on the streets and the blocked drains after a rain storm and the smell of dust from all of the construction on the street. City smells... Nothing like them!

Six more months and I will give birth to a little boy or a little girl. My own child that I will love and care for and educate and promise to give as good of a life as I can to. A little being that is half of me and half of him that I already love more than anything or anyone I have ever loved in my life. Over the next six months I am going to get bigger, and happier, and grumpier and more and more tired of the city. I am going to continue being a vegetarian (I mean it's been 17 years already), as the idea of ingesting any meat or fish still makes me want to vomit, but I am a lot more aware of what I eat nowadays and what I should be eating more of. And I also had forgotten how happy I was when I was sober (minus the times that I felt alienated and alone because all of my friends were out drinking and partying). I am so much more productive, and sleep better and just am generally happier. Of course, this time round I am sober for a very different reason than I was last time, and it makes it all the more exciting and important. Right now in my life there is nothing more important than this little munchkin that is growing inside of me. I've also noticed that my bullshit acceptance tolerance factor has lowered itself so much that I don't accept any. Not anymore. Either I will walk away or just open my mouth and tell you quite plainly to stop bullshitting and to leave me alone. It's quite liberating, this telling people exactly how I feel and think about things. I should have tried it much earlier!

Once again, herbal tea has replaced the post-work beer and shot, and bed with a book (and crackers and crisps and string cheese) has replaced hanging out until 4am. And nothing feels better than sipping that chamomile tea, knowing that this is life as it is going to be for the foreseeable future (minus the crying and the lack of sleep that will come in six months). To be honest the whole idea of even being in a bar at 4am just made me feel like vomiting. Thanks morning-which-should-be-called-all-day sickness!

Love is Everything

This is the story of a story that could have never happened, or at least could have not panned out the way it did, and still is. One day, last Valentine's Day to be more precise, you and I had a night that we thought would only be that: one night. Instead it turned into a few nights here and there, and then more frequent nights, and then days, and then it was us. You and me together, for real, in a proper relationship.

I can't imagine not waking up next to you every morning and tickling you so that you wake up too and kiss me and tell me that you love me. I can't imagine going to sleep at night without you holding me tight and making sure I dream special dreams. I can't imagine spending any holiday without you. And I can't imagine life without the rapidly growing little human that we created inside me. And then life together with our little daughter, loving her and loving each other.

Who would have thought last year that by Thanksgiving of this year I would not only be telling a man that I loved him and meaning it with all my heart, but that I would also be pregnant and so very, very, very happy?

Who would have thought that Christmas would have been spent together, that you would bring me a tree home late at night as a surprise and that I would show you all my own personal Christmas traditions? This one was just a taste for all those that will come in the future together: you, me and our child.

This is not a story that can fit on one page, two or even three. This is the beginning of a life time of stories and anecdotes and images and changes. This is one that will be updated as life goes on, with additions and departures, with moves and with aging. This is the story of two lives and then three and maybe more, together under one roof and bound by something that had up to now only played hide and seek with me. What used to be torturous and unfair is now what makes my heart beat every day.

Our next steps are being created together, a home for us and a home for our child, a place of peace and quiet and music and art and creativity, a place where we can be ourselves, together or alone. Space that will be for everyone. Clean and pretty and happy and most importantly: ours.

It's finally time to live life to its full extent: no regrets and no more running away. This is what it was always meant to be like; it just took me a while to make my way here.

One more cup of very strong coffee please

It's been exactly a year. Exactly a year since I had that dream that I was having a baby, a year since I woke up and ran to Walgreens in my pajamas. A year since I went to Planned Parenthood and listened to the nurse give me the results of my test. A year since my life turned upside down and most definitely for the better. Our little Luna is now four months old and I actually can't imagine my life, our life, without her in it. I wake up in the morning thinking of her, I go to sleep thinking of her, I dream of her, and every waking moment is with her. I don't WANT to be without her. She's our little wonder, our munchkin, our actual reason for living.

I say "our life" because that is what it is. Me, you, her, us. We now form a unit, a united front, together as one. I don't care if that sounds soppy or silly, it's just what it is. And we couldn't be happier! This is what it was always meant to be like. And I really, really hope that everyone finds this in their lifetime, because everything I may have lived before this just pales in comparison.

I Disagree Doctor

One thing I really procrastinated about at the end of my pregnancy was finding a pediatrician for Luna. It was on my "to do" list forever and I kept pushing it back. My nurse at the clinic told me not to worry and that they would assign us one at the hospital and I could change at a later date if I wanted. But then the head pediatrician at the hospital ended up telling us we had to find one closer to us as they could only assign in the Fort Greene area (where the hospital was located) and not in the Flushing area. I had noticed a pediatrician's office on the route to the subway, and we ended up making an appointment with her for Luna's week 1 visit. I could barely walk for the first 2 weeks post partum, and as I was sleeping about an hour a night and Cesar was working 80 hours a week neither of us really had the energy to research any further.

I do like Luna's doctor. She's very competent, she is extremely likeable and friendly, and Luna obviously likes her. She also speaks fluent Spanish which was important for us, and where we live Spanish is not the second language. Her office is literally less than 10 minutes away by foot. The first time we saw her was exactly a week after Luna was born and after I told her that I was exclusively breastfeeding she mentioned to me that she had exclusively formula fed her own kids. I didn't really see it as a problem, and although it isn't really, if I had known better I would have been more proactive about finding a breastfeeding-friendly pediatrician.

It bugs me that I actually have to say that. Shouldn't every pediatrician be open to both ways of feeding your child and support you whatever you choose to do? Isn't the health of your child more important than the way the child is fed?

For me there was never any doubt I was going to breastfeed, and both Cesar and I know how we want to raise our child. I don't mean that in a "we know better than everyone else way", but in a "we do our research and make up our own minds" way. This means that Luna will be breastfed past her first year, we won't be introducing solids until 6 months and even then it will be just for fun as per AAP recommendations, we don't agree with any form of physical punishment nor do we agree with any form of sleep training that requires letting a child cry for any amount of time. When Luna cries she gets picked up, as fast as one of us can. This is how we roll, no judgment on anyone else's way of doing things. I'm also pretty stubborn, and when I know that something is right for my child and for us, then it's going to take something huge to sway me away from it. If this means that I only get 5-6 hours of interrupted sleep for a while, then so be it. This is pretty much what I signed up for when I became a parent!

So I got a little annoyed yesterday when we went for Luna's 4 month check up. Luna now weighs 16.5 pounds which means she has more than doubled her birth weight. She's 25 inches long, which means she has grown 7 inches in 4 months. All this goes to show that she is getting more than enough nourishment via breast milk. She's also hitting all of her milestones and obviously super alert and happy.

After a few minutes into the check up Luna's pediatrician actually tried to tell me that I should give her formula to "give myself a break" (when did I ever mention I needed a break?!), and also in the same sentence not to give my breast milk away as I should keep it for Luna (confusing?!). I don't need a break. Yes, we could have got Luna used to a bottle so that Cesar could take over some of the night feedings using my pumped milk, but at the same time he works over 60 hours a week and I don't work right now, so I think it's pretty normal I would be the one getting up to feed the baby. Also, I don't see why formula NEEDS to be used?! Her theory was that breastfeeding was done in the past, but now we have developed excellent formula that mimics breast milk. Fine, if that's what you want. I'm very happy doing what I think is best for my daughter, which also happens to be completely, 100% tailored for her needs and completely, 100% free.

Anyway, moving on, I knew her thoughts on breastfeeding, so I just brushed it off. My body is producing more than enough milk for Luna so I shall not be supplementing with anything else. A little bit later she asked us if we had started solids yet. I said no and that we were going to wait for a while longer. I kind of anticipated what was coming as she had already suggested I add rice cereal to a bottle of milk at her two month appointment to help her sleep better (this by the way is something I would never do and told her so at the time). In my opinion that is the equivalent of eating a load of wet sand so that your stomach stays fuller for longer (but only because you are filling yourself with something your body isn't ready to digest).

She said that we should, and when I told her that Luna was in no way ready (she can't sit up unassisted and her tongue still does the pushing out thing – although that has changed over the past few days I have noticed). So she said that we could actually make that change by trying every day. By this point I just didn't want to say anything anymore so we just nodded while mentally telling each other that nothing had changed.

Yes I could have told her to stop and tell her that I didn't think she was right. Or even that it wasn't what we were planning on doing (which would have come across as me telling her I didn't think she was right anyway). But who am I to tell a pediatrician who has years of training that me, first time mum Jade, doesn't agree with her? It was just easier to listen and move on. I'm just lucky that I do my own extensive research and that I also don't see the need to change something that is working fine for now. Why try to force food on my child when she doesn't need it yet (and then have stinky poop diapers to look forward to and an onset of tummy complaints)? And rice cereal has no nutritional value anyway, so we will be bypassing that and starting things like mashed avocado, pureed carrots, peas, squash, banana etc. One item at a time per week. I want to make it into a fun pastime, not a chore. Food IS fun, not something I want to force onto my child!

Ugh. This IS my fault, I should have been more proactive about choosing a pediatrician before Luna was born. But at the same time, I didn't realize that breastfeeding was such a big issue here! Was I supposed to call around to different doctors asking them if they would support my breastfeeding? Why would it have to be an issue? I can totally understand a pediatrician suggesting supplementing with formula if the child is not putting on weight, but saying that to a mother of a big, healthy baby? That's just weird! I'm quite happy to be in charge of all feedings. Cesar has had a million other opportunities to bond with Luna, and she is such a Daddy's girl too.

I also know that pediatricians are not nutritionists, and also that the recommendations do keep changing. What used to be considered a good age to introduce solids (4 months) is now considered too early. Some people say that it doesn't make a difference. I don't know if it does, but again, if my child doesn't need it yet then who am I to force it down her throat? And if this means more chances of avoiding allergies and stomach problems in the future then fabulous!

I'm not going to change doctors right now as she IS a good doctor and she is very conveniently located a few blocks from us. She is the one who detected Luna's heart murmur and who immediately referred us to a cardiologist. She is also available 24/7 and was able to explain to me what the weird breathing noise Luna sometimes makes was, and how she will continue to monitor it. And I actually like her as a person. I just don't agree with everything she says or some of the advice she gives...

That said, if I had to do it all again I would have researched much better and used those last couple of weeks of waiting for Luna to make an appearance more productively than sitting on the couch watching every single episode of *Call the Midwife*. Then again, maybe this is just normal... You just pick and choose what the pediatrician says? Who knows... I guess we will continue to do as we have been doing since day one. We seem to be doing an OK job so far!

(I am actually looking forward to making Luna food from scratch and introducing it to her little by little. Just not for a couple more months).

62

Sleep (or No Sleep)

You know how people tell you to get as much rest as you can before the baby is born as you won't get any afterwards? I kind of get it now. You can't stockpile sleep and tap into it at a later date, but you can remember back to the days when you could get hours and hours of uninterrupted sleep with a smile. A good memory. I actually can't remember the last time I had a real, good 8 hours straight of pure sleep. I WISH I could have rested properly during those last weeks of pregnancy! But I was literally up every few hours to pee or because I was thirsty, my heartburn was absolutely horrible, and it was really, really hard to find a comfortable position to sleep in! But now I wish I had just stayed in bed during that 41st week, with books and magazines and snacks at hand, forcing myself into such a relaxed state that I had nothing else to do but close my eyes and REST.

I've never been a good sleeper. Or I can't remember when I was. I've always been one to sleep late and wake up early naturally and not be able to go back to sleep again. For years I was able to go out at night and go to work in the morning and be a productive as I needed to be. Years and years ago when I spent a year in Israel I would party all night with the other volunteers and kibbutzniks, go to sleep around 5am or 6am and be up around 9am unable to go back to sleep again. And don't even talk to me about naps. What are they? I can count the number of naps that I've successfully had during my teenage and adult years on one hand. I've never really felt sleep deprived though (apart from those times that I was really burning the candle too hard on both ends – but that was easily remedied with a couple of "normal" nights of sleep).

You know how they tell you to rest after you have given birth and you are in hospital? Well that's just pure BS. I was woken up all through the night by doctors and nurses coming to check on the baby and me. Next time I am going to give birth in a birthing center where I can go home with my baby within hours after the birth. It will be possible to get a little bit more sleep at home without all of the interruptions. Seriously doctors? Do you HAVE to do your rounds at 5am, just after the baby has gone back to sleep and we are about to slip into a slumber? Does my temperature really need to be taken every two hours?!

The first few weeks after the baby is born is the hardest in relation to sleep deprivation. I was prepared for it in a sense, but not prepared for literally being awake 23 hours out of 24 every single day. They tell you to sleep when the baby sleeps, right? Well that is absolutely fine when you are a person who is able to sleep on demand, fall asleep when you tell yourself to. It doesn't work when you are like me and need about 20 minutes to be able to put you to sleep. During those first few weeks if you are breastfeeding you are supposed to feed your baby every two hours. Not two hours after the last feeding, but two hours after the feeding starts. I guess I was lucky in the way that I never had to wake myself up to do it as either I would be awake anyway or Luna would wake me! And of course, once she was asleep there were always so many things that I wanted to do, especially shower or get something to eat that was actually cooked and not just a (unhealthy) snack.

You know what? You get used to it. It's amazing what the body can do when necessary. It's amazing that you are able to function on a couple of hours interrupted sleep, look after your baby, do laundry, shop for groceries, cook dinner, respond to phone calls and emails. And it does get better... Somewhat. Until you hit a sleep regression at 4 months when it all goes back downhill again. Our better was 4/5 hours-3 hours – 2 hours – 2 hours. Of course the longest stretch would happen in the evening, not when I was asleep. And we only got this because I resigned to letting Luna sleep in the swing. She hated the bassinet. She hated the swaddle. She spits a pacifier out. Luna loved, and still loves, to be held, cuddled, to nurse, and now to jump around in her door bouncer. She dislikes napping, being asked to go back to sleep when she wakes up wide awake and not being in our arms. You adapt, so we did. A baby needs sleep and so do the parents, so you do what you need to to get this sleep. If it's the swing, then so be it. If it's cosleeping, then so be it. I actually felt like we were all getting some sleep and it was great.

Then we hit the 4 month sleep regression. You know how bad it was when your child was a newborn? Well this is worse. Only you expected it when she was a newborn. It was also worse because she was literally waking up every hour, all night, and wouldn't nap during the day. Granted I have a fussy child who literally resists sleep all the time, but this was out of control. From what I have read, around 4 months a baby's sleep pattern changes into a more mature sleep pattern, like our own that we have now. However, when we wake up in the night we just turn over and go back to sleep again – a baby doesn't know how to do that yet. So they wake up. It lasted all in all about three weeks from start to finish and I feel like it is finally getting better again. The only issue is that now the swing isn't cutting it anymore. We are slowly getting there with the crib, a little bit longer every night and all naps, but the only way we all get some real sleep is when we sleep in the same bed. And the full size bed that is just fine for Cesar and me is now not big enough. Thankfully we now have a big room with more than enough space for a queen sized bed, so once we can afford one, it will be our next big purchase. One thing I am grateful for being in Flushing is that the rents here are still affordable and we have a big one bedroom apartment.

Also, Luna is one of those children who seem to be going through one continuous growth spurt, and when she is learning something new really doesn't like to sleep. I don't think I will get a real night's sleep for a few more years yet... Right now I am just aiming and hoping for a schedule along the lines of 7:30pm – 7 or 8am sleep with night time feedings at 11:30 pm and 4am. And three one hour naps during the day. Not too much to ask for, right?!

I'm typing this at 10am, while my boyfriend and child are both sleeping peacefully. Why am I not taking advantage of this and napping myself? Because I know I won't be able to. I'd therefore rather spend this time doing something productive, instead of tossing and turning for 20 minutes and getting frustrated when nothing happens.

And you know what? It's all worth it. This is what we signed up for. And I firmly believe that as Luna is a fussy infant who wants to stay close to her mummy and daddy all the time she will be a calm and peaceful toddler, right? ;) And as much as it can be tiring to get up over and over again during the night, there really is nothing like holding your baby in those wee hours, in the silence, and reflecting on how amazing your life has become.

Healthy Body Image

I wrote a piece on weight gain after pregnancy a while ago, and how I was dealing with that. I personally have never had any real issues with my weight in my life. By "issues" I mean anything spanning from being under or overweight to eating disorders. Of course, there have been times in life where I have wished I were skinnier, or where I have wished I were a little bigger, but I have never held back from eating, or at the same time overeaten (unless you count giving me a bag of chips... I really must eat lots of those!). In our family we eat mainly healthy, simple foods, but like to indulge at times, but all in all we have a balanced diet. Now that I am home I am also trying to expand in the kitchen somewhat, nothing too over the top right now as Luna doesn't really let me spend too much time cooking, but my plan is to make everything from scratch all the time at some point (even bread if possible). But basically, food has never been an issue, unless you count the times when I was really poor and needed to figure out how to make those pennies stretch until the next pay check.

I think that I have always been lucky enough to go through life eating what I want, with a healthy attitude towards food (part fuel part pleasure). I do thank my mother for this, for introducing me to all types of food as a child, and then for letting me become a vegetarian without any questions, and for helping me find a balanced diet that way. That's the way it should be, right? Is it all about education, or is it because I am just lucky? I have been known to utter the words "I'm fat" now and again, but never really believing them, just because I feel a bit larger than I am normally. At the same time I have been known to say the words "I'm too skinny" too, when I've been stressed out and worried about things and spent too much time drinking coffee and smoking cigarettes and not eating enough. But all in all I've mainly felt comfortable in my body, even during those teenage years when we never feel good enough for anything.

Since becoming a mother I have questioned many things, and one big one is the ability to teach my daughter to always accept who she is and what she looks like. When I was a kid we didn't have any form of social media, photos were taken with film and you didn't get to see them until they were developed. The word "selfie" didn't even exist. Today I scroll through my Facebook or Instagram feed and see so many of these "selfies", people taking pictures of themselves at the perfect angle, with the perfect pose and the perfect lighting. We've all been guilty of it now and again, but I feel that it's really becoming an epidemic; natural, fun pictures are being replaced by posed pictures of someone's face. "At the beach!" has gone from a picture of the beach to a picture of someone posing with a little bit of water and blue sky in the background. Anyway, in the end it doesn't matter what I prefer, people can post what they want and I can choose to look or not look at it, it just worries me. Not for me, but for my daughter.

You watch the TV and you see so many commercials containing "perfect", flawless women. Open a magazine and it's the same thing. Trends change over time, when I was a skinny teenager Kate Moss came on the scene and I was happy that my shape was fashionable again. Nowadays I am a lot curvier and I actually love it too. Skinny or curvy, slim, fat, chubby, everything is human and everything is beautiful. What bothers me is the "perfection" attribute. With all the photo-editing on photos nowadays, there are no imperfections, nothing that actually make us human. I get that this is done on models in magazines, but people can nowadays do it on their own selfies before posting them to the internet. Again, this worries me. Not for me, I actually prefer the completely natural look in my photography, preferring to catch someone off-guard and am not one for much editing. But it worries me for my daughter.

How am I going to be able to ensure that my daughter grows up with a healthy body image when in fact we are surrounded by people and images and fad diets that are trying to make us think otherwise? Where do you draw the line between healthy and unhealthy? I know that at home I can teach her to have a healthy relationship with food, by introducing all types of food, maintaining a healthy but interesting diet and at the same time not withholding treats. We don't use non-fat in our family, that's not how we were raised and I am fully convinced that the full fat version of something tastes better and is more filling than the non-fat version. We eat sugar and butter and eggs and cream and cheese here, always have and always will. But we also eat beans and veggies and fruit and rice and hummus and pasta. We eat a healthy amount of anything and don't restrict ourselves (although I don't eat meat or fish as I just don't like them). No food is "the enemy", just as no food is eaten in excess. I would love for my daughter to see fruit and veggies as something delicious like I do. Of course I would also love her to prefer a salad to Taco Bell. And it is entirely up to me to make sure that happens.

At the same time, as much as we, as parents, can educate our child to have a healthy outlook on food and body in general, how can we make sure our kids are strong enough to not be influenced by negative images or people in the outside world? How does one go about telling a child what is "normal" and what is "not normal"? I don't even want to use the word "normal"!! I can't even imagine what it's like nowadays, growing up with all of that immediate communication around you, Facebook, Instagram and the likes. I struggle with it a lot myself, I like to share photos of my gorgeous little daughter with my family (which is spread out around the world) and my friends, I share my writing, which is often very personal, with the public, but I like to control what I share and what people know about me. I especially dislike being checked in to places online… Why on earth would I like random people to know where I am?! It took me a while to learn what I do and what I don't want to share though, and a while to learn to keep personal writing and photography OFF of Facebook proper by only linking it from other platforms. And I suppose that one day I will be able to help Luna learn what to keep private and what she can make public, but how do I teach her how to weed through everything she sees online and see it for what it really is? That all of those articles containing images of the "perfect woman" are not real life and all of those pretty selfies are usually posed and not real life. That nobody is perfect, and anyway what is perfect? What those magazines tell us? That's not even real.

It was hard enough growing up without being bombarded by images on the internet every day, so I can't even imagine it now! I don't want to keep Luna from being exposed to any outside or negative images, but I do want to give her the tools to be strong enough to know that she is wonderful just the way she is, and that so are other people, and that we don't judge people on what their appearance is. I've made a conscious decision to make sure I don't say things like "oh my god I feel so fat today!" and the like anymore. If I make it sound like I don't accept my body, then how on earth can I teach my daughter to? And that also goes for anyone that she is close to – I shall be asking them to be aware of what they say about weight and food and exercise, about themselves or about others. And if they can't or won't, then I'm afraid that contact will become limited.

I know that may sound a little over the top, but I grew up so aware from such an early age, with worries and fears that I should never have had, so I just want to bring my child up so that she doesn't go through the same, or at least never, ever thinks that she isn't good enough. Maybe I'm worrying about things a little too prematurely, or maybe a little too much, but when it comes to the happiness of my child I want to make sure I'm prepared to get rid of any obstacles!

Ode to a Fussy Child

I have learnt that "fussy" is not a bad word. That having a "fussy" child does not mean that said child isn't a happy child. I've also learnt that the word "fussy" tends to be used to describe a child who doesn't sleep through the night after two months, who won't learn to self soothe around the same time, who needs to be held constantly and who gets frustrated and cries when they aren't fully comfortable.

Nowadays, at 5 months, I can leave Luna to play on her floor mat for 15-30 minutes, and she will play quite happily, as long as I am sitting nearby and she knows that I am not just leaving her there (if I go to the loo or to the kitchen she usually realizes it and makes it heard). I can now put her in her bouncy chair in the bathroom and have a shower (long gone are those days when I would get her to sleep, put the shower on, start getting undressed and hear her crying, or those days when I would wake up after one hour of sleep to shower before Cesar went to work). But these moments won't last longer than 30 minutes, as she starts to miss being in my arms, or she just gets frustrated with something on her mat and needs a cuddle.

Back when she was a newborn it was easy to distinguish between her needs and her reasons for crying: hungry, tired, dirty diaper, gassy tummy. Once we hit the three month mark there were times that she would get grumpy just because she was bored or wanted to be held. I've heard too many people mention that you shouldn't pick up a baby every time that you hear them cry as it will spoil them. That's not the way that we work in this household. If Luna cries, she gets picked up. Even if it is sometimes annoying and I am dying to pee or to finish writing something I started 10 days ago. This is when those perfect things like slings, carriers, wraps come into play. Without them we wouldn't get anything done. First off, I can't bear to hear her cry, because crying means some kind of discomfort and I don't want my child to feel any discomfort. Secondly, by picking her up I think we are showing her that she is always going to be secure with us, and can always ask us for anything. That is so much more important than worrying about possibly "spoiling" our child (which I don't agree can happen anyway). And... There really isn't anything that can make you happier than knowing that your child feels happy, secure and loved in your arms.

One day in the very near future she will decide that she doesn't always need my help and my cuddles. She will want to play by herself and with her friends, choose her own clothes and go to the loo by herself. I want to take every single advantage of this time when she wants to be held 24/7. I know I will be a little happy-sad when she gains more independence, so I am going to cuddle and hold her as much as I can right now. Everything else (cooking, cleaning, writing, showering etc) just goes on a backburner in these moments. For example yesterday I was trying to help her take a nap and she was screaming from being overtired and refusing to sleep (one of our ongoing issues), when she finally relaxed and fell asleep in my arms I didn't want to take her to her bed and risk waking her. So I stayed on the couch for 90 minutes while she slept peacefully and read some of a book on my phone. And those 90 minutes of sleep were so important because they set the tone for the rest of the day and night (yes, sleep does beget sleep somehow). All that to say that she is not spoilt, just cared for in the way that she wants to be cared for. And if she needs to sleep with us until she is one then so be it.

I actually dislike the phrase "fussy child". I would rather use the word "sensitive". I think that some children are just more sensitive to change than other children, and it affects them in different ways. I know for a fact that when Luna is trying to learn something new she wakes up all through the night. Once she is comfortable with the new "trick" (finding her arms, rolling, finding her feet, babbling etc), she will go to sleep easily and rest properly. I started tracking her sleep tendencies and she will usually have one good day and night and 3 terrible nights. By terrible I mean that she will wake up on the hour, and if I make any sign that I am awake (apart from nursing her) she will think it's play time and refuse to go back to sleep. She has started making up her own babbling words and sings them all day long "lalalamamamagagagadadadalalal". Last night she woke up in the middle of the night, rolled over, looked up at me and said "mamamamgaga", and then went back to sleep again. As we need to save for the new bed, we recently transformed the crib into a type of cosleeper, meaning that she can roll over to be closer to me, but still be sleeping in her bed. If she had been in her crib on the other side of the room last night she would have started crying as she needed me. But instead, she went back to sleep because my presence close by reassured her. And that is honestly the most important thing for us all right now – sleep. Because sleep means healthy baby and healthy parents.

Babies are all born as different people and not all the same and I feel like we should be in tune to their sensitivities and not make them follow our routines. This is, of course, my own personal opinion. Some babies are "easy" and "calm", others cry constantly, and others are "needy" or "fussy". Instead of trying to make a child conform to what we think should be right I am completely convinced that we should bend our own rules or preferences or conveniences so they work with our child's. I really really doubt that our children are going to become spoilt brats because we rocked/nursed them to sleep or picked them up every time they cried for the first year of their lives. I suppose you can come back in a few years and ask me if I was wrong. I believe that every time a child cries it is for a very specific reason and not to be "annoying".

I used to be one of those people who hated making plans and then canceling on them, but nowadays I have been canceling more often than I feel comfortable with. But I came to terms with the fact that I have a sensitive baby and sometimes it's hard to go places when I am tired and when I don't know if she will be comfortable. She really, really dislikes the heat and especially having the sun in her eyes, so at least it's a lot more pleasurable to go out and about in September. Luna is also really bothered by her teeth, and I cannot wait for those first teeth to come out so she can catch a break! That said, she doesn't really cry very often, she gets grumpy and yells, but doesn't really cry. Maybe because I just don't let her. And if that's a bad thing then I will just continue doing this "bad thing". I'm pretty sure my mother did the same with me, and her mother with her.

And you know, we will do exactly the same thing over again if our next one is just as sensitive, because I completely believe in fully showing my love to my child. I really doubt that she will want her face covered in kisses by the time she is 5 years old, so I might as well do it now when she enjoys it. I guess I should just apologize to those we have canceled on in the past 5 months. It's just easier to stay at home sometimes. My "fussy" child has already taught me so many new things about myself and the world.

The Return of Social Awkwardness

I was a really shy child. I preferred my books and my journals and my stories to people. I got nervous around other people and never felt quite "right" in any kind of situation, apart from the times that I was with my closest friends and didn't feel like I had to hide anything. I was shy as a teen too, but that kind of changed into rebellion once I hit the age of 15. I could hide behind my hair and my cigarette smoke and my loud music. There were so many times that I wanted to say things in certain social situations, even amongst my closest friends who I trusted with all my heart, but I just couldn't. Mainly out of an irrational fear of looking like an idiot. I remember a friend of mine once saying that it is better to look like an idiot than come across as stupid, and that helped me come out of my shell slightly, but never as much as alcohol did. In hindsight you know that awkwardness is a prevalent part of life as a teen, and people deal with it in different ways, but when you are actually living it, it feels like you against the rest of the world. You know that feeling where it appears that everyone has it together and you are the only one who hasn't figured anything else out? That. My journals from 15-18 are filled with angst-ridden posts, really well-written stories that I thought would never be good enough for anything and so many questions.

I wasn't one of those people who was too shy to speak, who hid away from everything. I actually tried to hide my shyness as much as possible, and it did help that I had a wonderful group of friends and that we all felt a little like outsiders. I have so many good memories of times spent growing up with my friends, doing stupid things, drinking too much, having endless conversations about things that mattered so much to us. But my self confidence was always super low. It was never really because of something that had happened to me, more just part of me – I had always been quiet, even as a child. It was just a long and torturous path, trying to accept myself and live the life that I really wanted to live.

There were those months when I didn't want to leave the house and doing the daily tasks such as classes and work were the only things I could actually do – anything else made me feel physically ill. And then, finally, there was the time that I let go, and just started to be myself. After a year of feeling so lost and with no idea where I was going with my life I went to see my aunt and her family in Israel, and ended up staying there for a year, for the most part as a volunteer on a kibbutz. The experience completely changed my life – I was in a place where no one knew me or my past and where I could be myself and believe in myself. And it worked! I finally used my voice, had a lot of fun, made sure I experienced so many different things and made some lifelong friends. It was in my mid twenties that I learnt to be myself in front of everyone, in all social situations. I forced myself to do things that I absolutely hated (speaking in public, still hate it, won't do it again, but it was great to actually do it).

In my early 30's I learnt to be myself without any aids such as alcohol. I managed to confront all types of social situations sober, which was a great accomplishment. It was hard, but had to be done. And even though I did start drinking again for a while after three years, I didn't lose any of the confidence I had found. It took me to turn 30 to finally be completely happy with whom I had become. Of course, there were moments that I doubted myself and moments that I wanted to crawl into a hole, but I wasn't afraid to open my mouth and speak anymore.

Before I gave birth I could talk to anyone, voice my opinion when needed without any worry, carry on interesting conversations with people, act on impulse, and conquer the unknown, without any fear. Large social gatherings were not a problem, telling annoying customers (politely) to eff off out of my bar and restaurant, just part of a normal day. I even had no problem speaking in public. I would never have been able to do any of this in my teens and with a pit of fear in my stomach during my early 20's. I will always remember the day I had to present my MA thesis – I don't think I had eaten for days before and was literally a nervous wreck. I sometimes wish I had known then that it didn't really matter anyway. Ah hindsight and time and age, there are times that I could have benefited from it in my youth, just to quell my nerves a little.

A few days ago a friend of mine posted a Facebook status about how she felt like an alien in social situations since she had had her child. It totally hit home because that is exactly as I have been feeling! It's such a strange feeling, and I couldn't put my finger on it until now. It's not really that all the shyness I had fought to conquer has come back again, I still feel the same, don't have a problem going into social situations, speaking my mind or going out and about. I'm very confident as to how we are raising our child, and taking her out and about into busy areas, breastfeeding her in public. But I often feel like a deer in headlights when I am in large social gatherings and find it really hard to find the exact words I want to use when I'm trying to have a conversation with someone! It's a mix of postpartum baby brain and a light form of anxiety that I can't quite put my finger on. Someone will ask me a question and I will look at them all wide eyed and stumble over my words. I'm not anxious about going outside or being amongst other people, I just feel exactly how my friend so aptly put it, like an alien.

It's possible that no one can see it; I have become pretty adept at hiding my shyness since I was a kid, but I feel so awkward! What happened to that person who could actually string an interesting sentence of words together and interact in public? Is it possible that all my energy is spent on interacting and stimulating and tending to my child that I just don't have any left for public interaction? I'm so glad I can still write – I don't know how I would express myself otherwise! At least I have time to think about a sentence for a day or so, so that it actually makes sense and doesn't sound like "that thing I was talking about the other day, remember that?" I suppose sleep deprivation could also be part of the cause, although that is getting a lot better nowadays that I have resigned myself to going to bed at 8 or 9 and getting a 5 hour stretch at the same time as Luna.

I'm assuming it shall pass with time and I shall become as funny, witty and engaging as I was before, but until then just pretend you understand what

I mean when I stare at you with wide eyes and mutter something about that thing that I have wanted to talk to you about for ages. It was important, I promise!

Ho, Ho, Ho and a Bottle of Whiskey

The first time I had a "real" drink (as opposed to sipping the foam off a beer, or that half a glass of champagne at a parent's party) I drank a bottle of white wine, a bottle of cider and ¾ of a bottle of Baileys. It was a New Year's Eve and I was 16 years old. My mother was at a friend's NYE party and my sister and I had a few friends over, smuggled the alcohol in and some of us drank (come to think of it, the younger ones didn't really drink; only the "older" ones – we were still kind of responsible). Needless to say, my head was firmly welded to the toilet seat within 90 minutes, and I rang the New Year in by crawling to the phone and trying to pretend I was fine when my mother called us to see how we were. It served as a lesson. A big lesson. Just not the one you are probably thinking.

Never mix your drinks. If you want to keep your head out of the toilet and with the party, be smart. Stick to one type of drink and you will be grand. That was the lesson I taught myself. And after that one incident, during the next 20 years of drinking and not drinking, I threw up from alcohol less than 5 times. Great accomplishment, no? I cannot, however, count the amount of times I blacked out, said stupid things, acted very drunk, cried in a bar or probably made a fool out of myself. Black outs are scary. One moment you are having a blast, and the next you are waking up in your bed, in your sleeping clothes, wondering how on earth you got home. What happened between the last moment you remember and waking up in the morning? How did you make it home by yourself in a cab, pay the cab, get into your apartment, fold your clothes and put on sleeping clothes? It's as if your brain shuts off and your body goes on autopilot. Very, very scary when you think of it.

During the past 20 years I have had times when I will drink now and then, times when I am completely sober, times when I drink a lot and am fine and times when I drink a lot and am not fine. I've been sober for over 16 months now, and that Guinness and that shot of Jameson I had right at the time I guessed I was probably pregnant are the last drinks I will probably have in a long time, maybe forever. I have learnt to never say never as it often comes back to bite you in the face, but I have always made a promise to myself that if I ever become a mother all drinking and partying goes out the window. This is a personal choice based on my childhood and in no way to be seen as anything else. I also don't see this anymore as being sober, just as part of my life that changed when I got pregnant. Everything is different now, and that is not a bad thing. Nowadays what I really, really crave, instead of a cigarette and a shot, is a really good cup of coffee.

My up and down relationship with alcohol has been a love/hate, thwarted and twisted, calm and happy, relationship. Paradoxical, I know. Alcohol gave me wings, or so I thought. In the beginning alcohol helped me get past my shyness and be a more vocal, more fun, more extreme version of myself. Or, actually more truthfully, alcohol allowed me to show who I was without hiding behind my shy exterior. It enabled me to let go of that façade and just BE. We were all doing it, all of us in our teens and early 20's. My group was a little more extreme than others, maybe because we were all pretty much outcasts and never fit in anywhere, but we were in no way over the top. The only drugs we ever did as kids were to smoke hash. I never knew of anything really being available anyway, and drugs always scared me. I never wanted to become like my dad, let drugs ruin me. But alcohol never scared me. So many stories of drinking wine in the streets of Grenoble, sitting on statues and singing, hanging out in parks at night and crashing random people's parties just for fun. Wine meant some kind of freedom, a slight loss of control but not enough to feel out of control. I never blacked out in those days.

Then came a time when I just stopped drinking, for a few years, a time of terrible social anxiety and depression and too many existential questions, and all I had the energy to do was finish my MA thesis, go to work and read novels in bed. I think that all started with a bad reaction to only a few drinks in England that summer, a panic attack that I had never had before, but that would often come back to haunt me later on in heavily stressful periods of my life. About a year later, after I had been in Israel for a few months, I finally felt at ease enough to drink again, and not so worried that I would have another panic attack, and guess what? It was wonderful. Pure, straight vodka. Amazing. I danced all night, had so much fun, and didn't even have a hangover the next day. We liked to party, us volunteers at Kibbutz Evron. Every Friday night we would get the liquor and the beer (10 shekels for a cheap bottle of Russian vodka – bargain!), crank up the tunes and dance at the volunteer house until it was time to go to the pub. Every Saturday we would sleep in the sun and try to get rid of our hangovers. My affair with vodka lasted for years. I drank a lot in Israel, some in California, a little in London and a LOT in NYC. I think the amount of times I left half-drunken glasses of Stoli-on-the-rocks at Darkroom or at Motorcity is in the hundreds, always running between one and the other. Vodka made everything OK. Running up and down Ludlow Street on vodka-fueled energy became a normal part of my life.

Vodka was also very, very bad for me. Especially once I was living in NYC. What was always fun and easy became very difficult. It became a vicious circle, I was stressed at work and felt trapped in my job so I would stay out all night drinking, trying to forget about it. But once the morning arrived, I would have to go back to work on little or no sleep and act as a responsible and hardworking adult. The more stressed I was, the more I went out. The more I went out, the more money I spent on stupid things (who has time to do laundry when they need to sleep and party at the weekends; new clothes can just be purchased at Urban Outfitters down the street anyway). The more I went out, the more I blacked out, until I felt, and probably acted (seeing as I don't really remember), like I was going crazy. And I felt like one night I did. I don't remember anything, but it was a few nights after a wonderful New Years Eve party that I remember all of. My friends were worried about me, took me out for dinner to talk to me about it, but I had already made up my mind that I was done with it all.

While drinking was all about losing control, sobriety was all about maintaining control.

The first few months were very, very hard. I had the support of family and friends, but at the same time I felt very alone. My friends were all still doing the same thing as before, going out and partying, and I wasn't going to ask them to change just because I was, but it was often hard. I had to force myself to deal with work stress sober. I actually threw myself into work as a way to counter the need to go out and drink. I started writing more again, took up photography. I would go out to visit my mother who lived on Long Island at the time, every weekend, just to get away from all of the triggers. I lost weight from my already slim frame; I smoked even more and drank even more coffee than before. Little by little I eased myself into public situations that I used to deal with tipsy, and made it through them. After all, I could always leave and go home if it got too much. I would like to say that I got more sleep, but that isn't actually true. I slept on and off, erratic nights filled with stress and anxiety. And then, about 6 months into it, I felt much better. I was myself. I was myself all the time, everywhere. I talked to people. I even went on a few dates (awkward). I laughed, I cried, I had a few minor panic attacks, but I was finally feeling healthy and able to face everything full on again. Birthdays became a little more inventive and I felt like I was being really productive too. I saw an old friend who I had been very close with a few years before, who had moved away and who had stopped drinking too, and he told me something that struck me. He knew I would always be OK, because as much as I was going to strike rock bottom it was because I wanted to, in order to climb back up again. He was right in a sense. I had actually really liked that dark freefall, losing control and falling into a strange abyss, but I was all the more happy to climb back out of it, one step at a time.

Sobriety became a main part of my life. Once I hit the one year mark it wasn't even something I thought about that often anymore. I just didn't drink. I worked harder than I had before, sometimes pulling all nighters because I was stacking up the projects and always feeling overwhelmed. I still went out a lot, not wanting to give up the night life because I wasn't drinking anymore. I actually didn't even WANT to drink. I liked the control I had over myself, over my life. I thought I had a good rhythm going, work, friends, fun, writing, photography. Lots of time spent with my mother in her house on Long Island, early mornings, late nights, books devoured and many a 35mm film developed. After 2 years it was just my life, I had so much to feel grateful for, but in hindsight I never thought about why I was drinking just about why I had to stop. Instead of drinking to alleviate the stress I was feeling and the constant worry that I wasn't doing what I had always wanted to in life, I used work as an excuse. I took on too many projects, never said no, never drew any borders or limits. I would check my email at all time of the day and night, made myself constantly available 24/7, and literally drove myself into the ground. I would wake up in the morning after a few hours sleep where I had dreamt of ongoing projects and issues that did or didn't exist. I tried to write, but nothing except resentment came out. I tried to take a step away but there was always someone who needed me, a call to take, an issue to figure out. And then one day I just couldn't live like that anymore, and I walked away. It took me a long time, but I finally gave myself the strength and the reasons to live my life as I had always wanted to. I don't think I would have been able to do that if I hadn't have been sober, or I may have done it in a very different way and not have been able to pick myself up and figure out my next steps afterwards.

In any case, I remained sober for exactly 3 years. I had been working in a bar for a while with absolutely no pull towards drinking when one day I just said "oh fuck it, a few won't hurt, will they?". A few weeks of that and I decided to try AA. It helped, slightly, but I felt like it never really was for me. I had had my moments, but I could easily stop, right? I mean, I was never going to be as bad as I had been before... Right? I wasn't depressed because of my job anymore, so I wasn't drinking for all of the wrong reasons. So it wasn't going to hurt me anymore, right? Well, you see, this is where it gets tricky. For some these may be questions that you can easily answer with a yes or a no. I can't, and I shall try to explain why.

It's not hard for me to stop drinking. It's not hard for me to have just one drink and go home. It's also not hard for me to have a lot more than one drink and stay out way past closing time. It's not hard for me to drink and be a normally functioning human being. It's also not hard for me to get so drunk that I don't remember how I got home. All of the above never depended on how much I would drink, but always on the frame of mind I was in when I was drinking, or if I had slept enough the night before, eaten properly, etc, etc.

A break up, sad news or an argument with someone would usually mean a black-out night. Happy times would usually mean fun times. But sometimes it would get blurry, and as much as I would tell myself I could control it, I couldn't always. Sometimes I could. Some weeks I could, but then it would slowly spiral out of my control again. I could easily work without drinking, and have a lot of fun. But it was just as easy to drink while working, have just as much fun, if not more, and finish up the night pretty sober. Or drunk. I didn't like to get drunk at work though, it was just better to have a little buzz to get through the night and then maybe get drunk afterwards. Or not. It's a lot easier to work back to back shifts without a hangover. But it's also easy to get rid of said hangover with a couple of shots of whiskey. I love bartending, always will, and have never had an issue with bartending sober. Or drunk.

I've had a lot of fun drinking. I've also had a lot of fun sober. I've had moments when I wasn't much fun drinking and moments where I wasn't much fun sober. I've been depressed when drunk and depressed when sober. I've been a happy drunk and a sad drunk and a crazy drunk. I've also been happy and sad and crazy while sober, just a lot more contained about it. At times I have been a worry to myself and a worry to others. From day one alcohol was a way for me to express certain feelings and actions and sides of me that I was too shy to expose to the world. It was a tool to liberate myself from certain binds that I had tied around myself. I always promised myself that I wouldn't let it get the better of me, not like addiction had done to other people in my family. I was stronger than that.

Maybe I was, maybe I wasn't. But I can say with conviction that that life is behind me now.

The day I found out I was pregnant was the day that I consciously made significant changes in my life. These were not changes that were only meant to last 40 weeks, but different paths that I wanted to take in my life. I've known for a very, very long time that I cannot always control my drinking when I am drinking. I've also known for a very long time that for someone with a slight frame I can ingest way too much alcohol and still function (this is not really a positive thing, believe me). I have also known for a very, very, very long time that I will not be raising a child and subjecting her to my drinking habits, even if they are contained and few and far between. So when I immediately stopped drinking and smoking due to my pregnancy it was for the long haul.

As I said earlier, I can't or won't say the word never. I can't say I will never have a drink again. I can however say that I will never be that person drinking whiskey in a bar at 5am again. I don't want to drink again. I don't feel like drinking again. I don't even think about drinking again, and I'm not even kidding myself about this. I love bars and pubs and nighttime, and I am more than comfortable hanging out in them sober. I'm not doing this for anyone else but myself – I didn't stop drinking for my daughter or for my boyfriend. I stopped drinking for myself, so I could be the mother I always dreamed of being. I will never be perfect, but at least I can strive to avoid showing what could be the worst side of me. I've now been sober for over 16 months and although for 9 of those months I was pregnant and for the rest I have been breastfeeding, it's been very easy. And if it ever gets hard then I will go to a meeting, find a sponsor and stick with it. I will never lie to my daughter about who I am and what I have done in my life, because it's a part of me and a part of my past and my education, and I won't lie about my reasons for not drinking either.

I feel that I have only really touched upon the subject to be honest, there is so much more to say about it, but maybe that can be said in all of the little stories and anecdotes and essays that I have slowly been compiling over the years. Sad, happy, funny, silly, compelling, embarrassing, lovely, heartwarming and interesting stories. I have many of them that should, could and also maybe shouldn't be told.

Autumn Time

A year ago I was in California for my brother's wedding, enjoying the time with my family, seeing old friends and loving the gorgeous weather. I was also missing Cesar terribly and 16-18 weeks pregnant. It was about that time that I had started showing, and I knew that it was the last time in a long, long while that I was going to be able to have a holiday where I could really, completely relax, all by myself. It really was lovely – I even had a pedicure twice, and made the most of the time I wasn't working to sit around and read a lot, as well as go around taking photos of ghost towns, Día de los Muertos celebrations and pumpkin patches with my mother. I was going to try to take Luna out there before Thanksgiving but it's just not possible right now. There are so many things that are on the more-necessary to buy list before plane tickets, and Cesar just can't take the time off right now... Maybe early next year, after the holidays.

So this year we are setting up our own Día de los Muertos altar at home, a tradition I really wanted to start with Luna. I love Halloween, always have, and I love bringing a tradition that is part of her father's heritage into our home. I also love having a boyfriend who is super creative and who can pretty much make something out of nothing, and make it look really cool at the same time. I really wanted to get some real sugar skulls, so we went to Corona yesterday (only a couple of subway stops from us) and found skeletons and pastries and pan de muerto. We ate huge burritos but didn't find any sugar skulls. I will have to actually make some next year... Luna had great fun hugging the pumpkin for photos and seemed to love the Halloween playlist I compiled a few years back. I promise, I do balance out her music! We were listening to Mozart the other day! She seems to enjoy absolutely everything at the moment, apart from sweet potato but that is a story for another day.

I've been doing some freelance writing work here and there, and am finally beginning to get more offers. I just did a paid test for a company that runs a really cool website. The projects are not something I would normally do, but it would be really great to get the job as it's fun and different. Ten to twenty hours a week, work on my schedule, decently paid... More information to come if I actually get it, but fingers and toes crossed. I'm finding it hard to make time for anything outside of looking after Luna at the moment, so I need to figure out a way to be a little more productive if I am going to work at home regularly, continue writing my personal stuff and make sure the house is clean and that we are all eating correctly. And sleeping. Still very important. Sometimes I don't know where the days go! We are often out and about as I want to make sure we do things outside of the house and see people and that I maintain adult interaction, but it leaves less time in general for writing.

I think that's why I got a little frustrated with myself the other day. I want to make sure I post something on my blog every couple of days. But then I don't want to post just anything... I have many half-written essays that I need to finish, reviews I want to write, photography projects I would love to do, short stories that are waiting to become fiction, and they will all be released and realized at some point, along with many pieces that will eventually flock into my brain as they are wont to. It's always a catch-22 with me though: on the one hand I think I should be able to reach a wider audience, but on the other I wonder why anyone would want to bother reading what I write anyway. I mean, I created a Facebook page for myself as a writer so that I could keep it separate from my personal page. But I don't want to invite friends to "like" it because I don't want to seem pushy. Yet I write about very personal things at times and share them with the world. Yes, I can be very silly at times. Another reason why I would love to have a crack at this potential job – my name would be attached to everything I write. This is all part of my resolve to start doing more and thinking less. Actually, less procrastination. I quite like thinking to be honest.

Doyle, my old roommate Beth's dog, has been staying with us this past week. He's such a sweetheart, an old soul, and is content to sleep on the couch and not be any bother at all. We think he had a very stressful life before he was found running around a dog park in Fort Greene, and he is such a happy, lovely dog. As much as I thought Luna would want to play with him, she is still much more interested in Joey and pulling his tail. Cesar has decided that he needs to prove to me that we can have a dog (as well as a baby and a cat and another baby at some point) and has been taking care of most of the walks, as despite all of Doyle's wonderful sides, he loves to pull on the leash, and it's hard for me to walk him when I am also carrying Luna. So we are coming to a compromise, because I really want a dog too… It has to be a rescue that is very good with children and cats, and we need to get pet insurance from the bat. Dogs are a lot more expensive than cats, and we already have enough expenses as it is. I have always wanted a bull terrier to call Bullseye, just like Bill Sykes' dog in *Oliver Twist*. We shall see. It won't happen right now, but at some point we will have a doggie. I bet we will end up getting a dog and then find out I am pregnant with triplets or something like that. (I hope not). But if we have a dog, he or she needs to be seriously well trained, and I just don't have the time or energy to do that. But Cesar at least has the energy to, so I won't need to worry about that part!

I read some of my first (and last) parenting book, *Bringing up bébé*. Where on earth did all these labels for parenting come from?! It's crazy. Am I supposed to categorize myself into a parenting camp? (That was a rhetorical question and the answer is NO). I found the book fun to read at first, as I grew up in France and completely related to a lot of the descriptions in the book, but I didn't relate to the author at all. For me everything she was learning was common sense. And then during the sleeping chapter I started to think we had done everything wrong and I had ruined Luna for life… So I shut the book and returned it to the library. Oh… Actually I lie. I have read parts of another book, one that a friend lent to me and that I should probably return, but that one was a general baby book with great breastfeeding and bedsharing tips. But anyway, that was my last foray into parenting books and we will continue how we started.

And I will spend my precious reading time reading something way more important like the newest Alan Furst.

I'm nowhere near as tired as I was a few months ago, although I still dream of a long night of interrupted sleep. I've just learnt that trying to cram everything I want to do between the time Luna goes to sleep and when she wakes up is not actually that beneficial to me. It's just better to go to sleep early and get some semblance of rest. Nowadays I also avoid phone calls after 6pm. I know it's easier for many people to chat in the evening, but it's the only time I actually get any "me" time, when I can let my brain sit in silence or drown itself in music or words, and I need that time to be a happy mummy. I do like our little non-schedule that we have set up these days with early mornings and breakfast, favorite TV shows and baby naps and mid-morning food and walks and talks and more naps and play time (alone and together), and cooking time and cleaning time and outing time and finally bath and bed time. It's flexible and predictable at the same time, something that seems to work for all of us. I think becoming a mother has really calmed the internal anxiety that I used to always carry around, as much as I still worry about things, I do not let them nag away at me incessantly. Basically, I just feel more relaxed nowadays. Not a bad thing really!

I should probably finish this before Luna wakes up again and I accidentally fall asleep next to her... The amount of times I wake up around 2am, fully clothed and wondering what happened, is more of a regular occurrence than not.

Día de los Muertos

I love holidays and birthdays and celebrations of all sorts, to organize parties and dinners and decorations and cakes for others. I feel that everyone should have a cake on their birthday and should be made to feel special for at least a few minutes. I love all the traditions that my parents started with us and that I hope to continue with my daughter. I love that over the years I have adopted French traditions and holidays and US traditions and holidays, and now, thanks to my boyfriend, Mexican traditions and holidays. Last year when I was in California I learnt more of the Día de los Muertos (Day of the Dead) traditions and really wanted to make sure that we celebrated them too. Halloween is one of my favorite holidays (nothing surprising there), and I feel this is an awesome way to extend the holiday by a few days with the celebration.

The Día de los Muertos tradition can be traced back thousands of years, to the indigenous people of the area that is Mexico today. Although it may have more modern religious connotations today it is really mainly a tradition where one celebrates the dearly departed over the days of October 31st, November 1st and November 2nd. People usually create an altar with photos of dead family members and friends, with candles, offerings, skulls, sugar skulls, flowers, poems or stories, pan de muerto (special bread made for the occasion) and anything else that may be relevant to the people they are celebrating. Traditions differ from family to family, region to region; some people use the day to clean the graves of their beloved, others remember them in different fashions. We decided to create our own altar at home and will probably build on it every year.

We found pan de muerto and skeleton cookies in Corona (Queens), cardboard skeletons and spiders in a decoration shop and black and red candles at the dollar store. We used pumpkins, scarves, purple lights, a really real-looking skull, cards and black cardboard backdrops. And most importantly, we printed out photos of loved ones who have passed away, family and friends, and made them the centre part of the display. Then we also printed out pictures of our favorite musicians who are no longer with us and added them to the altar. While Cesar was mainly in charge of the design and lay-out, I wrote two pieces, and put them in the coffin-shaped cards that we found. In the end it looked really, really cool (even after Joey jumped on it and sprayed the carpet and himself with black candle wax). I think it's so important to remember and talk about those people who are no longer here, and I would really love for Luna to think of her grandfathers and great-grandparents who have left us as if she had known them. And of course, aesthetically both Cesar and I just love this whole idea. Next year I would love to make our own Catrina dolls and dress them up! Maybe we could all go dressed like that for Halloween... Who knows...

We dressed Luna in her adorable little vampire bat costume for Halloween this year and spent a while taking cute pictures of her trying to maul a pumpkin. No trick or treating as she can't eat candy yet, let alone walk, so I really don't see the point. I have enough candy at home anyway! We already have an awesome costume idea for next year when she will hopefully be on her feet and be able to talk a little and actually say "trick or treat". We took some photos outside after lunch, and then after Cesar went off to work, I spent the late afternoon and evening watching The Addams Family and Beetlejuice, and dancing to the Rocky Horror Picture Show with Luna. Actually sounds like an average day or evening in the Castro-Hughes household to be honest. Maybe next year I will have to do the opposite and play movies like Mary Poppins and Annie, just to be contrary. And we could dress up all in pastel pink and white and listen to happy pop music... Sounds a little torturous, but could be fun. So many ideas!

Here is the text that I wrote that now resides on our Dia de los Muertos altar:

You are our fathers, our grandfathers, our grandmothers, our aunts, our uncles, our dogs, our cats and our friends. All gone too soon from our lives, because never is not an option in life. We love you and think of you often, even after years and years have gone by. There will always be the memories, the photos, the good times and the bad times. The first steps and the last steps, the mountains and the valleys. The cities and the villages, the desert and the ocean. England, France, Mexico, California, NYC. The words, the thoughts, the barks, the meows, the hugs, the kisses, the love that is everlasting. Rest in peace our friends and family members and beloved pets. You are always with us, your spirit lives on in all of us and all around us.

Some of you comforted us in our childhood, during our tumultuous teenage years, on into adulthood. Others appeared earlier, or later, but all of you left us with a firm stamp on our hearts and a lasting impression in our brains. You sang us to sleep, you appeared in our dreams, you helped us through our tears, you made us dance all night and you always made sure we never felt alone. You still do all of that. You may not be on this earth anymore, but you are in our hearts and we will pass your music and your words on to our children, and our children will pass them on to their children, just like our parents passed your creations (at least some of them) on to us. Music lives on forever and without the music you left us with we wouldn't have all of the memories it helped create today. Rest in peace Tim, Jeff, Kurt, Janis, Freddie, Peter, Mia, Lou, Marc and all of you who have left us with sounds that shape our lives.

We Will Just Celebrate Thanksgiving Next Week

Don't read any further if you don't want to hear about projectile vomiting and baby viruses!

Well, we did have plans. Cesar had both Wednesday and Thursday off, and we were going to do grocery shopping on Wednesday and then spend Thursday, Thanksgiving, cooking delicious food, watching movies and cuddling. Maybe Luna could even taste a new food. We were going to cook chicken pot pie for Cesar, vegetable pot pie for me, roasted carrots, potatoes, parsnips, brussel sprouts, mashed potatoes, Yorkshire puddings, pecan pie, key lime pie (our favorite). It was our first Thanksgiving as a family of three, and with Luna being the only American among us, we wanted to start our own little traditions. Well, all was not REALLY lost – we did watch a lot of movies and we did all cuddle together for the most of 4 days. All day and all night.

That scene in The Exorcist comes to mind. You know, the infamous projectile vomiting scene? Just picture a 7 month old baby doing it. We have been blessed with the fact that Luna has not been sick at all for the first 8 months of her life. No unexplained fevers, no ear infections, vomiting (she barely spat up, ever). No, she decided to save all of that up and just get a really horrid virus that in itself was harmless, but at the same time pretty scary. A virus that lasted the most part of a week, and that week happened to be the week of Thanksgiving.

Tuesday morning I took Luna in to the pediatrician's for a booster shot, but she already had a slight temperature so we decided to postpone it. She had some kind of viral upper respiratory infection so the doctor gave her some medicine for the fever which she proceeded to vomit right back up all over me and the floor. We tried again and she kept it down (little did I know that that was the first of many times I would be changing my clothes over the next few days). By Tuesday evening her temperature was over 101 and all she wanted to do was nurse, and nurse, and nurse, but couldn't sleep. At around 11pm we FaceTimed Cesar at work, and 10 minutes later she started (literally) to projectile vomit. Her poor little face looked so surprised at what was happening, probably matching the look on my face. And that set the pace for the next 3 days… Fever, nursing, vomiting, crying, cuddling, no sleep, nursing, fever, Tylenol, vomiting, nursing and so on. By Thursday evening we had all slept about 3 hours in total since Monday night. I told Cesar that if we all didn't get some proper sleep sometime soon we would all collapse… That didn't happen (the collapsing that is), and Luna's fever broke on Friday morning after a good few hours of sleep. Yay!! Finally over! I did the (huge amount of) laundry, Cesar went off to work in the evening and Luna had a good few naps. And then she barely slept again. We got up early on Saturday and Luna was in seemingly good spirits when all of a sudden she developed a red rash all over her body and started vomiting profusely and was acting very lethargically which is completely out of character. I had already called her doctor around noon when the rash appeared but by 2pm she hadn't called back so we just went to the ER.

Luna's sees her cardiologist at New York Hospital Queens so we went to the ER there (Flushing Hospital is actually a little closer, but not by much). The nurse actually rushed us through due to the rash but once she had been assessed it was determined it was most likely Roseola. We were sent to a room to wait for the (lovely) attending doctor who confirmed it was indeed Roseola (also known as Sixth Disease). It is apparently a common and highly contagious, but harmless infection that can happen in young children, usually before the age of two. Basically it starts as a viral infection like a cold, with 3-5 days of sustained fever and the day after the fever breaks a full body rash develops. FULL, HEAD TO TOE, BRIGHT RED BODY RASH. That coupled with the vomiting was enough to warrant a hospital visit in my opinion, especially as her pediatrician hadn't even called back yet.

The doctor was a little worried about dehydration and had me feed Luna 2 oz of Pedialyte along with a few short nursing sessions, and had us wait to make sure she kept it down and peed in a diaper. By this time Luna had totally perked up again. Cesar had had to leave us a while before that as no one could cover him at work and at this point I just wanted to go home and get Luna to bed, so the doctor released us. Luna ended up sleeping about 11 hours with a couple of very short dream feeds, and has napped most of today, so I finally feel like this is all going to be a distant memory very soon, and we will all be able to catch up on some sleep... Although I feel like I am coming down with something now, which would be just my luck!

Oh, and Luna's pediatrician did call me back, six hours after I left the message with her receptionist, just to tell me that she thought it was Roseola. Pity she couldn't have called me back between patients to tell me that... As much as I think she is a nice person, we need to change doctors. She is obviously overworked and it might have avoided the visit to the ER if she had just quickly called me earlier in the day. I'm not one to rush to the hospital with any random ailment, I'm actually not even one to rush to the doctor for myself, but when it concerns my daughter I tend to worry. I mean who wouldn't? It was scary enough to learn about her CHD, but at least that is asymptomatic for now and won't require surgery until she is a little older, but it's something that is always in the back of my mind. But a sudden body rash is also scary, at least for first time parents who have never experienced this before! I'm so happy that I am still breastfeeding as nursing is obviously a comfort to Luna, and I don't know if we would have been able to get her to drink anything else.

So, we shall be celebrating Thanksgiving a week later, with pot pies and roasted veggies and pecan pies and key lime pies, and hopefully no fevers or projectile vomiting or sleepless nights! And I am very, very thankful that this illness is over and hope that we won't have to go through that again for a long, long time (never is probably too much to ask)!

Adapting

The other day, out of the blue, Cesar asked me if I ever get lonely when I'm at home alone with the baby. He works long hours and has a 90 minute commute each way, so he is often away from the house for 12-16 hours at a time. The question brought me back to the early days, about two to three months after Luna was born, and I started to compare that time to today. I don't feel lonely at all today. Sometimes I don't actually feel there is enough time in the day to get everything done! With looking after Luna, writing and delivering assignments on time, keeping the house somewhat clean and tidy, grocery shopping, and cooking food, I sometimes wish that I didn't get so tired by 11pm and could work later into the night on my own personal writing! It's not like the old days when I could subsist on a few hours of sleep a night; with breastfeeding and running after a very active 8 month old all day, I need at least 4 hours nowadays. Not that I get much uninterrupted sleep yet, but that's another story… When I feel I need more adult interaction, or just a change of scenery, I make plans with friends, go into the city or call someone. Friends come and visit and I love to go out on visits myself. Luna is a real city child, she loves the subway, loves interacting with other people and is comfortable hanging out in the Ergo all day, sitting in restaurants and walking around.

When I think back to 5 or 6 months ago I know I felt a little lonely and isolated at times. If I had to do it all over again I don't think we would have moved to a neighborhood we didn't know at all, in the middle of the worst winter in a while at 34 weeks pregnant. There was so much snow and I was still working 50-60 hours a week so we never really got to explore the neighborhood before Luna was born. And then after the 39th week it took so long for me to waddle anywhere! During those first few weeks after Luna was born I was way too sleep deprived to even care about conversing with anyone. Cesar was working upwards of 80 hours a week and when Luna was about two months old and I started feeling normal again I suddenly realized that the days would often stretch out. I would try to go to the city when I could but there were so many days that it all seemed too tiring, or it was too hot, or Luna was cranky. We would go for walks in the neighborhood, go to the Rite Aid around the corner or the Chinese supermarkets and made friends with the people working there, just to have an actual conversation with an adult human being. Some friends came to visit; others kind of disappeared off the face of the earth. Nothing wrong with that (the latter), I've been in the same position before and probably not made as much as an effort as I could have done. It's part of life.

In hindsight those few months were really all about adaptation. I went from working in a busy restaurant until I was 39 weeks along to being at home with a tiny baby in a neighborhood that I didn't know. I was used to running around at work and talking to many people every day. I was used to spending all my time with Cesar, at work and out of work. Orchard Street was sort of like a family and it was a little strange not seeing all the regulars on a daily basis. I didn't miss going out, I didn't actually really miss anything, I was really just trying to adapt to my own new life. Spending more time with other friends who have children, getting into a new kind of routine, figuring out how to find time to be able to write and freelance. Getting to really explore Flushing and actually learn to love living here. You can only imagine life with a newborn, but you never really know how it will be until you are living it. And even then it has a tendency to change every week! And you just learn to relax and adapt accordingly. The emotions, the worries, the laughs and that love that is unlike anything you have ever felt before. Of course, like with anything, there are still some days when I miss the hustle and the bustle of working in a restaurant, but on those days we make a quick trip into the city to visit everyone, and by the time we get home I'm happy to be home again.

I'm still me. I still like the same things, dance to the same songs, read the same books and wear the same clothes (although maybe a size or two larger). I still have the same thoughts and dreams; they are just a little bit bigger nowadays! On top of everything I was before I am now a mother too. And it's the most amazing role I have ever had to live. But it's not always easy, and if anyone ever feels lonely or isolated contact me and I will be over as soon as I can, or call you for a chat if you aren't nearby. Sometimes we all just need someone else to talk to.

Christmasses Past, Present and Future

And while Luna sleeps curled around my full belly, that sleep that only babies have when they have had their fill of sleepy mothers milky, I reflect on Christmasses past, those of many, many years ago, those of not that far ago in the recent past.

Those times in the tiny village in England, a few decades ago, a pretty Christmas tree and snow on the ground, listening for Father Christmas from the top of my bunk bed, wondering if I would be able to hear the reindeer land on the roof. Pillow cases full of presents under the tree on Christmas morning, playing in the snow with Daddy and eating our full of dinner made by Mummy. The same food that I continue to make at Christmas today, in some shape or form.

There was that Christmas is Holland that wasn't really Christmas because everyone celebrated Sinterklaas on December 5th, where we felt a little strange and out of place, as if Christmas had just been postponed for a year and would be back the next when we flew back home to be with the rest of our family. England just always felt just the way it should at Christmas with the lights and the bells and the shops and the TV shows and the tinsel and the songs. While I spent many a Christmas in France growing up, amidst the snowy mountains, a fairytale Winter city, nothing beat the Christmas feeling in England. Mainly due to nostalgia of those Christmasses spent as a child waiting for Father Christmas to surprise us, leaving mince pies for the reindeer and school plays with The Snowman song in the background. Watching Scrooge (the one with Albert Finney and Alec Guinness) and listening to The Pogues and Wham and Band Aid.

Then came the time when I would travel across the ocean to California to spend Christmas with my family, discover new friends and new traditions, Christmas in the warmer weather and the sun, everything so much newer and cleaner and bigger. A strange type of Christmas which felt paradoxically home-like and very, very foreign. There was one Christmas spent in Israel where 12 of us all banded together and had our own Christmas dinner and party in the volunteer house, the kibbutzniks helping us have a merry Christmas away from home, in a country where the majority of the population does not celebrate the holiday. A mix of different traditions and foods from all around the world, celebrated altogether. A Christmas Day spent on the beach in Tel Aviv, sunshine, falafel, bourekas and sachleb, with bare feet in the sea.

And then, 10 years ago, New York City became my home. The city that brings Christmas to life like no other. Christmas trees for sale on the streets, beautiful lights all over the city, pop-up ice skating rinks and beautifully decorated trees, snow and ice and shows and laughter. Christmas parties and Christmas dinners, the search for Christmas crackers and Mr Kipling's mince pies. Every year new traditions were created, until this year when for the first time in our lives, I spent my first Christmas with both of my loves together, my wonderful boyfriend and my beautiful daughter. The excitement at finding that perfect present, wrapping it up and putting it under the tree, waiting to see how she would unwrap it on Christmas morning. Devising menus for Christmas Eve and Christmas Day, based on our own childhood traditions and ones that we wanted to create. Waking up together and dressing up, just because we felt like it. Wishing people a Merry Christmas on our walk and feeling so happy and blessed, as this is how life should be.

While I reflect on all of those special moments in the past and this Christmas that has just gone by, I also have to think of those in the future, and how one day I hope that Cesar and I will be able to sit back and watch our children and grandchildren create their own traditions. Christmas will always be my favorite holiday, and there will always be something so special about it, something that transcends the gifts and the food, a feeling of happiness, joy and gratefulness.

And Then There Were Four

Less than a year ago we had just found our new apartment in Queens and were getting ready to move. I was in my third trimester and looking forward to make our new place into a home before Luna's arrival in April. And now this January Luna is 9 months old... And I'm nearly 10 weeks pregnant with her little sister or brother! It was no real surprise to us as we have been talking about having another child for months. I know it may seem like I was only just pregnant with Luna and we are already having another child, but they will actually be 17 months apart, which to Cesar and I is a decent age gap. There are 23 months between my sister and I and we are very close. I would love for Luna and her sibling to experience that closeness too!

I had an amazing pregnancy with Luna, and I missed those little kicks, the hiccups, the good days and even the bad days. I loved reading up on what was new with the baby every week. I embraced the changes that my body went through and also loved thinking about the unknown that would be labor, delivery, postpartum recovery and living with a newborn baby. I'm really excited to experience all of that again, this time with more knowledge and insight, and probably with some surprises along the way too. Some things are already very different, I have been suffering from debilitating "morning sickness" (which should actually be called "all day and night constant terrible nausea that makes it extremely difficult to function as a normal human being") for the past three weeks now, and it's a lot worse than it was when I was pregnant with Luna. There is no way that I would have been able to hide this like I did with Luna in the restaurant! Nothing helps alleviate it this time around, and as I don't want to take any kind of medication I am just going to wait it out. It's not too bad staying at home and around Flushing – I have quite a bit of work right now and Luna needs a lot of attention so our days are pretty full!

I am definitely calmer about certain things with this pregnancy but at the same time more stressed about others. We have a lot to think about (and a lot of time to plan), and I am adamant I will not have the same experience during labor and delivery as I did the first time. Even though I thought I was informed, it was nothing like I expected. I doubt everything will go according to plan this time around either, but at least I am taking a different approach, and feel that I can open my mouth and voice my concerns and wishes a lot better. We also have to have so many more tests this time around. Some of them because I am now 36, which means over 35, and therefore of "advanced maternal age", which does make me feel slightly old! As long as the tests are non-invasive we are having them (an NT scan at 12 weeks and a blood test). I will not be doing any type of invasive testing as this is just not for us. We will also be having several fetal echocardiograms after 18 weeks, because Luna's heart defects went undetected until she was three months old, so we now get more tests to make sure it doesn't happen again. Not that that bothers me, the more often we get to see our little baby the better!

There are so many thoughts racing through my head, I look at Luna and my heart bursts with so much love and I wonder how it will be when I have another little blessing in my arms. I wonder how I am going to make sure that Luna gets the same amount of attention she gets now while at the same time I give the new baby the same amount of attention I gave Luna. I wonder if he or she will be a "bad" sleeper like Luna, or if he or she will fall asleep whenever he or she is tired. I wonder if I am going to be able to breastfeed both of them together as there is no way Luna is going to self-wean just yet (and I'm not interested in weaning her so early). So many thoughts and so many moments wondering about everything. I actually love those moments in the middle of the night, when I have just fed Luna and she has gone back to sleep, those moments before I go back to sleep when I imagine a hundred different scenarios. Wouldn't it be funny if this baby looks just like me, but with Cesar's skin tone and auburn hair? Will we have a boy or a girl? How fast will this year go by?

I'm so excited… And nervous and overwhelmed and ready for this, altogether. I can't wait to document the continuation of this amazing journey that we started with Luna!

What a Difference Two Weeks Can Make

Two weeks ago...

I feel so brain dead! I haven't read a book in weeks now as it hurts my tired eyes to read on my phone's Kindle app (and I still haven't learnt to read in the dark next to my sleeping daughter who still wakes up on average 3/6 times a night to nurse – although I am pretty sure 90% of the time it is to comfort nurse and who am I to deny her comfort?). I haven't written anything in a while apart from a few assignments here and there. It's not that I don't have the time; I just don't have the energy. While Luna's first trimester was full of nausea and fatigue and worries, this new little one's first trimester has been full of debilitating, constant nausea, insomnia and extreme fatigue. I've been falling asleep early, often into an unintended slumber around 8pm with Luna, only to wake up around midnight or 1am, wide awake, to finally get back to sleep around 4am... Only to then wake up at 7am by kisses or slaps in the face, meaning that Luna is awake and ready to party. I've never been a good sleeper, but I really need this extra sleep, because not only do I have a little munchkin growing inside me, I'm also still breastfeeding Luna pretty consistently through-out the day.

So bring it on second trimester awesomeness! I could really do with some of that boosting energy and glow right now! It would help if winter would take its long yearly nap and leave spring to take over. These days of negative one million degrees, of ice and snow were tedious enough when I was 9 months pregnant with Luna last year, but they are even worse when you have an infant who screams at the whisper of an icy wind on her face. So while we have been cooped up in the apartment for too many hours and too many days, Luna has developed a severe bout of separation anxiety... And there we were, thinking that we had got past that stage unscathed. Oh no... I can't even go to the loo without her breaking out into eardrum-piercing screams, the end of the world as she knows it. It will pass, as will the sleepless nights and the constant need to nurse through-out the night. I mean, she's not going to want her milky when she's a teenager, is she?! Ha.

Today...

It's amazing how things can change over just a few short weeks! Spring is coming in fast, the mounds of ice and snow have practically all melted, and I am now 16 weeks along, into my second trimester and feeling so much better! The nausea finally started to wane around 14 weeks, and now only rears its ugly head if I don't eat often enough through-out the day. While I packed on the pounds really fast with Luna, things are a little different with this one. I was already bigger than I was before I got pregnant with Luna (not hard there), but I'm also still breastfeeding, and plan on continuing through-out the pregnancy if I can. Luna has shown no signs of giving it up yet anyway! So I don't feel like I've put on TOO much weight yet (or I am refusing to admit it). I've read a lot on the subject of breastfeeding while pregnant, asked a few friends if they have done it, but funnily enough not too many have (I actually only know one person who was able to nurse through-out her second pregnancy!). The ladies at the WIC office were at a bit of a loss as they didn't know how to counsel me properly (which gave me the incentive to do the training to become a breastfeeding counselor after this pregnancy). While I know that my milk supply will probably diminish substantially over this trimester, I hadn't noticed a difference until last week. Luna started waking up with a dry diaper, she was fussy and grumpy, and started wanting to nurse through-out the night again. At the same time she had really started to eat more regular food, so I thought that that was it... I tried to give her some formula but she spat it out and continued to nurse (I tasted it, it was disgusting so I totally understand the spitting it out)... This week everything seems back to normal again, so I guess either my supply really dipped and she knew it, or it was actually a growth spurt and I was just too worried about having to stop nursing her before we both wanted to.

So we shall continue as we have been and hope to make it at least another 3-8 weeks, past her first birthday.

I've finally been feeling a lot more motivated again, to write, read, think, imagine... With the temperatures rising slowly, the days getting longer and the knowledge that in less than half a year now we will be four and not three anymore, I feel that there is so much I want to accomplish! Write more, save money, sort out different administrative things I keep putting off, plan for what our life is going to become during the second half of 2015. I have no doubt that it is going to be hard. Yes, amazing of course, but it will be hard. When Luna was born I had nothing to compare it to, and now I know. Granted, Luna has always been a high needs baby, but at least we will be prepared for two high needs babies together! And while I am so excited about having another child, I want to make the most of these months where Luna will still be an only child, these months when my attention is focused solely on her and her needs and wants. I feel like I was a really boring mother during the first couple of months of this pregnancy, when I could barely move due to nausea, and we ended up spending many an hour in her play are reading books and making up silly stories to pass the time. Now that the sun is out we need to make the most of it and get some much needed Vitamin D!

I don't know if it's because things change in the space of a couple of years, or because I'm getting better prenatal care this time around, or just because I'm 36 and not 35 anymore, but I had an NT scan at 13 weeks (an ultrasound meant to check the size of the nuchal translucency behind the baby's neck, a larger than normal accumulation of fluid can be a soft marker for a chromosome abnormality, but can also be a sign of a heart defect). I also had a blood test to check for signs of Downs Syndrome. All came back as looking fine. Not that it would have made any difference to us anyway, but I guess it's good to be prepared. Because I refused any type of invasive screening they offered me one of those new non-invasive fetal blood screening tests which are about 95% accurate. Turns out everything looks good and we are having another girl! For some reason I was sure we were going to have a boy, but now we get to use the beautiful name that we had picked out for a girl months ago (and will only reveal when she is born).

And while this is the time to kick back, relax and enjoy the second trimester, I will still be a little antsy until we have the fetal echocardiogram and then the anatomy scan in the beginning of April. I feel a little jealous thinking back to Luna's anatomy scan, and while we were nervous, we were more excited about finding out if she was a boy or girl. Now I just want to make sure that this little one's heart is fully formed and functioning correctly. Funny how sometimes ignorance is bliss...

What Did I Learn?

I was thinking about writing this piece around 3am this morning when I couldn't get back to sleep again. Thinking about how April 1st last year, how it was (and will always be), my little brother's birthday, but last year it was always Luna's due date. She didn't actually make an appearance for another 8 days, but during this week I shall be reflecting on the past year a lot, thinking about what changed, what didn't and what I learnt through becoming a mother and living through the first insane, intense and overwhelming year. So what did I learn?

- That my body can survive on little to no sleep for a VERY LONG TIME. Let's be truthful about it. I haven't really slept for a year. Luna has never, ever slept through the night (even when you use the true meaning of sleeping through the night which actually means 6 hours straight). And while not completely typical she is definitely is not alone. Some kids' sleep is affected more than others by a multitude of things (growth spurts, teething etc), and no amount of sleep training or trying to fill them up more at night or trying to replace the boob with water is ever going to change this. Sleep training is not for us, I refuse to leave Luna to cry, because she won't put herself to sleep, she will just cry until she vomits. Not that it had ever been an option anyway. We just figured out a way to make it work for all of us, and my body functions fine on an interrupted sleep. And I'm not one to complain either; she is growing well and thriving, so we must be doing something right!

- I never imagined the depths of love that open up the moment you hear your child's first cry. The amount of time I have spent just staring at Luna in amazement at the fact that Cesar and I created this beautiful little being! The times I have not been able to go to sleep because I'm content listening to the sound of her breathing right next to me, ready to anticipate when she will wake up next to make sure that she doesn't cry. Watching her go from rolling over to crawling to standing up to practically walking. That first time that she looked at me and said "MAMA!" and wanting to tell everyone in the world how it made me cry and laugh at the same time. And there is so much more to come!

- That sometimes you will get thrown a curveball that you never saw coming, and that it will hit you right in the face, but with that you keep on moving, keep going forward and continue to fight the fight. I would never, ever want anyone to have to go through finding out your child has a congenital birth issue, in Luna's case her heart, but it is really difficult to understand if you haven't been through something similar yourself. It's like you have a ticking time bomb continuously going on in the back of your mind. You check your child's breathing rhythm more often, her skin color, her temperature. When she stops gaining weight but is eating every couple of hours you start worrying if it is her heart. Will she need her operation earlier? How are we going to keep her still during the next echocardiogram? Why is she not sleeping properly anymore? You don't make a big deal out of it because your child is going to live life like any other child, but it's always there in your thoughts.

- That you don't need to listen or follow everyone's advice, especially when you didn't ask for it in the first place. We have instincts for a reason and they should be followed in my opinion.

You know your child better than anyone else, so you should know what is best for him or her! If I had listened to one OB that I saw before choosing another back in January I would have had to stop breastfeeding under the sole reason that I was pregnant again and you can't breastfeed while pregnant. Well I knew that was absolute BS and now have a doctor who totally supports the fact that I will not be weaning my daughter when it poses absolutely no risk to my pregnant self or baby. I'm also a big proponent of following what YOU feel is best. If my child is crying I tend to her needs, even if it means she just wants to cuddle and nurse all day; but at the same time I let her figure things out by herself too. Sometimes they fall, but it is all part of learning, you just try to make sure that any fall isn't going to be too bad. Sometimes they pick up dirt from the ground and put it in their mouths, so you just try and make sure that you vacuum once a day. Germs aren't all bad, we need them to build up a strong immune system. And you know what? Your house is not going to be clean and tidy every day anymore, and you learn to be OK with that. Somewhat anyway!

- That it is OK to want or need a break now and again. This is one of my main issues in all parts of my life: I refuse to acknowledge that I sometimes need a break from things, until I get so overwhelmed I don't know what to do with myself. And being the mother of a high needs infant really teaches you that it's OK to need a moment alone here and there, a moment to write, to read, to shower alone without a little monkey standing at the end of the tub babbling to you. It's actually pretty necessary sometimes! When we decided I wouldn't go back to work full-time, but that I would stay at home and freelance I knew that I would most likely need a break here and there, but I didn't realize how necessary it would be until Luna was about three months old. Even just a 10 minute walk does the trick. It's important to remember that you are still you, and you need to look after you, mainly because if you look after you, you are also looking after those you love.

- And then, the main thing is that I never knew such happiness could really exist. I learnt that even with the sleep deprivation, the moments of sheer panic, the tough moments and the moments of real joy, that life before being a mother was wonderful, but nowhere near as wonderful as it is now. To have found that great balance which comes with being with someone who you not only love but who is also the perfect partner and companion for you, and then both of you bringing a child into this world to love and nurture is something so special. And we love it so much that we are crazy enough to do it again!

Halfway There Already

We are already past the halfway mark! The first trimester seemed to really drag by, probably because I felt so sick every day and it was so cold outside that we were stuck inside. This trimester is already starting to break into a sprint and I want it to slow down! While I don't feel like there is as much to prepare for as there was with Luna (new apartment, entire set of necessities for baby, mental preparations as what to expect after expecting), I still want to enjoy this part of pregnancy as it's the best part! After the sickness and fatigue and before the heartburn, discomfort and Braxton Hicks, this second trimester is very similar to what I experienced with Luna: energy, pregnant glow despite not sleeping anywhere near enough and constant appetite! Oh, and I feel like my belly is so much bigger with this one! I don't think the baby is any bigger than Luna was at this point (according to our anatomy scan last week she weighs in at 11oz, on point for 20 weeks gestation age), but maybe she will be. Luna was of average weight (7.13 lb) but way below average in height (18in), so it will be interesting to see how this one will be! While I don't mind going past full term again, I would love to go into labor naturally and not resort to pain medication. As I now know, my body takes a long time to recover from medication that it is not used to, and I am more than happy to deal with contractions if it means I can leave the hospital the next day and walk home (even Pitocin contractions if need be).

The hospital is actually only a 30 minute walk from our apartment, and I feel that the care I have already received there has been so much better than at the hospital where I had Luna. For each scan I have never waited more than 10 minutes, I have been able to follow the technicians on my own screen, and everyone has given me a play by play during the procedure. We had our fetal echocardiogram last week and I am very happy to announce that the baby's heart is fully formed and working correctly! The echo was performed by Luna's pediatric cardiologist's colleague, and he explained everything very clearly. So this is one thing I will not need to worry about anymore! We then had her full anatomy scan a few days afterwards and she has all her limbs and fingers and toes. She moved around a lot and I think there were a few things that the technician couldn't get good photos of so I have to go back for a follow up ultrasound in 4 weeks... As long as it is not because something else looks wrong, but I haven't heard anything from my OB yet so I assume not. And we get to see her again which is always exciting!

I started to feel what I call the "popcorn popping flutters" a few weeks ago, and a few flips here and there, but nothing consistent. Last week I finally started to feel little tiny kicks on the inside, nothing that you would be able to feel on the outside yet, but it's so reassuring to feel my growing child moving inside me! With Luna I had an anterior placenta and felt flutters way after 20 weeks, and didn't start feeling kicks until 28 weeks! And I was super slim at the time, so weight has nothing to do with feeling baby movement. Although once I felt that first kick she didn't stop moving, and still doesn't sit still for a minute today. I can't wait to see what Luna's reaction will be when you can start feeling the baby's kicks on the outside! Luna already does this absolutely adorable thing where she cuddles my belly and strokes it if I tell her to "come and say hi to *babyname*". Who knows if she will actually be that affectionate when the baby is born, but it's very heart melty right now!

Just like we did with Luna we shall not be revealing the name until after birth, mainly because we love keeping it to ourselves until then. A few people have guessed it and I have told a few more, but for all you others you will have to wait and see. It's a little harder than with Luna though, because we called her Munchie all through the pregnancy (and sometimes still do), but while we started calling this one Cachito/Cachita it never stuck as well and I keep calling her by her name! Probably a good job that I don't see everyone on a regular basis anymore otherwise the cat would have been long out of the bag. A few hints is that we will be remaining somewhat within theme with the first name, both names can easily be pronounced in English, Spanish and French, and the second name will also refer to a classic movie actress that I adore.

I've had to pretty much give up on wearing Luna on a regular basis for the time being (only when it's absolutely necessary, like on her birthday when she wouldn't nap anywhere else), and she is finally getting more used to a new stroller my sister kindly bought us (rear facing – she seems to be much happier being able to see us), so we have been venturing out into the sunshine again. I quite frankly need the exercise and she needs the fresh air! And just thinking about it right now, I really, really want a bagel from Whitestone Bagels Factory… SO DELICIOUS. My only cravings up until now are eating sandwiches and bagels outside in the sunshine – and we are lucky that we live in an area with a large choice of little parks. Which reminds me! I met with my dietician a few weeks ago (an awesome perk that comes with the clinic I go to), and I had lost weight, which apparently is not advised in the second trimester, especially as I am still breastfeeding. So, just like Luna, I have been told to eat more. It's hard though, because I already feel like I eat tons! We will see what she says next week. That said, I am still a lot bigger than I was with Luna, although I probably see myself as being huge when I am not really. I'm all belly again! But then again I know that my body is carrying more weight than it has ever been used to and it worries me a little. I'm not overweight by any means, but I am not used to being so much bigger than I have ever been in my nearly 37 years on earth. I'm going to make a much bigger effort to lose it faster this time around and get back into some sort of shape. Although I have a feeling it won't be that hard with 2 littles under 2! I had better get around to actually posting this as otherwise it's going to be another week and then another and then I will be in my third trimester!

Little Kicks, Little Bumps and Big Steps

We have about 15 weeks left now, and strangely enough everything is feeling a little surreal. Strange because it is more than obvious that there is a little baby growing in my body! She's growing very well too, at our last ultrasound she was weighing right on target at about 1.9 pounds. I have been thinking for ages that I was so much bigger with this one than I was with Luna, but actually that isn't really true. I combined photos from 25 weeks with both girls and they are very similar, even in the way I carry. I'm therefore assuming that this little one will most likely be around the same height and weight as Luna was (7.13 lbs and 18 in).

That's kind of where the similarities end really. This pregnancy has been a lot tougher on me than Luna's was. I think it's a combination of things, still breastfeeding Luna, not sleeping enough, and also due to some issues that are out of my control really. At our 20 week anatomy scan it was discovered that I have some kind of mass on the placenta, most likely a cyst or a blood clot. It isn't actually causing any issues now, but I have been told to rest as much as possible, avoid extra activity, lifting etc. I'm being monitored by hospitals ultrasounds on a monthly basis and additional OB checks every two weeks. Best case scenario it disappears by itself, worst case it gets bigger and restricts the umbilical cord from doing its job. Right now it doesn't seem to be doing anything, so it can stay like that too, as long as it doesn't do anything to restrict the baby from growing. It is weird to have to stop and rethink every movement though. I really want to go through all of the storage closets and purge everything, but I have to ask Cesar to pull boxes out, which is something I am so used to doing myself!

Maybe all this resting will make for an easier recovery? At least this time I am giving myself more time to review all types of pain management techniques. I worry (unnecessarily) that the little one won't turn around soon (she's in the breech position – Luna was always head down so I never worried about that with her), because I would really, really love to have the birth experience I wanted with Luna and didn't really have this time around. I feel a lot stronger and more confident in the whole process, and now have doctors who support my requests, but I always have a niggling worry in the back of my mind that it will all go haywire again! In the end all that matters is a healthy baby and mama, I know. I would just love to not go through the hell that was my recovery with Luna again. At least I have 15 more weeks (I hope!) to make a nice long playlist full of happiness-inducing music such as The Cure, Bauhaus, Varsovie, Thought Forms and Nick Cave…

The little kicks! Even though I have an anterior placenta again, I have been feeling good kicks for a few weeks now, low in my belly, which is normal as her head is up under my ribs right now. She's more active in the afternoon and at night, and I can already see my belly move when she gets all excited! Luna loves to rub my belly to say hello to her little sister and likes to rest her head on the bump when she's tired. This reminds me! I will most likely jinx myself here, and it's not a continuous success, but Luna's sleeping patterns have become a lot better in the past month. She wakes up a lot less and sleeps better, especially as she now has a huge king size bed to spread out in (which she does, very often). How does such a little monkey take up so much room?! Between her and Joey the cat they usually take up about ¾ of the bed! Add another child in the mix and Cesar and I should probably just resign ourselves to sleeping on the floor! We aren't going to force Luna to sleep elsewhere for many reasons, but if baby number 2 doesn't sleep in the crib either we will probably transform it into a toddler bed so Luna can start sleeping in her own bed. We aren't worried, it's kind of special, waking up with a foot in your face and little kisses from a well-slept little munchkin. We only have a little span of time when this will actually be possible, so we may make the most out of it. I'm not going to put any of us through the stress of crib training when I know that all it is going to lead to is lots of crying. Might as well save that stress for potty training, something that we are going to start working on pretty soon. No reason not to start early in my opinion, if it doesn't work we will just wait a little longer.

Work has been going pretty well, I'm quite happy with the regular, ongoing projects that I am working on, and with the new projects that are popping up here and there. With Luna finally sleeping better in the evening I am able to get a few hours of undisturbed writing in, and am trying to keep weekends for my own personal projects. I think I may take a week off when the baby arrives, but no longer as I don't want to lose my clients, and most of the work can be done during what will be many, many cluster feedings and sleepless nights. Hopefully at some point I can build it up so that when the kids are at school it will be a full time job. In the meantime it helps with all the extra monetary needs that come in week after week. And it helps me feel like I am doing something for myself too, which I think I always need.

Luna is coming to the point where she loves being around other kids now and I wonder if we should maybe put her in daycare for a few hours a week. It's so expensive here, but I think we could wrangle a few hours, especially if it's beneficial for her. She loves going to the park and always cries when we leave! I still don't know anyone with kids in this neighborhood, but we are going to go to baby and toddler times at the library from next week and hopefully make that into a more regular occurrence. Luna actually plays really, really well by herself, with her cat and her teddy bears and all of her toys, but she really does light up when she is near another child (especially her favorite friend Xavier). I love watching how she becomes more slightly more grown up every day... And it's interesting to see the development of tantrums too. I have a feeling those won't be disappearing for a while! I think a lot of it has to do with her not being able to communicate with words, so shouts, screams, whines and crying is the easiest way to get a point across. And she has a pretty good, loud scream, I can tell you that!

So, 15 more weeks of me growing bigger and 15 weeks left of Luna being an only child... Probably time to start sorting out baby clothing again, and getting some things set up for when this is all going to happen! I'm hoping

Luna's wonderful godmother and my best friend Meg will be here when I go into labor so she can watch Luna for us for the time that it takes to deliver the baby. If not our lovely Henna will be able to help, and I'm sure Ashton would love to too. We have a lot of wonderful friends. I hope that everything will go perfectly fine so that we don't have to stay in hospital for more than 24 hours. I'm much better at home where I feel comfortable, even if this hospital is a LOT nicer than the one I gave birth to Luna in!

I'm sure I shall provide another update within the next 5/6 weeks, when I am in the third trimester and starting to feel like a waddling hippo (do hippos actually waddle?!). We also have a doctor's appointment coming up for Luna so we can see if she is finally putting on weight or not (fingers crossed she is because if not I am going to have to take her for some blood tests and I'm not too keen about going through that hell again so soon). In the meantime we shall enjoy the spring weather and the picnics in the park!

Those Little Fears

It's nearly 9pm, baby girl is sleeping and the other is kicking up a storm and all I want to do is relax on the couch and eat ice cream. The apartment is in dire need of a good cleaning, and I should probably get a head start on this week's work, but I honestly just want to breathe and not think about anything. Of course this is the moment when you think about everything and when your mind starts to conjure up silly thoughts and worries. I don't usually scare very easily, to be honest I've been through a lot in my 37 years, and seen many things, but my attitude has mainly been that if you can get through one thing you can get through anything. When faced with the inevitable fact that I was going to become a mother I felt a little scared, but mostly excited. And I guess I'm not doing such a bad job. I am scared of the future, of the world that we are raising our child in, but at the same time I think that every mother fears this. We just try to do our best to raise a new generation of people who will take more care of their home the planet and who believe in the equality of humans and will not judge another based on religion, sex, skin color or anything else. A generation who will see our mistakes and hopefully not follow in our footsteps.

I sometimes fear that I will fail at all this at some point. I see my own limits and frustrations and have to get past them calmly. Breathe and move forward. There is no more room for letting go in the spectacular fashion of years before, the whiskey and the barhopping days, nowadays it's more of a "let me just lock myself in the bathroom for 10 minutes and listen to some very loud music". I don't want to be the person who gets angry for no reason, or who doesn't react calmly in a situation that warrants a rational reaction. I've always been one to see things through clearly and to work out a solution, but sometimes the lack of sleep makes me more irritable than normal, or the fact that I haven't had a moment to myself in days builds up inside until it becomes a silent scream. I am a very happy person in general, so when I feel this way I often feel like I am failing somewhere, however much I tell myself that it's completely normal. Sometimes it's hard not to create such levels of high standards that are difficult to attain on a regular basis, because it just leads to a more spectacular fall. Somewhere in the middle is good. And yes, mac n cheese is fine as a meal now and again during the week.

I used to fear that I would always let people walk all over me. At the same time I used to fear that if I spoke up I would be shut down. I don't fear either of those things anymore. I'm just not very tolerant these days, and I don't feel the need to deal with idiotic dramatics and attention seeking actions. If my feelings are hurt I will say so and move on. No one needs unnecessary hurt in their lives, right? To be honest I think once you start a family a lot of things that once felt important fall by the wayside. A lot of my attention is now focused on my immediate family, and the rest on my extended group of family and friends who I love with all my heart. But nowadays if I feel like I have been crossed once then I don't need to make any further effort with that person, be they family or friend. I have to spend my energy on making sure these little ones get everything they need and more from me! I would rather spend 20 minutes kissing the beautiful cheeks of my sleeping daughter than trying to figure out why someone is yet again creating boring drama in their lives. We are way too old for that! And too tired. Way too tired.

I suppose this brings me to one of my main fears, one that has been niggling in the back of my mind since this new little baby was just two lines on a pregnancy test. A fear that gets a little more real with every passing week, and one I know is irrational and silly, but that is still stuck in my brain, waiting for me to confront it. I worry how we are going to cope with having two children under two, how I am going to make sure Luna never feels like I have abandoned her, while still making sure the new baby feels as loved and cared for as Luna does. And also making sure that in the middle of all that Cesar and I remember to exist too. I read articles that are titled "how to survive 2 under 2" (or something along those lines) and wonder if it really has to be all about survival? And then I see beautiful pictures of mothers and children and families on Instagram and wonder how they all have it together and how they make everything seem so easy and seamless. Maybe I am looking into this too much. It's not something that constantly bothers me – I went into motherhood with a "go with the flow" attitude and I'm going into having another child with the same attitude. While I have always been the one to prepare, I also love being impulsive, come what may, and seeing where we end up. What can we really prepare anyway? The basics, a place for the baby to sleep, a place for her to play, a way for her to stay wrapped to me so I can play with her sister and cook and clean and write. Other than that nothing really. We don't know what her temperament will be like, we don't know if she will be feisty and loud and needy like Luna. We don't know whether she will require round the clock feedings or will be relaxed and Zen and go to sleep by herself (one can always dream, nothing wrong with that). My fear isn't about making sure my children's physical needs are met, we won't have a problem with that, it's about me being able to give them everything I want to give them emotionally and physically, all of the time. The stories, the cuddles, the songs, the walks... Writing it out sounds a little silly, which in the end was the whole point of laying it out there. My way of confronting it, really. Of course I will be able to give them all they need. I just don't want to see it as "survival". Maybe more as a challenge? It's more than an experience, it's my life, and their lives, and Cesar's life. Our lives. So no more reading about "survival" and more just living. Because even with the sleep deprivation, this is all a pretty cool way to live really.

I think we will be OK. If not there is always ice cream, anyway.

Ten More Weeks To Go

Luna is napping peacefully next to me, and while I know I should take advantage of it and nap too, I can't seem to switch my brain off today. I have a lot of work to do and could also be doing that while the house is peaceful, but instead I am just browsing through photos and thinking of friends and realizing that we only have 10 more weeks left of Luna being an only child. I want to make sure we do something special with her every week, something that we all enjoy as a family of three, before the insanity of being a family of four takes place. A few weeks ago we went to Queens Zoo in Flushing-Meadows Corona Park, which happens to only be a 30-45 minute walk from our house. The weather was perfect and the timing wonderful as we missed the school kids parties and had the entire zoo practically to ourselves. I finally got to see the Unisphere in person and we ended up taking a lot of pictures on the Holga, something I'm really excited about right now! (Although the place I took the photos to be developed at managed to completely botch the development. At least we got a few nice pictures, and found some old ones from Cesar, Henna and me on the beach in Sept 2013, when I was just a few months pregnant with Luna).

Luna seemed to enjoy everything, from the big cats to the beautiful tropical birds, and Cesar even took her on her first carousel ride, where she bravely sat on a horse and even ended up enjoying herself, squealing at the horses in front of her. We were all exhausted after a long day walking in the sun, but it was so worth it, just to be together, happy, watching Luna discover new things and adventures. I really wanted to brave the Bronx Zoo before it got too hot, but I think it will have to wait until later this year when Luna is a little older and I can walk around for hours without trying to jump into the water with the rest of the happy hippos. Yes, I feel huge. Belly-wise I'm not really any bigger than I was with Luna, but all-over-wise I am definitely. I guess that comes with the territory of having back to back pregnancies, and if this is what my body needs to do to carry a healthy baby then so be it. And kickboxing lessons will be happening in the autumn ha!

Everything is actually going very, very well. I continue to have sonograms every 4 weeks to check up on the cyst and its growth, and for now it has remained exactly the same. Little baby weighs approximately 3.5 lbs, so right on target for 30 weeks, and has now turned into the vertex position, head down, which is one less thing to worry about. She is a big mover and loves to kick and pummel me all night! I however actually sleep better than I did when I was pregnant with Luna, maybe just because my body is so bone-tired anyway that it just doesn't care if I have a body pillow or not, it just wants to sleep for 2 hours straight! I know this isn't going to last much longer, as the days when I will need to roll myself out of bed are looming, so I am just making the most of it. Luna is having quite a few issues napping lately, so I've taken to napping with her in the afternoon, which really does seem to help both of our moods in general. And it's so hot outside that our park visits have been relegated to the morning or the late afternoon, or on the days when I know I will have enough energy to run after her every time she tries to join a group of teenagers hanging out at the edge of the playground.

Anyway, I passed all the mid pregnancy tests again fine this time, no gestational diabetes, normal iron levels, still breastfeeding Luna, although to be honest it's not as easy as it sounds when pregnant. It's painful and can be slightly annoying, especially when she wants to nurse for ages at night due to teething. In the end it's easier than forcing her to wean now when I will only be starting again in 10 weeks, so we might as well continue. At least I hope it will be a lot easier this time around with the new baby. We have finally started getting the little bits and pieces prepared for her. I have some of her own Aden & Anais blankets arriving this week (the best baby swaddles and blankets and can literally be used a million different ways), her little Rock n Play arrived today (we have no idea where she will want to sleep and I am not stressing about it like I did with Luna... Our bed is big enough to accommodate all of us and the cat if need be), and we chose her first outfit out too. Her name has as much meaning to us as Luna's does, which will be obvious when we tell everyone. I love keeping that part a surprise. Now I just need to finish spring cleaning all of the closets and start packing away the little one's first few months of clothes in the dresser, schedule a Salvation Army box pick-up for the amount of things we have to get rid of, and stock up on everything for those first few weeks post-partum.

Trying to find the time is a little difficult though! I haven't written much recently as I have been completely swamped with work (a good thing), but as I work from home around Luna it can often be a little tough making sure I get everything done. And Cesar has recently taken on a second job, so we have both been juggling busy times with making time to just relax and all be together. You know, all of the general life things that most people go through! I hope we are able to have at least a week together when the baby arrives, but we may have to do some juggling there too. As long as we can make sure that Luna feels extra special during that time to make sure the transition goes as smoothly as possible. I think that's my main worry!

It's funny how I am less worried about making sure we have "all the stuff" this time around. As long as I have my sling to carry the baby around when I'm playing with Luna and somewhere for her to nap consistently then we are all set. Oh and a couple of big play mats for the floor so they can both hang out together (and hopefully Luna won't try to feed her sister, or pull her head off or something along those lines!). In any case we have pretty much everything for another little girl, including a year's worth of clothes! I don't think either of us has been kidding ourselves that it's going to be easy, but I refuse to worry about it too. We both come from long lines of highly adaptable families, so I doubt we will have too much trouble adapting!

Expect the Unexpected

This is about a week late, not because I was being lazy but because there were some things that happened that were completely out of my control last week and I'm still in a bit of a haze because of it all! I compare both pregnancies quite a bit, and so far this one has been a little more difficult and definitely a little more stressful. I didn't, however, think that there would be a chance that my daughter would be born at 36 weeks. My family has a history of having babies well past their due date and Luna was no exception, so I thought it would be more than likely that I would go to 42 weeks with this one. Especially as my doctors and hospital will not induce before 42 weeks unless it's a medical necessity.

So I hit 36 weeks last Monday, feeling fine, the heat getting to me a little, lumbering rather than prancing around, but otherwise great. I drink around three liters of water a day so I was definitely staying hydrated, even though it was boiling out. I saw my OB on Wednesday morning and she had a little trouble finding the heartbeat, but found it eventually, and when I mentioned that the baby was moving a little less she checked placement on the sonogram machine and sent me to the hospital for an NST and fluid check. It was over 95 on Wednesday but I decided to walk anyway (it really isn't that far), and I thought it was quite pleasant to have a little more "me" time than expected seeing as Henna was at home with Luna...

An hour later I was in the process of being admitted to L&D to be induced due to dangerously low amniotic fluid! As I mentioned earlier, my doctors do not like to induce unless they think it's necessary, so they started a slow induction later that night, and had me on a continuous IV for 24 hours.

After two doses of Cytotec overnight and regular but not strong contractions it was obvious it was going to take a lot more to get the baby moving (she was and still is pretty content in her little home), and the IV fluids had actually helped build the amniotic fluids back up to a much better level, so it was decided to not push the induction, let little munchkin cook a little longer and have me come in for NSTs every other day.

What a rollercoaster of emotions! I went through an hour of crying because I just wasn't ready to give birth, because I wasn't going to have the unmedicated birth that I wanted, that I hadn't made more of an effort to hug and kiss Luna before I left her that morning. And then it moved to acceptance and that if I relaxed I would be able to guide my body through an induction without pain meds, with Cesar and my awesome nurses help. And then it lead to excitement, we were actually going to meet our little one! I was a little worried about NICU time, but the nurses reassured me that most 36 weekers are born without any issues at all. And then I couldn't stop thinking about all the things that we still needed to do! The apartment still needed deep cleaning, I still had assignments to finish, we still haven't finished buying everything, nothing was READY! Luckily we have a little longer. I bet after all this she will decide to come out all by herself at 42 weeks, just for a last laugh!

So here we are now at 37 weeks, baby is moving well again, I have swollen feet and hands due to the IV and woke up with a swollen face this morning (ugh), I feel a little under the weather, but I'm determined to make the most of whatever time we have left, and to also help start the process naturally by walking as much as I can every day. As it stands it could be any day between now and the next 5 weeks. I may talk a lot about the pregnancy and how I am feeling and everything around it, but I like the labor and delivery part to stay quiet. It's a time of such intensity and I just would rather it be Cesar and myself getting through it and then Luna meeting her little sister before telling anyone else. Well, I mean obviously Henna will need to know as she will be watching Luna! She did a wonderful job the other day, just taking everything in her stride and making sure Luna was safe and looked after. And then Ashton dropped any plans she had and came over to babysit on Saturday so I could go for my NST. We have wonderful friends! Luna is not easy to babysit, but I feel like she is getting a little less high maintenance. Or maybe that's wishful thinking, it's not like I'm here while she is being babysat!

I can't even remember what I wanted to write about last week now after all of that happened! Most likely just a minor update on how there were just 4 short weeks left and about how I was feeling and everything we still had left to do. One good thing did come of last week and that was that I now know that this hospital is like night and day compared to where I delivered Luna, exactly what I wanted. Nurses basically run the show and deliver babies unless a doctor is needed. I actually mainly saw the (wonderful) nurses and PAs most of the time, and the doctors just popped in to see how I was doing. They are completely pro-breastfeeding and skin to skin, and will do everything to help me get through labor without pain meds. The main problem about being induced for me is that you need to stay attached to an IV and monitor so that they can monitor the baby's heart and your contractions. This means that you can't just get up and walk about with every contraction. Being stuck in bed is much harder to deal with, so everyone keep their fingers crossed we will still get the birth that I really want. I know it might seem a little frivolous and that the main point is that we both get through it safely (of course), but I would love to be somewhat in control this time.

It's quite bittersweet, getting to the end of the pregnancy. On the one hand I can't wait to meet our little munchkin, for our family to be complete, but on the other this is most likely the last time I will ever feel little kicks from the inside. No more measuring the growth of the belly, no more waddling around, no more wondering how long I can get away wearing those clothes before they don't fit anymore. I still love being pregnant, I still love knowing that the little bean growing inside of me is one day going to be a fully grown person who will make me laugh and cry every day. But now it's time to get ready for a new adventure, that of having two kids under two, tandem nursing, and learning how to be even more patient and also forgiving of myself. And also figuring out how to continue working nearly full time from home around the littles. Challenges galore!

Internet Rabbit Holes (so DISGUSTING)

I think this is probably going to be a post full of real ramblings, thoughts that have been running through my tired brain over the past few days. I will try to remember what I was thinking this morning, and yesterday morning, but it's a little difficult seeing as my brain may be turning to mush. Blame it on the impending arrival of Baby no 2, or the insane amount of work that I have been swimming through (maybe that's why I feel at a loss today as I am waiting for new assignments and edited work, but nothing to do right now, which is kind of weird). 39 weeks today and I feel like my body is really stretched to its limits. I don't know if the baby has much more room to grow really. The bump appears to have reached her optimal size and I'm really hoping that we don't have to wait too much longer. I trek to the hospital every 3 days for an NST and fluid check and every time it's always the gamble of "OMG is today going to be the day?!" and then I get to go home. I made a wonderful playlist for labor and now we just WAIT.

I see that it was World Breastfeeding Week last week and I did get stuck down some random internet comment rabbit holes that tend to drive my blood pressure up more than anything else (or at least give me the impression that it is rising). Comments such as "if the child can hold a cup then they don't need a boob in their mouth anymore" or "cow's milk is healthier" (yes, that's why cow's make milk for humans and humans make milk for cows, right?!). Another one was "breastfeeding a toddler is DISGUSTING". OK lady, why is it disgusting? Because your boobs belong to men? Well sorry about that, mine belong to me, and as long as they belong to me they will feed my child. My gosh... I now avoid participating in any type of online breastfeeding discussion because so many people in this country think it's normal to see Victoria's Secret billboards all over the place but get offended by a woman breastfeeding a 1 year old in public.

There is room for both! One is not "more acceptable" than the other. I kind of have to blame my brother for getting worked up this time as he was the one who mentioned being sucked into a ridiculous comment thread, so I HAD to go and check it out myself... Even though I knew what I would be reading before I even did. Silly me.

And then, amidst things like a huge explosion in China, continued attacks against people in Syria, debris of that Malaysian plane turning up, a drought that isn't ending in California and you know, probably a load more deplorable and inhuman acts against humanity, a woman causes "outrage" because she decides to run a marathon on her period without wearing a tampon. Once again I started getting caught in internet comment hell, and learned, yet again, that this was DISGUSTING. Men and women pee and poop themselves while they are running (this is pretty common knowledge), but a woman knowingly had her period and decided to run without anything to catch the blood, well that's just wrong, isn't it? Blood, like breast milk is just so DISGUSTING when it is in the public view. Nevermind that this lady, Kiran Gandhi is her name, did it for reasons of raising awareness, no, according to some people she just wanted her "15 minutes of fame". Oh and this is the US where women have access to sanitary towels so "why would she want to raise awareness here? Can't she just send a box of tampons to a third world country?" (even though it happened during the London Marathon, which still happens to take place in England if I am not mistaken). She probably could, but if she sent a box of tampons to a third world country would anyone be talking about it? Would the few people who actually looked past the DISGUSTING side of it and saw that she was trying to get people to focus on what period shaming really means in certain countries, then maybe they would understand what she was trying to do.

Think about it this way. Most women between a certain age have a period every month that lasts for about a week. Where we live we don't need to stop our lives, yes it's annoying and uncomfortable and sometimes a little painful, but we aren't stuck at home for a week every month, hiding, or washing out pieces of cloth to reuse them, are we? Now place yourself in another country where women may not have access to tampons or pads, where they aren't allowed to do anything when they have their periods except stay at home and wait it out. How would you feel if you had to live like that? So while what Kiran Gandhi did may appear as "DISGUSTING" to you, all she ended up with were some ruined running trousers and a lot of internet comments from women who don't understand why she did it. But hopefully a few more people will talk about the real reasons why she decided to do this. And think about it, there are many other ways to get your "15 minutes of fame"... I doubt this was her objective. But you know, it's DISGUSTING, so why even try to look past that? Just read through some comments for a laugh really. It's quite incredible how people think. It reminds me of the famous scene in Carrie when all the high school girls are taunting her to "plug it up". DISGUSTING. Because the blood that runs through our veins is DISGUSTING. Reminds me of the time when my mother went to pick up all of the photos taken during my brother's birth, and someone at the photo lab had put black crosses through them all. They were private photos, only intended for the eyes of a few but blood on a newborn was supposedly too DISGUSTING for the photo lab worker to deal with. I hope they never had to deal with childbirth; their stomachs may have been too weak for it.

Which makes me think about how DISGUSTING some women are with each other online. You don't have to like everyone per se, I sure don't, but some people really need to get their head out from under a rock and start looking at the world that surrounds them. It's a lot bigger than you think it is.

In other news I am going to spend the rest of today playing with Luna and trying to stop her from eating crayons and playing with a pair of scissors that I am positive I keep hiding on a top shelf but keep reappearing, and watching Call the Midwife again. Which happens to be my only real preparation for childbirth, again, apart from the awesome playlist I made last week. Other news in the outside world is that our beloved Rhynan has finally finished his extremely tough 9 weeks of chemotherapy, started his senior high school year 2 days after his last treatment and is quite the embodiment of the super teen. We all have our fingers and toes and anything else that can be crossed, crossed that the next scans come up clean and that he can go back to living a normal life again. **Now THIS is something that is DISGUSTING: a 16 year old who has to go through a summer of chemo because he has a rapidly developing form of cancer.**

So, back to the couch while I muse upon the question that if my waters break in public will I be considered DISGUSTING, and maybe next time I have an update it will be as a mother of two. Maybe. My babies tend to enjoy staying past their due date. Kind of like me in my 20's when I never wanted the party to end, even though it was closing time.

Adapting All Over Again

A while ago I wrote about adapting to life as a mother and not feeling that isolation and loneliness that some people often mention. I've been thinking about this a lot again recently, especially with Cesar taking on another job and being away from home for longer hours again, and with another little one expected any day now. Will I feel more isolated now? Or will I just be even busier? I have my friends that I try to see on a regular basis (and who have been awesome in coming to visit me and Luna these past few months), I made a new friend in Flushing who I hope I can see more of when we have both had our little ones, and hopefully we will all be able to get out and about again as soon as possible.

I love September in NYC. It's my favorite month. Still hot, but not as humid, the beaches are not packed and you feel like you can breathe much better. The nights slowly start to get longer as you head into October, but it still feels like late summer and doesn't yet have that nostalgic feeling that October does. I hope we will be able to go to the beach, for picnics in the park, for trips into the city and story time at the library. I hope that we will be able to enjoy this last month of summer together as a family of 4, little miss Luna being a daredevil at the ocean front with her Daddy and me watching from a nice comfortable spot on the sand (under a parasol) with little miss number 2. I promise her name will be revealed soon, as the doctor said yesterday it cannot be any longer than 2 weeks now. Which, you know, you kind of grind your teeth at and smile grimly because after 40 weeks two more weeks sounds like an eternity. An eternity of achy hips, waddling marathons to the shop on the corner and the joys of wondering if every twinge is the start of labor. I've come to the conclusion that my babies just don't ever want to come out by themselves, so I am now content to wait. And scrub the bathroom floor with bleach again.

So, back to the whole adapting topic, I think that it's very important to have friends that you can reach out to, people who really get it. Even if you don't see each other that often, a simple text or call with a story to tell or a question to ask goes a long way. Kids playing together while you chat and eat food or no kids and catching up on all the gossip that has been happening. And also, time to organize nights out here and there, as a couple, or off with friends. Not a break, just an opportunity to see some live music or meet up with other friends you never see. I think now that we have come to the conclusion that two kids is enough for us right now, I am more able to start planning for the next phase, that of being a mother of two little girls and how much fun it is going to be. Beach trips next summer, constant cuddles, shopping trips, teaching them how to read and write, watching movies together, drawing, painting... A thousand fun activities that I can think of. Playing with friends that they have grown up with too!

I remember the only times I really felt sad or isolated in the first few months last year was when a few friends that I had spent the best part of the past 7 years with just kind of... Disappeared. But it's actually what happens. Life changes happen and some people just don't follow, they go off on their own path. And that's fine, it hurts a little, but at the same time you meet others who are on a similar path to you and with whom you bond and become friends. That's kind of why I have a love/hate relationship with those Timehop and Facebook memory things: sometimes they show photos from fun times years ago and they make you a little nostalgic, and wonder if you should reach out and see how these people are doing... And then you think, why? When did they last reach out to me? Life's too full of amazingness to worry about this anyway. I am thankful for all the wonderful times spent over the years and I hope everyone I have ever been friends with is as happy and content in their lives as I am. Because, yes, after 37 years on this earth I can say with utmost confidence that I AM happy. And that's such a wonderful feeling.

So while we try to wait patiently on the arrival of yet another little girl who doesn't want to be born (and the signs are pointing more and more to the fact that she is unfortunately going to need a little push at 42 weeks), I'm going to enjoy the time we have left with Luna as an only child and continue to wonder about how interesting and fun it is going to be to adapt our little routines and quirks to a newborn's first weeks. I'm so excited to discover if she will look like Cesar or me or Luna. To watch that little startle reflex again, to document first smiles and rolling over and little mannerisms. To watch Luna grow as a big sister and teach her little sister all of the good and the bad things you can do to really annoy or scare Mummy (jumping on furniture is one right now).

In terms of adapting, I think some just adapt better than others. I've never really had an issue with that, moving around to so many different places, discovering new traditions and blending them with my own. Also, feeling out of place. I have discovered that you can feel as out of place in California as you can in your country of origin or in the middle of the Israeli desert. It doesn't really matter where you are or where you are from, sense of belonging or not don't seem to be attached to a place or a time. I do know that I have never felt out of place in NYC, although I have in some situations here of course, which is most likely why I am still here. I'm not scared of change; in some cases I even embrace it. You can't spend your life trying to avoid any type of change, or fighting against it, because in the end it is going to happen whether you like it or not. Being mentally prepared just makes it easier in the long run. Going from a lifestyle of bartending and restaurant managing and drinking and running around like a crazy person to that of a stay at home freelance writing mother was strangely easy. I doubt adding another little one to the mix is going to be a huge change. Or maybe it will, and then we will just adapt to that.

While I am in this period of limbo between 40 and 42 weeks I shall just finish rewatching Call the Midwife, scrub things again (as they are already not as clean as they were last time I scrubbed), and not do much else because even walking has become difficult. Oh and if you feel like asking where the baby is, please don't. She's still in my womb until further notice.

Aurora Vivienne's Birth Story

Ever since I had Luna I was convinced I would make sure my next birth story would be different. While I was happy we were both healthy and had no real complications, there were so many things that I would have done differently had I known beforehand. Fast forward to 7 months later and I found out I was pregnant again. After pondering the idea of a birthing center (nixed because it was already full) and a homebirth (nixed because I couldn't find a midwife who would take my insurance AND be available at the time), I ended up just making an appointment at the Family Health Clinic in Flushing, affiliated with the New York Hospital Queens where Luna has her cardiology appointments. It's funny because I remember saying to Cesar the first time we were there that I wished I had given birth to Luna there. There is just something very calming and peaceful about the hospital.

I never waited more than 10 minutes for a prenatal appointment at the clinic. Everyone was so kind and friendly, and made sure that we had all the sonograms and NSTs that we needed when we hit upon some complications. They were all aware of my wanting a med-free, natural birth, and immediate skin to skin and breastfeeding (which is hospital policy anyway), and reassured me that I didn't have to worry. Even when the baby was in a little distress at 36 weeks and they tried a slow induction, my doctors ended up figuring out a better way to fix the issues so I could carry the baby a little longer and hopefully deliver at term. Aurora Vivienne was born on August 29th at 8:06am, weighing 7lbs and 14oz and measuring 21.5 inches. Apart from being 3.5 inches taller at birth, she looks exactly like her older sister did, and has some of the same little mannerisms already. Her hair has streaks of blonde through it, but otherwise they could be twins! Aurora's birth was however the opposite of Luna's, and probably the most intense experience of my life.

While I had been having some contractions and cramps for a while, at my

40 week appointment I was still at 1cm and Aurora was so high she didn't seem to be anywhere near ready to arrive. Not only that, during her NST and BPP on Thursday (August 28th)her fluid had magically gone UP after weeks of being way too low. I was sure she was going to just hang in there until the last minute.

On Friday I felt the same as I had every other day: pregnant maybe for eternity. In the evening I had some strong Braxton Hicks and mentioned to Cesar that she was probably coming over the weekend. We went to bed at 11 as we were both exhausted (the first time I had gone to sleep before midnight in a while). I woke up at1:30amwith a real contraction and some spotting, but nothing too painful. I started timing them and they were only about 15/20 minutes apart and completely bearable. I knew that I was finally in labor, let my mum know it was time to purchase that ticket, let Henna know that we would possibly need her in the morning and decided to get some rest, preparing for a slow ramp up. At3amthe contractions were every 6/8 minutes, never lasting more than 40/50 seconds and still what I logged as "bearable". I was too antsy and uncomfortable to lie in bed though so I went to relax on the couch. I completely downplayed the contraction pain to Cesar too, deciding it was best to let him and Luna sleep, seeing as we obviously had hours to go. I got in the shower around4amwhen the contractions started getting closer, around every 3/5 minutes, still no longer than 40/50 seconds and painful enough to make me cry. At this point I just thought I was being a wimp and that my tolerance to pain was not high enough and that I wouldn't be able to do it. It was at this point that I all of a sudden felt exhausted, as if I could fall asleep on my feet. I decided I needed to go to the hospital to get an epidural so that I could sleep for a few hours. If I had actually listened rationally to my thoughts I would have realized that I was actually pretty close to delivery, at that point when all your willpower goes up in the air... But no, I was just being a wimp and didn't care anymore. I was obviously not thinking straight and in transition, as it's around this time that I kept wanting to vomit. I'm just glad that I didn't put the hospital trip off any longer though.

I got a cab just after 6am (poor cab driver he was probably glad to get this moaning British woman out of his car ASAP), and was admitted to Labor &

Delivery triage just before7am. My favorite doctor was on call (this was perfect timing on Aurora's part; I was hoping she would be the one to deliver her!). She checked me and announced that I was at 7cm which was practically too late for an epidural. At the rate I was going I would be fully dilated shortly. My nurse pretended that I could still get one I think just to calm me down as at this point it was as if I had been taken over by a groaning monster. I'm usually quiet when in pain. Apparently not when in labor. It all gets a little hazy from then on. My body just took over. I didn't care about what I was wearing, where my stuff was or what I was saying. The contractions were still coming every 3 or so minutes and not lasting longer than 50 seconds, but they just took over. When I look back now it was as if I had a real split personality – I would be chatting like a normal person about my nurse's grandchild or my doctor's triplets and then turn into the groaning monster, and then back again.

Not even 10 minutes later I stood up to get in the wheelchair and announced that I needed to push. Right then. There is no real explaining the feeling about from an intense pressure pushing your insides down. It's not painful, just strange! Within seconds I was whisked into my L&D room, doctors and nurses were putting gowns on and prepping tables and beds while I was already on the bed pushing, going between breathing through each push and moaning that I was never going to be able to do it, and chatting about the weather. My doctor broke my waters and it was a short feeling of relief followed by an intense need to get this baby out RIGHT NOW. I heard them mention "meconium" through the haze in my brain (part focus part not believing what was happening) and this made me determined to have this baby as soon as possible. I didn't want the risk of her aspirating her own poop.

It's amazing how you know exactly where the baby is and how many more pushes you are going to need. It's also amazing how your body just takes over, no need for anyone to tell you when to push, your body just does it naturally. There is no stopping it. In any case, I pushed Aurora out in less than 6 minutes. There was literally no time for me to even mess my hair up, for the nurses to place monitors or get an IV in properly. It was all over and done within the space of minutes! I was able to hold her immediately but they did have to take her to one side to make sure she hadn't aspirated the meconium and check her breathing. 5 minutes later she was on my chest and latched on immediately. This was about the same time that Cesar made it to the hospital - 20 minutes after the birth! As he walked (ran) into the hospital he received my text with Aurora's photo. Henna was ready to come over at4amwhen she finished work but I told her to go home and sleep for a few hours... She was jolted awake at 7am, saw our calls and made it to our home at7:35, but even then it was too late for Cesar to make it. For some reason I was convinced that I would end up giving birth alone, and I did. And I did it. I wish he had been able to be there, but it literally all happened so fast!! It makes me a little angry how the doctors made me wait an hour to push with Luna when I was fully dilated – I now know that if I hadn't had an epidural my body would have dictated her birth, not them.

Aurora was taken off to the nursery to be washed and checked over and my nurse was finally able to admit me and then took us to my room in the maternity ward. Less than an hour later Aurora joined us and from then onwards we spent the time breastfeeding constantly and cuddling.

I was able to shower, walk around, eat, communicate and still feel good, although tired, pretty much right after birth. My main issue with Luna's birth was how long it took me to recover, and this is the why I wanted a med-free birth. And it's true, I felt like I could walk home quite happily24 hours after birth. Not shaky, alert, a little sore but not anything crazy. I suppose my pain threshold is a lot higher than I thought it was... My doctor told me that if we ever have another kid I had to come in at the first contraction as I would never make it to the hospital in time otherwise!

I did everything I wanted to: I labored at home, went to the hospital and had the birth I wanted to. I just didn't expect it to be THAT fast or that intense! When you hear those stories of women giving birth on sidewalks and in cabs you just assume they waited too long... Not anymore! I see exactly how it can happen! This also might sound a little silly, but it helped me feel more at peace with myself. I doubt we will have any more children, and this was the perfect way to end a long and somewhat interesting pregnancy.

It was a very emotional moment when the little sisters finally met each other. I still don't think Luna completely understands what this little being is doing in her house, taking up her mummy's time, but every day is getting a little easier. I am still nursing both of them, so that takes a little juggling and patience, but we are working it out pretty well!

In any case, we are so happy to welcome our little Aurora Vivienne into our lives, another special little being who already makes our hearts sing and pound with happiness!!
Super moon baby!

Readjusting the Harmony

Change, whether chosen or accidental is always going to come with a learning curve or an adaptation period. Sometimes longer or more difficult than other times, but at some point or other the change blends into normal life and you stop thinking about it, moving on and challenging the next change to rear its head. I hope that at some point in time this is how change will seem to Luna.

It's not been so difficult for me, I have just taken everything in my stride, but then again Cesar and I made the choice to have a second child so soon after the first. Luna did not choose to have a little sister demanding mummy and daddy time. And she has definitely made that known! But the way I see it is that while these first few months may be tough on everyone, they are only a small speck on a lifetime of love and friendship. A small speck that neither child will remember consciously. Luna will most likely not recall that her little sister wanted to eat all the time, and Aurora will hopefully not remember the times her big sister tried to throw things at her head.

Luna has never been an "easy" child. She is highly sensitive and demands attention. This doesn't mean that she isn't independent, quite the contrary, but she does need a lot of physical and mental attention. She still wakes up multiple times at night and needs to be near one of us to feel safe enough to go back to sleep again. She still fights naps and needs to nurse when she is tired or upset about something. Aurora on the other hand seems to love a calm environment, sleeps well, just cries when she is hungry or wants to be held and literally closes her eyes as soon as Luna starts screaming about something and shuts her out. I try not to laugh...

So, it hasn't been easy, but that was to be expected. Navigating the bedtime routine alone, bathing one after another and trying to get Aurora to sleep long enough for me to get Luna to sleep has been full of trial and errors. Dealing with nighttime waking when one is hungry and the other wants comfort isn't always easy. Blocking out Luna's high pitched screams while trying to get Aurora to sleep can be somewhat trying. But day by day we are getting there, figuring out solutions and little things that work better than others. We have figured out that Aurora actually likes the swing and will sit quite contentedly in it, even if she doesn't fall asleep, so she goes in it when it's time for Luna to nap and sleep. It helps that Luna and I can have that cuddle time together too! Everything affects Luna's sleep, so if I can give her 30 uninterrupted minutes of my time before she nods off I know that she will sleep more calmly.

Luna kisses her little sister and then throws something at her two seconds later. She cuddles her and then tries to kick her... She's still learning herself so how can she really know that she is inflicting pain on her sister? How can she really know that her sister isn't like her doll? I used to pull the heads off my dolls while saying "head off!". Then one day I tried to do it to my baby sister... At two years old I had no idea my little sister's head wasn't going to come off just like my dolls did. So we just have to gently but sternly tell her "no", usually about 100 times a day. I'm sure at some point it will stick and there will be more kisses and cuddles and less tantrums and flying objects. We always have to remember that Luna is only 18 months old and is still learning how to communicate effectively.

Sometimes I feel like my body is being ripped in half, one half with one and the other with the other, and then all of a sudden we are all one, cuddled together on the couch or in bed, breathing in unison and feeling perfectly happy and safe. Sometimes I feel bad because I can't pick Luna up every time she wants something because I am feeding her sister. Other times I feel guilty because I can't carry Aurora around constantly like I did for the first 4 months of Luna's life. But mainly I feel so amazingly happy and in awe of these perfect little beings that Cesar and I created. Their beautiful little faces, the expressions on those faces whenever you look at them, the little kisses and the laughs and the first smiles and that huge, aching love that you feel constantly, the love that seems so wide and deep and fulfilling.

All those worries about spreading that love you have for one to two melt the moment your new child is placed on your chest, there is more than enough love to go around and around and around.

It's easier the second time around. Your body is used to the sleep deprivation and you don't stress about a million things anymore. It's also easier for us because Luna was a tough baby, hated sleeping and would fight it at every nap and bedtime. She still does. Both Cesar and I expected the same with Aurora, but she is more relaxed, calmer. Or maybe that's because we are just more relaxed and calmer? Who knows. It also helps that my recovery was a million times easier this time, no back aches or knee aches or extreme fatigue. No breastfeeding learning pains or completely sleepless nights. No stressing about the state of the apartment - it will get cleaned when we have time, in the meantime these little munchkins get all of my attention!

I have even managed to carve out some me and some us time which is quite miraculous, usually both babes are asleep by 9pm, sometimes 10pm, which leaves a few hours to work, cuddle, chat, read and watch movies. Or clean up or eat if necessary. It's lovely to have a few hours like that, when everything is peaceful and calm, little children sleeping and grownups just relaxing.

It's all perfect in its imperfections. I never thought I would love life as much as I do today.

Let's Talk About Postpartum Depression

I think it's great how the TV show Nashville is portraying Hayden Panettiere's character, Juliette Barnes, as someone suffering from Postpartum Depression (PPD). PPD isn't talked about often enough and it's good to see a popular TV show actually show how bad it can get and not make light out of it. Mental illness isn't on the top of the totem pole at the best of times, but PPD never really sees the light of day in mainstream media. I'm pretty sure that most people don't really know much, if anything, about PPD unless they have been pregnant and/or spent a lot of time doing pregnancy and recovery research, chatting on message boards such as BabyCenter or What To Expect, and/or had a great doctor or midwife.

The thing is, while Nashville's writers have implemented this hard-hitting and pretty sad storyline, Juliette's life is far from the life of an everyday woman. She obviously feels very confused and alone, and is countering her depression with drugs and alcohol, in a very visible, and scary way. She is not however a mother of 4 living in the Bronx who is showing no outward signs of any problems until one day she throws her infant out of her apartment window. The two stories are a little different... One is a portrayal of PPD in a glitzy show, great for raising awareness and starting a discussion, the other being real life, as hard as it is to accept. PPD can hit anyone, no matter your age, income or familial structure, and while both cases listed above may be on the more severe side of the spectrum, this illness exists and needs to be understood.

Over the past three months THREE babies have died after being thrown from windows by their mothers in NYC alone. The fact that these three infants died in exactly the same way at the hands of their mothers is a huge call for concern. It hurts me to even write about this but we must open up the conversation and talk about it, raise awareness and start pushing doctors, nurses, friends and families to look out for warning signs. And most importantly, let women know that they can ask for help. Throwing a child out of a window is not a typical act of premeditated murder. It seems to be a fatal and brutal act of impulsive violence; an act that happens on the spur of the moment without thoughts of the consequences, an act that may have been out of desperation and suffering. The point of this article is NOT to make what these women did seem less horrific, but to open up the conversation about depression and PPD and to hope that one day we won't see mothers harming their children and themselves so regularly in the press, that at least women will know when to ask for help.

I consider myself lucky that I haven't suffered from PPD after either of my pregnancies. I have suffered from depression in the past, a recurring issue which would push me to self-medicate with alcohol. Depressive times would usually equal many black outs followed by a period of sobriety. I am lucky to have learnt how to deal with these unexpected periods of darkness, and to not lean on alcohol to get me through them anymore. I have friends and family members who have had it a lot worse than me, but I think between us all we were able to help and educate each other. I had heard of PPD before my first pregnancy, but I didn't think it was very common, and didn't really think I was at risk. I was overjoyed to be pregnant and couldn't wait to meet my daughter. My life was changing for the better, so what did I have to be depressed about?! This was until I talked to a friend who was telling me about her pregnancies and births, and she mentioned that she had had PPD with her first. She had never been depressed in her life, was over the moon with her child and couldn't understand why she was finding it hard to bond with her daughter, was constantly crying and getting angry with everyone. She said that it was like seeing herself from the outside and didn't know how to make it better. Luckily she was able to talk to her doctor who prescribed her the meds she needed to feel like herself again. She stopped taking the meds after a few months and had no further issues, and her PPD didn't return after her second child.

It gave me a lot to think about after I had my first child. I cried quite a bit during the first few weeks, but then again, I cried a lot during my pregnancy. It wasn't from sadness, or depression, or even from frustration, I just clocked it up to hormones. At my 6 week check up my midwife asked me a lot of questions and pressed upon me to never hesitate to contact her for a checkup if I felt unlike myself, sad or depressed. That type of follow up is what should systematically happen during a 6 week postpartum check up. It unfortunately doesn't. I had a different group of doctors with my second child, and while the prenatal care as well as labor and delivery were more than excellent, my 6 week check up was practically in and out (granted I didn't see the doctor who had followed most of my pregnancy, but that shouldn't have mattered). I wasn't asked about my moods, about how I was dealing with my newborn, if I was sleeping OK. Nobody ever asked if I had any prior history of mental illness, depression or PPD. Had I no real idea of what PPD is I could have just walked in and out of there none the wiser, suffering from a mental illness that no one had detected, or even bothered to detect.

How many other women has this happened to? Doctors practically follow your every move during pregnancy, offering all types of tests and procedures to make sure mama and baby are doing well. Once a woman goes into labor she is offered all types of interventions and pain relief options, everything to make sure mama and baby have an easy and safe delivery. Two or three days later you are discharged from hospital, with stitches, bleeding and slightly dazed, and told to follow up with your doctor in 6 weeks to make sure everything has healed well. Can I tell you what happens in those first few weeks, especially as a first time mother? You need to learn how to breastfeed properly, and that isn't always easy. Babies don't "sleep like babies", they sleep whenever they want which may be all day and not at night. Your hormones are all over the place and you are worried about doing everything wrong. If you have other kids then you are learning to cope with the transition of adding one more to the nest, and not abandoning the others. Some women can't afford to take time off and rush off back to work still bleeding and tired as hell. Some women don't have the help of family members. Some women don't have a partner to help with nightly feedings or diaper changes. Some women have partners who work around the clock and can't count on them to help in the day to day routine. There are not many women who are able to really rest for those few weeks after delivering a baby, and it is in our nature to just get up and get on with it, never showing what we may perceive as fears or weaknesses. We talk about those with very close friends who have been through it all and with strangers on message boards.

We have become so good at hiding issues that it's very easy for PPD to go undetected. Especially if nobody bothers to check on you. If anyone asks me how I am, I always respond that I am OK, even if I am not. Not only is this my nature – it is also inherent in many women. Why would we say that we feel depressed when we have nothing to be depressed about? Why would we "complain" about our feelings when we should be bursting with happiness? Tired? Yes, that's normal. Depressed, sad and angry? No, that's not the way it should be.

So what exactly IS PPD? Let's review some facts and stats. The Centers for Disease Control and Prevention (CDC) has some general information on depression in women and PPD, not enough to my liking, but they do provide some statistics and some survey results and findings. All of the statistics from the CDC website come from surveys that you can find linked on their website. The CDC calculates the percentage of women who suffer from PPD at between 8 and 19%. Other stats provided give us an idea of how common depression is for women: 8% of pregnant women suffer from depression and 11% of non-pregnant women. These stats are all based on reported cases as well as live births, so women who suffer a miscarriage or still birth are not included. So who really knows how many cases of PPD there are a year? A fantastic website called Post Partum Progress takes these stats and fleshes them out a little. This quote really helps put into perspective how common PPD really is:

"According to the Centers for Disease Control, 11 to 20% of women who give birth each year have postpartum depression symptoms. If you settled on an average of 15% of four million live births in the US annually, this

would mean approximately 600,000 women get PPD each year in the United States alone.

In fact, more women will suffer from postpartum depression and related illnesses in a year than the combined number of new cases for men and women of tuberculosis, leukemia, multiple sclerosis, Parkinson's disease, Alzheimer's disease, lupus, and epilepsy."

I can hear many of you thinking "but it's only depression! Why not ask for help?!" There is no such thing as "only" depression. Depression comes in shapes and sizes and often hits you when you don't expect it. Many women who suffer from PPD have actually never suffered from depression in their lives! There are no "telltale signs" of impending doom. A black cloud doesn't appear above your head. Depression also often creeps up on you, little by little, until you are surrounded by a fog that just won't lift. There may be warning signs, but most women avoid picking up on them or acknowledging them before it's too late. PPD can be treated with therapy and meds, but it needs to be treated. While some women can get better without treatment, others may find themselves becoming more and more despondent, leading to a lack of self-care and a lack of care for their child(ren), and in extreme conditions to self-harm or harming their child(ren).

There are quite a few reasons for why women wil! not talk about depression or feeling depressed:

- The stigma of depression. Who wants to admit they feel depressed when they are supposed to be going through the happiest moments of their lives?
- No proper screening. Too many doctors fail to screen postpartum women correctly in order to diagnose PPD, or brush concerns off as "baby blues" and "hormones readjusting themselves". The baby blues are not the same as PPD. Most women go through them after birth, crying about silly things, but after a couple of weeks you stop bursting into tears at things like the sight of the

Clydesdales in the Budweiser advert. PPD symptoms tend not to disappear but worsen.

- Human nature. We are meant to be strong, tough enough to endure anything. Why would we complain about something as silly as a little sadness?! We need to get on and do things, because if we don't they will never get done. We are so used to multitasking, juggling and wearing different hats (with or without children), but the fear of falling off our paths or dropping a ball is always there, shimmering in the background. We just don't ask for help because we don't want to show that we are struggling.

Postpartum Depression is only one, albeit the most common, of a variety of perinatal mood and anxiety disorders. Others are Pregnancy Depression (depression during pregnancy), Postpartum Anxiety (while it's natural for new mothers to feel anxious during the first few weeks postpartum, PPA is more serious, including inability to stop worrying and the appearance of fears that will not go away), Postpartum OCD, Postpartum Panic Disorder (the onset of panic attacks), Postpartum Post Traumatic Stress Disorder (often after a difficult pregnancy or traumatic birth experience) and the rarer but very dangerous Postpartum Psychosis.

We all struggle at some point or another in life, and there should be no problem reaching out for help. Asking for help isn't a sign of weakness but one of strength. No one should be made to suffer depression alone.

What are the signs to look out for?

- Not sleeping well (outside of the usual lack of sleep that comes with having a newborn)

- Inability to eat properly

- Feeling overwhelmed on a regular basis

- Inability to take care of yourself and your child properly

- Issues bonding with your baby

- Feelings of sadness, anger and despondency

- Feelings of guilt

- Thoughts of self-harm or escape

- Thoughts of harming your baby

- Turning to alcohol and/or drugs to tune out reality

It's important to know these signs and to make sure those around you are aware of them too. In so many cases women will hide their feelings and thoughts because they don't want to feel like a failure in the eyes of others. PPD doesn't just happen to first time mothers, it can randomly happen at any time within the first 12 months after any child. It also doesn't always appear immediately after birth either – some women may feel fine for months until it rears its ugly head. While not as common, men can also suffer from a form of depression after the birth of a child, and it is equally as important to make sure it is taken care of with treatment and/or therapy. According the CDC website, 4% of fathers will suffer from depression during the first year of a child's life, and 21% of fathers will suffer one or more depressive episodes by the child's twelfth birthday. Not something to be swept under the carpet.

Certain women may be more at risk of getting PPD than others (hard time getting pregnant, complications during pregnancy and/or birth, premature child, multiples, pre-existing mental illness, child in the NICU for example), but there is just as much chance of getting it after a healthy and easy pregnancy and delivery.

Postpartum Progress states that "one in every seven women gets a perinatal mood or anxiety disorder like PPD" - if only half of those women get treatment, what about the other half? Do they suffer in silence? Do their children suffer because their mother cannot care for them properly? Growing up in the presence of a depressed parent is mentally harmful, and way too common. If you have ever let yourself in to your home after (elementary) school and made your own dinner, done your homework alone and tiptoed around the house, afraid to make any noise, then you know what I am talking about. So let's talk about depression, and let's talk about PPD, and let's remove the stigma that comes with asking for help.

While not every PPD case will end in such an extreme or horrific manner as the stories mentioned above; with proper, effective screening and education on the illness, we may be able to avoid such tragedies in the future. There is no need for entire families to suffer from a disorder that can be so easily treated. As I stated earlier, no one should be left to suffer alone, and we should not force ourselves to suffer alone.

It's natural not to want to take medication for a mood disorder and it is not always necessary. Some women who have PPD successfully manage it through therapy. There is not a one size fits all solution for the illness, just like there isn't for any mental illness, including depression. The most important part is the diagnosis and then an effective path of treatment.

If you feel like you may be suffering from PPD, reach out to a doctor or a counselor. Postpartum Progress also provides different types of support groups and help via their website, and if you are in the UK organizations like Pandas UK can provide help and support.

If you feel like a friend or family member is suffering from PPD or depression, reach out to them. Provide support in any capacity that you can. You cannot force someone to seek help for depression, but you can help make it easier to talk about, which is the first step towards seeking treatment.

Of Tough Weeks and Pretty Faces

To be honest this past week has been the toughest week I've had since Aurora was born, probably nearly as tough as those couple of months when I was so run down with all day first trimester nausea back in the beginning of the year. It started off with Luna waking up even more frequently at night (think every 20 minutes after I had finally nursed her to sleep), and then maybe getting a couple of hours tops in after I went to bed. We were both beginning to wonder when this awful sleep regression was going to pass (Google says that it can last up to 6 weeks), when I realized that she was also coming down with something. So sleep regression plus a cold equals a very, very unhappy toddler. And by unhappy toddler I mean screaming about everything toddler. We are lucky, the last time Luna was sick was exactly a year ago when she had Roseola. Since then no cold, no tummy issues, nothing! Hopefully some of my amazing immune system has rubbed off on her, because I can definitely deal with this only happening once a year. So anyway, Luna woke up in the foulest of moods on Wednesday and it hasn't really let up since then.

I feel terrible for her. She's obviously very uncomfortable, what with the whole not being able to breathe through the nose issue, but she refused to take any Tylenol for the fever (trust me, I tried everything) and wouldn't let me do anything to relieve her sinus and nose symptoms. Poor kid spent most of the days (and nights) whining, wanting to nurse and screaming about not being in my arms. She has perfected the tantrum to an all-out act of flinging herself on the floor with dramatic arm gestures and that terrible eardrum-piercing scream (which she practiced quite remarkably well in the Laundromat). I can't even imagine what this is going to be like when we hit the terrible twos, or threes. Actually I don't even want to imagine because at that point Aurora will also be a toddler and there will be some major double trouble action going on there. Of course, on Friday, I woke up with a sore throat and Aurora woke up coughing. Although I've had a perma-headache since Wednesday, it hasn't really got any worse, and while Aurora has a bit of a cough, other than a runny nose, she seems to be weathering this cold a lot better than Luna. I also feel slightly bad because our new neighbor moved in last week and when I saw him I said that the kids were usually pretty quiet. Ha!

I honestly don't think that my patience has been tried so much in a long time, and it's been a good learning experience about my own limits. I haven't been able to hand a kid off to Cesar because he's currently working doubles Wednesday to Friday and we barely see each other to say hello during that time, let alone be able to find the time for me to take a kid break. This schedule is tough, but at the same time allows us to have two uninterrupted days altogether (2.5 days this week with Thanksgiving), so it is worth it. I am just going to have to figure out fun activities to keep Luna occupied during the long winter months, because they are going to be long. We stayed inside for three days straight, but on Saturday I couldn't deal with it any longer, wrapped the girls up as warm as I could and went out for a brisk walk. Luckily the stroller winter covers arrived today, so now that it's getting cold out Luna won't be affected by the freezing wind hitting her directly in the face. In any case, this cold is still in her system and is really affecting her sleep, and therefore my sleep. Sweet little Aurora seems to manage to sleep through most of the screaming incidents, but that may just be because her way of fighting the cold is to sleep and she wasn't getting enough of it (my fault, I wasn't making sure she was napping enough, although she practically sleeps through the night right now). In any case, I decided to stage mini photo shoots to lighten up the mood, and to get back into practice again. I miss taking photos and I miss taking photos and focusing on what my camera is doing. This past year I have just been shooting and fixing, and not fixing then shooting. Too many blurry, badly focused photos, too many grainy iPhone photos. A change is needed! The best part about taking these photos was seeing the girls interact with each other, because it constantly makes my heart melt.

Moving Again

Two years ago Cesar and I started our search for an apartment together where we would start to raise our family. It broke my heart to have to move from Bushwick after nearly seven years there, but there was really no way we could afford to pay the rents there with the way they were rising. It would have been doable if I hadn't been pregnant with the intention of taking three months off work (and there is no paid maternity leave in the service industry... I was lucky that my job was being kept open). Anyway, I wrote about how we ended up in Flushing before, and it ended up for the best because I didn't go back to my job and ended up working on building up my freelance writing career while being a stay at home mum with Luna.

I've grown to love Flushing tremendously. It took me a while, but now that we are really settled and have found "our" little places, like our two favorite diners, our bagel shop, our preferred supermarkets I've really started to consider our neighborhood home. We've made friends at our different locations and I always stop in to different places for a quick chat when we are out and about. Through trial and error we found the best take-out places and I still have some Indian places to try out. I also love our apartment. It has been both Luna's and Aurora's first home, the place where Luna said her first word and took her first steps. The apartment is a good size, and while exorbitant for a 1 bedroom in most places in the US, very good rent-wise for NYC. It's not all perfect, it's an old building and we've had issues with cockroaches coming through the pipes and I'm sure there is a mould problem in one of the walls (even though the super assures me there isn't). Our upstairs neighbors have no regard whatsoever for the fact that they live above someone and they sound like a herd of elephants screaming at each other 24/7. (Seeing as I can hear them screaming and throwing things at each other all the time I sometimes really wonder if I should call the cops, but I don't want to be that annoying neighbor). I'm being serious though – I understand the sounds of their kid running around during the day and maybe early evening, but the stomping, screaming and throwing things after midnight? Not cool. Especially after he came to complain about our music at 4pm one day (it wasn't even loud). Also I think he may be a little evil and treats his wife terribly. But anyway, apart from a few issues we have been perfectly happy here. We are on the first floor which is great for getting the stroller in and out of the apartment, especially with groceries, and our windows look out onto the courtyard so we don't really get any street noise coming in. That also means that the apartment can be a little dark, especially in the winter which does bother me a little, but nothing a few well-placed lamps can't fix.

So, anyway, our lovely neighbors moved away in the spring and the landlord spent about three months completely renovating their old apartment. Around the same time that they started showing it to prospective tenants (October) we received our lease renewal form. Our lease isn't up until January 31st so I was a bit surprised and when I actually read it I thought I was having a nightmare, or at least in sudden need of glasses. They were raising the rent by over 40%!! Granted this place is great value but definitely not worth just under 2 grand. The apartment is old, the appliances are on their way to being ancient, the kitchen floor is peeling off and the bathtub is probably from when the apartments were first built. Our apartment is rent stabilized, but we have what is called a preferential rent agreement, where the landlord provides the "market rate" for the apartment and then halves it for this "preferential rate". Now, if I hadn't been 7 months pregnant and we weren't in dire need of an apartment when we signed the lease I would have researched it a little better. I guess hindsight is a bitch sometimes, but anyway, moving on. According to certain information I found thanks to some of my own and some friends' research, we could actually fight it, but neither Cesar nor I had the energy. (Something to keep in mind if you are presented with a preferential rent agreement in your lease).

So we decided that we were going to find a better place, maybe two rooms. There aren't very many affordable places in NYC anymore... Cesar went to look at a couple of areas in the Bronx and we were pretty sure that was where we were heading, and we already knew we were going to have to pay more for anything we looked at. And there was the eternal issue of having to save enough to move... At least one month's rent and one month security, which is fine if you aren't living paycheck to paycheck, not so much when you are struggling. But then our building manager asked us if we would like to stay in the building as a few apartments were being vacated, would be gut renovated and then put on the market again for $300 more a month. My initial thought was "eff off!!", but once we actually discussed it we realized that it would be cheaper than getting a new place elsewhere, because an extra $300 every month for a year would be equal or less than all of the initial moving costs!

So, in January we will be moving 4 floors up to a place full of light and no upstairs neighbors! I'm well aware that we are now going to become the annoying neighbors upstairs with stomping kids so we shall be putting rugs down in the hope that it will help somewhat! I'm excited – they have done a great job on the finished apartments... New electricity set up, new bathroom, new kitchen, new floors. I'm excited for the light and the view over this part of Flushing, and also for the little fire escape where we can start a little herb garden. And no need to change doctors and routines. It may be a little annoying trekking up and down 4 flights of stairs with two small kids but we will deal with that. I'm planning on locking the stroller under the stairs – I don't see how it could be a problem as it won't be a fire hazard or in the way. I'm looking forward to moving into a place that is going to be brand new and clean and light and bright! No need to scrub the bathtub and tiles with bleach just to see the black mould return within a few days. (I had a bit of a moment back when I was 38 weeks pregnant with Aurora and decided to scrub the entire bathroom with pure bleach. It wasn't very smart).

So we are good for another year, but how much more feasible is living here anymore? When I weigh the pros and cons of moving elsewhere, like Northern California, the pros have begun to outweigh the cons. Yes, I wanted our kids to grow up in the city I have learnt to call home, but now it's become more important to me that we can afford to rent a little house with a back garden and enough space for us all to have space. Room for Cesar to work on his construction stuff and artwork, room for me to work comfortably on my writing and room for the girls to run around and play freely. We would also love to adopt a dog. As I've said before, as long as we are altogether it doesn't really matter where we are anymore. And I'm so used to missing places that it should make missing NYC easier! Loving living here hasn't stopped me from missing France every single day.

So that's where we are now. Moving and saving and making plans for the future. A lot has changed in less than three years! Still in our castle-like building for the next year, but who knows what will be home after that!

Merry Christmas Again!

Everyone deserves a real family Christmas, akin to one spent as a child. We all have our own personal memories of Christmas, ones that we often pull through adulthood with us, nostalgia of more innocent days and memories of fun times trailing along with the tinsel every year. But I do think it is important to have some less than spectacular Christmases, in order to really appreciate those that are special. It will always be my favorite time of year, and nowadays, with two little girls and a partner in crime by my side, it has taken on an extra special kind of merriness and magic. After so many years of not being able to be near my family at Christmas and trying to recreate a semblance of it here it feels really good to not be constantly searching for that special Christmas feeling anymore. It's there, the moment that December rings its opening bells and Cesar brings the Christmas tree home.

The last two Christmases I was pregnant... We actually only discovered I was pregnant with Aurora on Boxing Day morning, but I already knew deep down that I was carrying another child. So this past year has been a little bit of a whirlwind really! It's as if half of the year was taken up by being pregnant, and the other half by learning to adapt to a growing family in the same apartment that we learnt to live together as three (or four, including Joey Ramone our incredibly patient and gentle cat). This Christmas we will cook and watch the girls unwrap presents (well, watch Luna destroy wrapping paper with glee), and spend time together, time that we don't get enough of nowadays. There will be a mix of Mexican and British Christmas music playing on a loop, many movies watched and plenty of food eaten.

We have so much to do before Thursday, and most of that will need to be crammed into one day. Sunnyside for mince pies, chocolate, crisps, Bisto,

HP sauce and bread, as well as a lovely Christmas cheer on the streets, Christmas presents for the kids and food shopping for the list of things that we are planning to make on both the 24th and the 25th. It's supposed to be unseasonably warm on Friday so a good brisk walk won't be out of the question, and Luna will be able to show off her pretty Christmas outfit. And I am planning on eating everything in sight because once the holidays are over I will need to start thinking about getting rid of this pregnancy weight that doesn't seem to want to budge by itself (I guess naturally slim doesn't always mean naturally slim after two pregnancies in less than two years). I'm planning on making oat roast, roast potatoes, roast veggies (Brussels, parsnips and carrots), steamed veggies, Yorkshire pudding, veggie stuffing (my mother used to always make me stuffing and roast it outside of the turkey), and Cesar will be making a roast beef. And of course, Bisto gravy! For dessert, mince pies and an assortment of pies and chocolate (not making any of that though, I don't have the energy and we don't have the kitchen space for endless baking unfortunately). Maybe some freshly baked croissants and scrambled eggs in the morning? On Christmas Eve we shall be making pot pies and mashed potatoes, and maybe Cesar can find some tamales on the way home from work… My mouth is watering even thinking about it! A vegetarian Christmas is super easy to create (although Cesar eats meat, everything else is cooked for the vegetarian in the house, so that I don't miss out), and seeing as the kids will most likely both be vegetarian until they choose otherwise, it's great that I can pass the traditions that my mum passed on to me on to them (if that makes sense).

We have already made our annual trips to the tree in Rockefeller Center and Santa (at the mall), and it was lovely to walk around the city, even though it was so warm it felt like we were in October, not December! Luna wasn't interested in sitting on Santa's lap, she actually used her banshee scream to let us know that she didn't like him, but it did make for another hilarious goth Santa photo, especially with little Aurora sitting in the middle, all calm and smiley. (And Santa really looked like he needed a double shot of whiskey; scratch that, the whole bottle!). Other than that I've not made much of an effort with Christmas cards and gifts this year as it's been a tough end of year financially with having to move and all, but I shall hopefully get back on that next year and be a little better (then again, who am I kidding, I wrote but forgot to send a bunch of thank you cards after Luna's birth and sent about 4 Christmas cards last year. For some reason I have become terrible at that and I really must try harder at being well-mannered!).

2016 is going to bring a lot of changes for us, some we already know about, and others that are sure to happen. I'm more than excited to take a step into the future and see what it has to bring us. We all need some changes, a spurt of new inspiration and drive, so I am looking forward to what we shall do with everything that life will hand us down the road in the next few months. I have a lot of plans, and I know that Cesar has too, and it will be wonderful to see them to fruition together. (And maybe a few more date nights and nights out in the future?!).

Goodbye and Hello

(A title taken from the second album of my most favorite singers of all time, Tim Buckley).

I never dreamed of NYC. I never even imagined moving here. My arrival in NYC happened due to a string of circumstances at the time. I never once thought that this city would become my home, it was a slight pause on my way to California. And then I got into a cab at JFK with my two suitcases and saw the skyline from the highway. My heart told my brain "this is home", and she was right. In the nearly eleven years that I have lived here I have never once regretted moving here. Wanted to run away at times? Yes. Never wanted to ever leave a 4 block radius? Most of the time. But I have no regrets at all, the random events that happened 11 years ago made this move a great choice of my life. This is why it breaks my heart to say goodbye.

I know that not a week will go by when I will yearn for a bodega coffee and a walk down the street with my camera in hand. But not a day goes by right now when I don't yearn for a walk up Orchard St, saying hi to friends along the way, popping into the French Diner for an omelette and to 200 for a pint. I walked down that block the other day and nearly burst into tears when I saw how unrecognizable it was. I felt completely disoriented and sad. 200, Taqueria, Bereket, all gone. The Sixth Ward empty and closed. But this is NYC, and this is how it goes, it changes constantly, she reinvents herself, evolves and as much as it saddens me, this will never change. All we have left are our memories, and they will always remain. This will not be an "I'm leaving because I can't afford it anymore" rant. This will also not be a heartbroken "I have to leave but want to stay" essay. While both statements hold some truths in them, it's a lot more than that. I dream of slightly different things now.

I dream of a back yard for the kids to run around in. I dream of a porch for me to sit on and write. I dream of a dog or two playing with the kids in the backyard. I dream of Cesar working "normal" hours and having time to play with his kids and hang out with me. I dream of being able to afford a place with more than one room, where the girls have their own room, we have ours and there would even be a room for guests. Our current super has lived in a 2 bedroom apartment in this building with his wife and three teenage kids for years now. That works for them. It isn't how I imagine our future. I dream of Cesar having his own area to paint and create and listen to his music full blast without me telling him to turn it down because a child is sleeping, or our upstairs neighbor is being an asshole. I dream of having my own writing space where I can cover the walls with quotes and pictures and inspiring pieces of paper.

I used to dream a lot about bringing the kids up in the city, just Cesar and me against the world, but over the past few months, especially after having Aurora, I have started to feel more despondent and the city has begun to lose her magic. **I never want her to lose her magic.** However much she changes, I want her to always hold that special feeling for me, the one that makes me sigh with relief and opens my heart. I don't want to leave with the feeling that we got run down by the hardships and the day to day life. Yes, life can be incredibly hard here; every day is a hustle for us. I used to love that hustle, the unknown, the idea that one always needs to fight to survive here, but now, with a family, I want more than just survival. My life has been full of spur of the moment choices and decisions that have helped make it into something wonderful and creative and spectacular at times, and this is just another step in the journey.

So we told our landlord to list the apartment he was holding for us upstairs, got one way tickets for us and the cat for the end of the month, and booked the movers. I'm nervous and scared of missing this city that I have called home for so long, but I'm also excited to see what the changes will offer us and what it will be like to be close to family again after all of these years being so far away. Apart from both my mother and my sister living in the city for a few years I haven't lived close to my family for over 15 years now. It will be wonderful for the kids to grow up near their Nana.

So there it is. I have way too many memories to fit into one essay. Enough memories for several novels, collections of essays and short stories. The good, the bad, the ugly, the beautiful and the in-between. Just life in general. With a little distance I may actually be able to finish something properly, make a real effort to continuously submit articles over and over again and not get discouraged by a "no" or a "maybe". Write a real book. And by the time the kids go to school actually make a real living from writing. (And yes, I know I need to start believing in myself a little more). I was so used to packing up and moving on before I came here, dipping my toes into the waters, sometimes even submerging my body, and then jumping out and onwards. I never once imagined that I would leave here a decade later with a family.

So, so long city I never dreamed would become my real home. You will always be my home, even if I have to lay my head elsewhere for a while.

California, Here We Are!

We have arrived! After a few weeks of stress, packing, working through a list of endless tasks that needed to be accomplished before we left, planning without really having a plan, we have made our way to California. And while that part seemed hard, the hardest part really starts now with job hunting and house hunting and getting settled in an area that couldn't be more different to NYC. Neither of us have a license, and I've actually never learnt how to drive so that's going to be a major task that needs to be accomplished. I have already taught myself how to install a car seat properly, both rear facing and forward facing, so I'm kind of a little proud of that! I have to admit that I'm actually a little scared of driving and even more so of driving with the girls in the car, but that is a fear that I am going to have to get over because otherwise we will be stuck at home for forever. Luna loves car rides now and Aurora hates them, just like Luna did at her age. Hopefully she will grow out of that soon enough.

I think we were all a little shell shocked when we arrived last Sunday. We spent two nights in a hotel on the Lower East Side and tried to see people and places as well as rest all at the same time and it ended up being extremely chaotic and tiring and a huge upheaval for the girls. I'm sure the owners of Dorian Gray will be adding a sign stating "no children allowed" after our few hours there last Saturday as we managed to turn the place into a kid's play area and breastfeeding station. Thank you to everyone who came out to see us and to those who contacted us – I'm sorry if I couldn't chat for long or was a little unresponsive, but I really, really appreciate all of your messages and words! I had told myself that I had really detached myself from the city already, but that wasn't really true. I think I will always love NYC and will always consider her home.

Sometimes you just need to make choices that help you move onwards and upwards and I think this was one of them.

We boarded our flight at 8:30pm, and luckily JetBlue have direct flights from NYC to Sacramento. There is however a federal law that doesn't allow more than one child under two in one seat section, due to there not being enough oxygen in case of an emergency. So we were seated on the same row, but with the aisle in between us. As the flight wasn't too packed we ended up having 6 seats to ourselves which sounds awesome, but when you have one toddler who only wants to nurse and an infant who had to nurse on take-off we really needed to be next to each other. Luna was OK while we were taxiing to take-off but that took forever and the moment we actually took off she started to scream and fight Cesar... I could already hear all of the poor passengers' thoughts, but luckily one of the flight attendants came over and allowed us to switch kids mid take-off. After that Cesar moved over with Aurora and the rest of the flight was completely uneventful. Luna actually slept longer than she usually does without waking and Aurora wasn't fussy at all. We were absolutely exhausted though, and it's not something that I would do often. Traveling with one now seems like a piece of cake, two is OK if there are two adults, and I really don't know how people travel alone with two tiny kids!

Of course, as soon as we arrived I got a horrid cold that has made me feel like a zombie for the past 5 days. Then Luna got it and now Aurora seems to be a little under the weather. And for the first few days the weather wasn't too good, but now winter has said goodbye to California and spring has come in with a blast! This is the California that I've always considered "my" California: bright sunshine warm and then hot on my skin, palm trees in gardens and streets, blue, blue skies and the smell of warmth and fresh soil, and occasionally skunk. I can't wait for the trees to blossom and the oleander to flower and for the ground to feel warm on my feet. I can't wait for us to settle, find jobs and eventually have our own little house with a yard. We have so many dreams and it's going to be exciting to make them all become reality, one by one.

My mother's new house is beautiful. She's only been here for three weeks now but she has managed to make it feel like a home already. Joey has met his new friend Muffin and I think he is trying to befriend her, but Muffin isn't having any of it right now! She's just a grumpy old lady anyway and he seems to have realized that it's best to just leave her alone and maybe she will come around at some point. In any case he has settled in like the cat king he is. He may even get to venture outside at some point, we will see how I feel about that when we have settled into our own place. My sister's home is also gorgeous and it makes me so happy to see her all settled in her own cozy place. Both Cesar and I love her neighborhood – it's quiet but still walking distance from shops and restaurants, and very close to the downtown area where Cesar will most likely be working. Houses are a little more expensive there, but I suppose we would be saving in gas and would only need one car there, so that's good. At the same time there are not that many rentals going. So we will see! Not going to get ahead of myself yet! But I would really, really love to live within walking distance of amenities.

The girls are settling in more or less, as I expected Luna is having a harder time than Aurora but she is getting there. She has already learnt how to unlock and open all of the doors in the house, find her way to me from our room, and she has the most gorgeous play room to play in with tons of toys. Now if she would just start talking to me again instead of saying "eh eh eh" that would be great! Sometimes it feels like every time we make a little progress we do something that causes a regression. All I can really do is continue to provide her whatever comfort she needs so that she feels ready to communicate via all of the words that she understands and can say. It didn't really help much that she has had this awful cold too and barely wants to eat any food and wants to nurse around the clock. We will get there; it's just a matter of patience and perseverance.

A Story of Nursing Two

A little over a year ago, or maybe more than that, I wrote an article on breastfeeding, after randomly reading an excellent article by Annie Reneau from Motherhood and More that popped up on my newsfeed. I was new to the whole motherhood thing and new to breastfeeding and having a baby attached to me 24/7. Breastfeeding was a no brainer for me while pregnant, my mother breastfed us all, and I was going to breastfeed mine. Such a natural act should be as easy as pie, no? (If the pie is one of those intricate models of patisserie artistry maybe). A couple of people warned me that it wasn't as easy as I expected it would be, and a family friend suggested I read a book before I gave birth to help navigate any difficulties with latching and all the rest, so I skimmed through it and hoped for the best. I've always been stubborn. In some ways it can be a downfall, but in many ways it just means I will persevere until I get something right. This trait really helped me in those early days.

And here we are nearly two years later, a 23 month old, still breastfeeding, and a 6 month old, exclusively breastfed. I breastfed Luna through my entire pregnancy and have now been tandem nursing for the past 6 months, with no end in sight really. Both births were very different, and so were the girls' breastfeeding stories. Luna's birth was long and difficult and breastfeeding was so hard for several reasons, Aurora's was fast, easy and completely unmedicated, and breastfeeding was the most natural thing in the world. Everything that didn't happen after Luna's birth happened after Aurora's: I got to see her crawl instinctively towards my breast and latch on without any issue. The latter was also due to several reasons, most importantly that I learnt what not to let happen. Breastfeeding is completely natural – but if you don't have the support of your medical professionals, family and/or friends, then it can become a lot harder than it appears to be. This support goes the same way however you feed your child – no one should judge a parent by how he or she feeds their child – as long as a child is thriving, healthy and happy, and as long as parents have found a way that suits them, then as fellow parents (or non parents) we should not provide unsolicited advice or "concerns". I've read way too many mean-spirited comments bashing mothers on how they "should" be feeding their children and it always makes me want to slap people. Exclusively breastfeeding as well as what is apparently called "extended" breastfeeding works for our family, and I hope to help normalize this again without insulting anyone.

After Luna's birth I got to hold her for a few minutes and then she was whisked away for a few hours. I was so overwhelmed and exhausted that I couldn't find my voice, and when she was finally brought to my room I couldn't get her to latch on. I had repeatedly asked to see the lactation consultant, but when she arrived she didn't do anything. Luckily one of the nurses was there and showed me what a proper latch looked like. From that moment onwards, by trial and error, Luna and I figured it out together, through being told I was starving my child by a nurse, through cracked nipples and pain, through clogged ducts and endless hours of nursing. Ten weeks later and all of that was forgotten, apart from the endless hours of nursing. Luna was gaining fast and breastfeeding had become a second nature to me. Nursing in public was hard at first as I was uncomfortable, and Luna would scream if covered (she still hates to be covered in any capacity, especially while sleeping), but in the end I gave up worrying about it. I sometimes received a strange look, but nobody has ever said anything to me. I suppose there is always a first, but I'm not concerned about that... Luna now can request to nurse herself by saying "dootie!!!" and requests it pretty often still. I say to myself that if we both managed to get through a pregnancy while nursing then it's for a reason. She's definitely not ready to give it up just yet.

Nursing through a pregnancy is interesting. Strange, normal and somewhat painful towards the end. When I found out I was pregnant with Aurora Luna was only 8 months old and I was so worried that I was going to have to deprive her of those last few months of breast milk. "As long as we can make it until her first birthday" became my benchmark. My (new) doctors had no issues with me nursing while pregnant (some OBs don't recommend it) and told me to continue for as long as I felt comfortable. Around 15 weeks Luna became very agitated whenever she nursed and I thought that my supply had disappeared but now I realize it was most likely the combination of a growth spurt on her end and a slight drop on my end. Everything evened out again and we made it past her birthday and all the way to 36 weeks where I had to spend a night in hospital, the first night that Luna spent without me. No issues, she went right back to nursing again, but at that point we were down to two or three times a day and night, before naps and bed time. I thought that was perfect – a great transition point. I laugh at myself now with hindsight as she now nurses all throughout the day again (but finally less at night). Anyway, if you have a tenacious child who will not give up then be aware that nursing is not comfortable during the last weeks of a pregnancy. Latching on is painful. Luna started putting on a little weight again so I assumed my milk had reverted to colostrum, and she didn't have an issue with it. I didn't really have any problems with contractions, some Braxton Hicks here and there but nothing real until I was in labor. I also think I am a great example of how the whole breastfeeding as birth control DOESN'T work. We followed all of the "rules", no bottles or pacifiers, breastfeeding around the clock (literally), exclusive breastfeeding etc etc, and Aurora still arrived a little over 16 months later…

Aurora's labor was so easy, so fast and so intense that I still remember it as a blur: one moment I was waking up to a contraction, the next I was in a hospital bed, half dressed with one part of a monitor stuck to my tummy, the other hanging on the side as the nurse hadn't had time to place it. As I mentioned previously, Aurora latched on all by herself and nursed for 20 minutes before she was taken to the nursery to be checked (she was born in meconium-stained waters). Cesar took a photo of me right then, tired but wide awake, so happy, and so peaceful. Aurora was brought back to me within the hour. I tandem nursed for the first time that afternoon, both children together, holding this tiny baby above my tiny toddler, hoping that I would be able to get the hang of it without any issues. With Aurora breastfeeding came completely naturally, she ate and unlatched when full, there was no round the clock nursing or cluster feeding – very efficient. From day one, despite her jaundice, she has thrived, weighing in at 20lbs at 6 months. I do feel that tandem nursing ensured that there was always more than enough milk waiting for both of them. Aurora started sleeping 6 plus hours a night very early, and Luna helped keep any engorgement at bay. I'm assuming that I will just keep nursing Aurora until she is ready to wean too, whether that be at one year, two, or three.

Tandem nursing isn't easy. I don't feel like a superwoman or powerful, but I do feel like it is completely normal. Sometimes though, I just want to sleep for 4 hours without having a child attached to my breast. Sometimes I want to be able to go out by myself for a few hours without worrying about a child who refuses to take a bottle. Sometimes I really want to be able to write for an hour without being interrupted by the words "DOOTIE!!!!!". Other times I am so grateful to still be able to comfort Luna whenever she needs it. And to make sure that she is still getting some kind of nutrition even on the days that she refuses to eat. I am happy that I can help Aurora through growth spurts, teething pains and any other worries she has by providing her with what she now feels is comforting. I am happy that I don't have to actually get out of bed when one of them wakes up. I'm really happy that I don't have to pack or clean bottles or have to worry about making sure that the diaper bag always contains more than a few diapers, wipes and clean baby clothes. I sometimes think that I must just be lazy, because I've made everything about ease for all of us. I'm so happy that I don't have to spend money on formula, because it's so expensive. This does also mean that my inability to actually make Aurora drink from a bottle results in me not being able to leave her for more than a few hours. And that Luna may rely on her "dootie" every time she feels even the slightest bit upset or uncomfortable, and every time she wakes up at night. It also makes me wonder how long I will be nursing two, because I am so adamant that I will let them self-wean, but at the same time I have no idea when that will happen. I think I need to find a cut-off point, maybe three years old, but at the same time I am pretty sure they will both be less reliant on me by then. Maybe Luna will decide in a few months that she doesn't need her dootie anymore. Who knows? I do know that I'm not interested in nursing three children at the same time, so if we do end up having a third then some serious decisions will need to be made. But we aren't there yet, and I'm not making any plans on that subject. I'm sure anything is possible though, women breastfeed triplets and quadruplets (I always wonder how they do it; it's so interesting and intriguing). In the meantime I feel like I should finally start working on that breastfeeding counseling course that I have wanted to do for a while, and obtain a certificate so that I can officially help people.

Nursing a toddler is both easy and annoying. Easy because you don't need to actually do anything, and there are no worries about making sure they are getting enough milk. It is annoying because it often becomes an acrobatic art, swatting away pinching fingers and feet that find their way kicking you in the head. And annoying because you lose the ability to "time" feedings yourself, or at least work your activities around nursing times. Most of the time Luna will all of a sudden drop everything she is doing, wherever we are, and demand "dootie" right then and there, for reasons unknown to anyone except for herself. Sometimes a "not right now love" works, other times the demands become more insistent and the only way to avoid a tantrum is to give in. Nursing a toddler is never boring and rarely relaxing.

All the above to basically say that breastfeeding can be hard but it can also be very easy. If you are a first time mother I advise that you make sure you are surrounded by people who support you, including medical professionals who understand that it is important for you and your baby. La Leche League is a great support group and you can go to a meeting before you have your child, just to make friends and learn from other mothers. And lastly, it's important to believe in yourself. Just because your baby is feeding every hour doesn't mean you don't have enough milk... If your baby is producing the correct amount of diapers and putting on weight there is no need to worry. Real supply issues are actually pretty rare as long as you nurse on demand, eat well, drink your water and try to rest and relax. I wish I had known a lot of those things during those first weeks with Luna; it would have saved me so much worry, stress and pain. I pushed through it, but it would have been so easy to give up too. Everyone is different, and every family is different, but if breastfeeding is really important to you, don't give up on a bad day. I've posted some links below to articles and groups that really helped me along the way, with the first few weeks, nursing in public, "extended" breastfeeding, tandem nursing, nursing through pregnancy and any other question that I may have had along the way. And I still have questions and feel very lucky that I have friends who also breastfed or still feed who I can call to ask for advice, give advice to or just to commiserate with.

And lastly, take pictures! I regret that I don't have many photos of breastfeeding both girls as tiny babies and none of me breastfeeding Luna as a toddler (must work on this). I love the #normalizebreastfeeding movement and have no issues posting photos of myself breastfeeding online now (I was very nervous about doing it a few years ago though), but photos don't have to be for the world, they can just be for you - these years are so fleeting and while one, two or three years may seem like a long time in the moment, they aren't in the grand scheme of a life. I love capturing memories on the fly, moments captured in time for oneself and for others.

Sorting Through My Thoughts

Sometimes I really wonder what I want out of being a freelancer. I know I want to write. I know I want to write about everything and anything. I know that writing makes me feel happy and that it makes me dig both inside and outside of myself to create something that makes my skin tingle. I also know how despairing it can be when you suffer from low self esteem and a constant lack of self worth. There is always an underlying question running through my brain, telling me that nothing that I write will ever be good enough anyway, so why do I continue to bother? And at the same time I sit there astounded by the absolute crap that some publications promote. I know that there is somewhat of a consensus that everything needs to be dumbed down nowadays, but is that because the people browsing content online require it? Or on the contrary because newspapers and blogs and other writing outlets are more intent in getting content out there as fast as possible instead of actually trying to produce informative and interesting articles? And when did the job title editor become "person who constantly misses typos on even the most prestigious news sites"? I remember a time when the BBC actually provided excellent news articles, well written and well researched. Nowadays they seem to mainly be written by toddlers with toddler attention spans.

So much is based on website clicks and traffic and "likes" and "shares" nowadays too. And this isn't limited to writing but to all types are artistic and non-artistic endeavors. If you can't generate a good, steady stream of traffic then people don't even bother to even read or listen to or look at what you do, because it is deemed of no importance. Yes, before the internet you would have to really go that extra mile to get published, have your demo listened to or get your artwork exhibited, but at least everyone was on the same level to begin with. Hard work didn't include getting people to click through to your website and leave again and hoping that what they saw sparked some kind of interest. And while you still need to pitch and pitch and pitch today, some people just don't care how great your work may be, they are just interested in how many people "like" you page and how many "shares" your content could generate. The amount of writing job proposals I receive that are more about creating clickbait content or writing fluff to boost SEO keywords is pretty insane. Or even better, getting paid to write content for your own website that actually contains an underlying advertisement to a company. These jobs can pay pretty well and are easy to do, but they kind of make me feel sick to the stomach (and yes, I have done a few). And then, if your website doesn't generate at least 500 views a day you aren't deemed good enough to hire.

Don't even get me started on all of those practically false clickbait article headlines! All they do is generate comments from people who haven't even bothered to actually READ the article (The Independent I'm looking at you here, amongst others). I do understand that everyone is trying to generate clicks and views mainly so that viewers scroll past advertisements that pay for the bulk of the publications' website and staff but I would honestly rather pay a small online subscription fee for say the New York Times and actually read some decent journalism and writing. Is it that hard nowadays to actually read through more than 500 words before getting bored and scrolling on? Is that all people want to do, be constantly assaulted by fake headlines and shock tactic images? Instead of researching a subject or a current event do we just want to blindly follow some website's information and assume that it's true, and maybe add our own misinformed comments to the stream of individuals who have very strong ideas about something they know little about? Maybe this is why I still have a hard time with Twitter. While I love the concept of having all of this information at my fingertips I find it difficult to navigate through the constant updates of snippets of information and dialogue. And I'm not one to post random thoughts on the internet all of the time, so after a few retweets and a few clicks I feel overwhelmed.

I know full well that a lot of my frustration in finding work and making headway in my writing career lies in my own inability to focus on one thing at a time and actually continue to push myself. I refuse to find a "niche" for my blog so it remains to be a bit of everything. I have been told countless times to find a "niche" and promote that, but I don't want to. I started blogging in 2003, on LiveJournal, but have been journaling since the age of 9. My blog was always an area where I could write about whatever I wanted to write, and it gives me the courage to put parts of myself out there. Every year I push myself to be a bit more open with my writing, to share things that I wouldn't have felt comfortable sharing with the world and I want to continue to push myself. I know there are many things I could be doing better social media wise. I know that I should be collecting articles and pitching to all kinds of publications. I know that what I really need is to set myself a proper schedule and stick to it – I've always thrived on a strange mélange of impulsions and routine, and I'm not where I should be right now. I feel like I am spreading myself so thin that I am not doing anything properly anymore. I try to write and breastfeed and play and entertain and eat and cook and write and tidy and do laundry and groceries and read and watch movies altogether and when you do too many things at once, nothing is done properly. I will have a hundred ideas all at once and can't actually sit down to really develop any correctly. I get frustrated with myself and with the world and then the moments of self-doubt creep up on me... What if I actually really am not that good? What if I actually fail at what is the only thing that I have really wanted to do in life? I can only blame so much on the internet and the quality of writing that people are looking for nowadays.

The thing is, I KNOW I can write. I just need to stop procrastinating and find a way to make things work again. One of my main stumbling blocks in life is that I always find it easier to concentrate my efforts on what is going on around me rather what I need to do for myself. And having two little children provides a great excuse for not getting anything done. So I just need to work out a new routine and make it work again, writing as much as possible, pitching as much as possible and working on my essays and short stories again. I have a huge pile of work that needs to be edited or rewritten and a lot of things that need to be written. I'm currently working on my travel memoirs series, I have a collection of essays around Orchard St and I plan to start one on Ludlow St. I want to finish off the collection of childhood stories and wrap a bow around it. Maybe actually start looking for an agent. I don't know. I just know that I don't want to continue to fight clients on pricing structures because they can "get cheaper elsewhere" and I know that I want to see my name right by anything that I produce. Not because I want to be "famous" or "recognized", just because it would be quite thrilling to see my name accompany my writing. I never wanted to be a ghost writer and even though I don't mind doing paid ghostwriting work, I would like there to be a balance.

So that's that. A rambling rant and some real progress. This is why I love to write – the written word helps me to sort through all of the thoughts that crash against each other in my mind, thunderstorms with pockets of sunshine, and determine next steps.

I'm still annoyed about how Facebook practically forces you to pay for ads to "boost" your content if you want people to see it though. And I have no idea how to incorporate keywords into my content to force it to appear in a web search. Isn't that what tags are for?! I suppose that's why people hire social media specialists...

Sometimes...

Sometimes I just need silence. There are moments when I wish I could close my ears as easily as I close my eyes, shut out the world for a few tiny minutes, bask in the glory of no noise. Or just place my headphones over my ears, turn the volume up, close my eyes and wait for my heart to soar. Just a few minutes, a few minutes to recreate the balance that has become top-heavy. Readjust the scales, put the thousands of noises and smells and visions and feelings that fly into me, clashing together en route, into their proper little boxes in my brain. Those boxes that are covered in colors that blend together to create a wonderfully multicolored life that sometimes, just sometimes, needs a little calm. A waxing and waning hurricane that requires a little rest by the ocean before tearing onwards and upwards towards its next destination.

Little voices need my ears and my arms, day and night; words ping onto my phone screen looking for answers or help or just to make me laugh; music comes from one side of the room and smashes into the sound of the cartoon that is playing on the other side. Peppa Pig and Nick Cave melt together, becoming one in my mind, and while the image itself is quite entertaining, the reality is a little jarring. Twinkle twinkle little star in my red, right hand. Can someone please ask Robert Smith to record a few lullabies?

Remember when as a child you would look towards adulthood and imagine that all of a sudden everything would change, you would suddenly become more responsible, know the answers to questions, even invincible? Then slowly but surely, as the years pass you realize that you are still the same child inside, your shell is a little weathered and your features more defined, but there was no adult awakening. Instead you continue to walk along your path wondering what being an adult actually means. I feel like such a fraud at times, playing at this game of "being an adult", accepting, embracing the role of parent but still protecting that shy, scared but strong willed soul inside of me. She fights back sometimes, urging me to just jump in the deep end with abandon while I weigh the pros and cons, balancing freedom and responsibilities on both palms of my hands. Adult is just a word for being over 21, nothing more than a word. I think we are all still searching for those elusive answers, some of us trembling inside, but determined not to show it. While the fears of earlier years have subsided somewhat others have taken their place, as simple joys have taken the place of the constant search for something more, something better. Nowadays it's all about the opening of a rose, the scent of freshly laundered clothes in the wind, a long walk down a country lane. Dreams are less of foreign travels and new discoveries and more of good health and happy children, but nonetheless still entwined. Priorities move around the board, hopping over each other to find a more advantageous spot in the game, and some wishes are stranded for a while until their turn comes round again. My main concern nowadays is to slow everything down, embrace all of the moments and let go of those that won't be coming round anymore. Some things are just better left to others, or, at least, better left in the past. Nostalgia will cover those memories in a soft, pink cloud, and will allow me to write about them later in a different light.

Ah, in the end silence isn't always necessary. A few moments to myself to pull these words out of my mind and onto paper also help balance those scales again. A little time with The Cure, singing at the top of my voice twirling a baby around the room works too. A long walk around, imagining life in all of the pretty houses surrounding us; hearing my eldest say a new word out of the blue; baking something delicious that makes others happy; and a long, hot shower with the birds chirping in the background through the open window. I don't need much, but sometimes I have to remember when I do need something to make it known. Silence can be as expansive as it can be harmful.

No More Two Under Two

A few days ago Luna turned two years old and that was also the last time I could say that we had two children under two. I use the word "whirlwind" a lot and I can say that the past three years have been a bit of one, but paradoxically they have also been a time of intense calm for me. Peace even (within, because that word has sadly nothing in common with the world that we live in today).

I used to rush through the days, packing in as much as possible, looking to always experience and learn and taste and feel. There was no time to spend doing "nothing", days spent in bed or on the couch watching TV resulted in a feeling of guilt. Guilt that I was missing out, guilt that being too hungover to move was a terrible way to spend one's short life. There was always something to do, somewhere to go, someone to see. I would rack up the hours at work in purpose, just to make myself feel useful. I would even thrive on the feeling of being overwhelmed. There was something satisfying with getting through an endless list of tasks that needed to be done simultaneously. Every so often I would stop and think about slowing down, but a day or two later I was back at it; "down time" was spent running from bar to bar, or running around trying to accomplish something or other, often left open ended when I lost interest.

These days I sometimes regret that I didn't pursue my writing and photography more during all those nights and days I spent either working or stressing about work or in a bar, or even just watching crap on TV, or even all those moments when I was reading two or three books at a time. Nowadays I cherish those moments when I have the time, like this, to write a few words down, the beginning of an article, an open ended letter, a stream of consciousness type rambling of words. But while I sometimes wish that I did have a little more time, it's all so worth it. Having kids or being a parent may not be for everyone, but it has been wonderful for me. More than that, it has been extraordinary and life-changing. The moment Luna was placed in my arms I knew that I had to live up to the person she needed me to be. And I've probably already failed a million times, but I will continue to strive to be better and better. Motherhood came completely naturally, so much that I couldn't wait to add another little being to our clan. Aurora just slid naturally into our arms and our lives, taking over our hearts just as much as her sister did. Going from one to two was actually slightly easier than going from none to one. Although each baby is completely different there are less of those new mama fears and worries when it comes to the second. I also had a much easier recovery from Aurora's birth, so that also has a lot to do with it.

That said, it has in no shape or form been easy. I still think that we were slightly (completely) insane to even consider having children so close together. Luna was only 8 months old when I found out I was pregnant with Aurora, and they are only 16 and a half months apart. This basically means that for 7 months we had two children under two. Luna has never slept through the night and still wakes up multiple times. Aurora slept for 6 hours in a row from about two weeks onwards but around 3.5 months decided that just wasn't fun and now also wakes up multiple times during the night. Neither have ever slept in the lovely crib that is at the end of the bed, well not really anyway, and I spend a lot of the night turning between the two of them to nurse them back to sleep. But you know what? It's OK. I've found that unless people know my kids they tend to think that I am exaggerating so I don't bother to say much anymore. We've had an extremely tough time with Luna, but at the same time I know that she feels secure and loved. All of the sleepless nights and battles and tantrums are worth it. I mean, how long is it really going to last anyway? How many sleepless nights did I have of my own accord, either by drinking them away in a bar or by stressing out about things that were never really that important in the long run anyway? THIS is important. Our children are important. And maybe I am just a big softie but that's OK, because now isn't the time for real tough love.

I've read enough articles and internet comments to know that everyone has their own stance on parenting, whether they are based on their own upbringing or their own experience, and most people feel very strongly about their own opinions. I learnt a long time ago to not listen to any of that. As a mother (or father) only you really know the best way to raise your child, what works for all of you and no one should be able to tell you any different. With motherhood comes a lot of insecurities and some people seem to thrive on making new mothers feel like they are doing the wrong thing. That's why it is so important to find that support group, whether it be your partner, extended family or friends, people who listen, help and only offer advice when asked. I can't even tell you the amount of times I heard "just leave her to cry for a bit" or "wean her now otherwise she will still be nursing whenever she needs some comfort". Those phrases tend to make even the strongest of people wonder if they have made a mistake and are raising their children to become "entitled brats". I don't know how loving a baby computes into raising an entitled brat, but there is a huge difference in picking a small infant up when they cry and doing an 8 year old's homework for him or her. Ah I could rant about this forever! All that to say less judgment and more compassion would probably help a lot of new parents feel more confident about their decisions.

Ah, those first weeks were full of changes and restlessness. Luna had a hard time accepting her sibling, which for a 17 month old is pretty normal. If you combine separation anxiety and the inability to communicate your wants and needs effectively the result is often multiple and pretty epic tantrums. I felt a lot of guilt during those weeks, guilt that I was somehow ruining one child's early years by forcing another child onto her. Even today, nearly 8 months later, there are moments when I feel that I don't spend enough one on one time with Luna anymore, or quite the opposite, that Aurora is getting the short end of the stick because Luna is just so demanding. And then for 5 perfect minutes in a day they will both "play" together around a pile of Lego, before Luna decides that Aurora cannot touch her toys or Aurora knocks down a tower that Luna has painstakingly built. But during those 5 minutes I know that it is all worth it.

I found it hard to juggle a needy toddler, a newborn and my freelance writing career. I couldn't concentrate on anything for more than 5 minutes, even during the evening or night hours when the children were finally sleeping. It's still hard, and most articles that I write have taken one, two or even five days to write and post. Anyone who says that by working at home they are able to be 100% there all the time for their kids is lying. When I am writing, I am concentrating about 50% on my writing and 50% on what my girls are doing. And usually have to drop the former for the latter, because that's just the way things are for now. It's hard to find time to actually talk to your partner about anything, and communication is absolute key in a relationship. Sometimes I look at the clock and am so excited about Cesar coming home from work so I can actually spend 5 minutes by myself in the loo, but then I remember that he has been out at work all day, dealing with a busy, often crazy, job and also needs a time out. There isn't always a balance and some days I feel like I am hanging from a thread... But then there will always be a miraculous moment of joy that brings everything back together again. A kiss, a new word, a milestone, dinner made for me or even just 30 minutes to get my thoughts down on paper. A beautiful flower in the breeze, a quiet walk in the park, an hour to listen to an album on my headphones, one or both of the girls sleeping longer than two hours in a row. A shower by myself! Most days I have both in the bathroom with me while I try to look decent – but I am proud of the fact that I have never gone a day without showering (the bathroom is set up with kid seats and toys for this purpose). So I suppose I can complain about not sleeping but never about not being able to shower!

All in all the tough moments are always outweighed by the wonderful ones. Seeing my children interact with each other, all of the moments of affection, the "I love you"s, the times when both children are sleeping peacefully together and Cesar and I can talk and laugh about how beautiful they are and how much we love them, running around the park, seeing them interact with their grandmother and aunties and old friends and new friends... If you asked me if I would do it over again if I had the choice I wouldn't even hesitate a second to say yes. If you asked me if I would do it again with another child I would probably say no, not so close together. Two this close is doable, three would be tough on us all. There needs to be at least a year or two between Aurora and another one. Tandem nursing is tough enough (mainly because Luna nurses as much as, or even more than Aurora), there is no way on earth that I want to be nursing three children of different ages in the near or far future!

I don't regret how I lived my life before having kids, but I sure as hell don't regret living my life as I do now. I'm so in love with my life, and with my little family, and feel like I can finally imagine a future that makes complete sense to me, and to my family. And I hope that one day when the girls are fighting about a pair of jeans or a CD that they don't hate us too much for having them so closely together!

My Tribe

Ever since I became a mother I have come across articles and social media posts where women talk about finding their "tribe". For a while, during those first few months of motherhood, feeling so insecure and alone, I wondered if I was supposed to find my own tribe; maybe one would miraculously appear in my life, surround me with warmth and hugs and reassuring phrases, telling me that I would be OK. Motherhood came easily to me, the love, the nurturing, the happiness, but adapting to all of the changes was a little harder. I would continue to read about women describing their tribe, see beautiful pictures on social media of women and their friends, all their children playing together happily and hope that one day I could do the same.

And then suddenly I realized... This "tribe" I was thinking of is no other than my best friends. **I already have my tribe; there was no need to find a new one.** Just because certain things shift when you have a child (or two in my case), doesn't mean that everything changes. Sometimes you just need to crawl through the fog to realize this. Just because you become a mother doesn't automatically mean you need to find a group of "mummy friends". You will make some along the way, most certainly, but those who have been with you through thick and thin still "get" you, or they do in my case anyway!

I've lived in many places, traveled to many countries, settled and then uprooted myself time and time again, and in every place I have left a group of friends behind. Some friends are there for life, an intricate bond that cannot be broken by time or distance, others are friends for a time, and with distance you lose touch. Some friends appear out of the blue and stay there for life; some come and go, weaving in and out of your path. Hearts are broken and sometimes healed again, friends are forgiven and forgotten; friends forgive and move on. Friendship is a give and take and there are always those where the give and the take are easy and seamless, and then there are others where it demands work, sometimes too much. I've always been a little wary of female friendships, having been burnt in the past by people, but those that I have really let in have my heart forever.

There is the one who became a mother at the same time as me, our children rolling, crawling and walking together. The one who knew I wasn't exaggerating when I said that I hadn't slept in three months. We would nurse our children for hours on the couch for hours, chatting about life, motherhood, or just bathing in silence. She is one who I can talk to at any time of the day or the night, who would come visit us in our apartment in Queens and bring treats and who I now miss terribly since we moved across the country.

There is the one who I met in a bar all those years ago and who I call my best friend. We've been through so much together and through so much separately. We have traveled through time together, angered each other, unintentionally hurt each other, held each other and laughed through too many wonderful, silly and exciting moments. She is still the first person I tell anything to, the one person who I know will always have a proper opinion or advice on something that I am struggling with and who will always write the best cards, be they for me or my children. Cards that I save and cherish. And she also happens to be the most wonderful baby shower organizer.

There is the one who I worked with, so much younger than me, but at times so much older than her years. A real free spirit, never to be held down by anything, that beautiful smile always raining down on you, making you feel so important and worthy. She will come crashing into your life like a bolt of lightning and wraps you in her relentless energy, ready to jump into any adventure that you are planning. She's the one I want to nurture and protect but at the same time need to let fly free as she has everything to discover and no boundaries will stop her. She was my Sunday afternoon partner, bringing food and stories, while let her rest her weary feet before her next adventure into the unknown. My little fiery wild child, so similar to myself at her age, but with all of the confidence that I lacked.

There are the two ladies who were my friends way before I was a mother, and mothers way before I even imagined having a child. At one point we were all thousands of miles apart, but that didn't stop them giving me advice and comfort when I needed it. One of them has the knack of calling whenever I most need to chat, and always making me feel like I am not going insane, and that everything is completely normal.

There are my Irish and English beauties, and even though we haven't lived on the same continent for well over a decade, we still communicate regularly, see each other when we can and support each other in our endeavors. We've known each other at our best and at our worst, we've partied together and been sober together, drank tea and eaten brunch, watched each other grow and shine and move forward and sometimes backwards. Sister from another mister and best friend, all three of us "met" online and became friends in person all those years ago.

Then there are the ladies that I have befriended through my writing and my thoughts, the kind and helpful ladies, the ones that encourage each other to persevere with their work and creativity, who always seem to appear when the going gets tough and you hit a wall. Kind of like an online cheerleading team, but one that cheers each other on, constantly. I never really feel alone anymore, even at 3am when everyone is sleeping and those silly thoughts of failure kick in.

And last, but not least, my sister, the one whose head I tried to pull off when she was a baby, whose obsession with Elvis lasted until well into adulthood and with whom I can have the most epic arguments and still talk to as if nothing happened five minutes later. I don't always believe that you have to be friends with your family no matter what, but I do believe in my sister as much as she believes in me. I hope that my girls will be able to love each other as much as we do.

My tribe, my "family", those people who never let you go, even when you push them away, and in return, who you will never let go either. I think back to those days when I thought I was supposed to do it alone, sitting there nursing endlessly through the night, wishing I had someone to talk to, and then feeling silly in the morning. I always had someone to talk to; my tribe was always there for me, just as I am always there for them. I had to learn that it was OK to reach out and say "I need you". No one is really superwoman, but we are all superwomen together.

Speech as a Milestone

Speech. Such a short word with huge connotations. We use speech every single day, a way to communicate, to express ourselves, to show emotion. So simple, but often so difficult. Before I had a child I would often consider speech a tough companion, because sometimes he was so easy to access, sometimes so hard, hanging out a few yards away waiting for me to stumble and wobble over, avoiding deep potholes that were always trying to trip me up. I would be so jealous of those who had no issues talking in public, or getting their point across to others.

Once I had my first child speech became a milestone, beginning in those little babbles that turned to "mama" and "dada" around 8 months, moving along to full words and then phrases a little bit later down the line. I spent my days talking and reading to a little baby who could only communicate with cries and babbles, hoping that it would all sink in and eventually turn into words flowing naturally from her mouth. I still talk and read to my kids all day long, a habit that I won't break until they demand me to.

When Luna turned one year old I expected to start hearing more than just mama, dada and "dat" (cat or dog depending on the animal, sometimes bird or squirrel). Instead we started to hear more and more tantrums, colorful moments of high pitched screams and streams of tears, snotty noses and sometimes so far as crying-induced vomit. A vocabulary that initially seemed so promising stalled and the eardrum piercing scream was perfected to a tee.

No matter how many talks we had, books we read or educational TV shows we watched, nothing changed. We used the excuse of being a bilingual family for a while, every time that people asked us why she wasn't talking, and were met with a few nods and a "ah ok that makes sense". I told myself that my brother didn't start speaking properly until well past his second birthday and now he's studying towards his PhD, so there was nothing to worry about. I thought about how I am much more eloquent in writing than speech and that maybe it would all click into place for Luna one day.

Luna hit 18 months and then 21 and there still wasn't any improvement. The tantrums got worse, especially as she couldn't communicate all the mixed emotions that were running around her heart and mind, sharing her mummy with another baby, having to wait in turn to be nursed instead of just cuddling whenever she wanted. I found myself having to curb my frustration with her more and more frequently, and began to wonder if we should start seeing a speech therapist to help her through this. I began to feel completely inadequate as a parent, on the one hand wondering what I could have done differently or better, on the other thinking that maybe I was making too big of a deal out of it. Luna has always been strong willed and demanding, emotional and caring, maybe she would find her own way with our gentle guidance, one step at a time. I stopped reading milestone blogs and started just trying to communicate differently with her, calming her down before another tantrum would break out.

And then it happened. Not long before her second birthday she started to repeat words to us, and every day she says one, two or three more new words. At 26 months she can now string two or three words together, tell me she is hungry, tired, sick or thirsty, ask me for a hug or for milk, tell me she wants to read a book or watch Peppa or Elmo, say please and thank you, tell me she loves me, name her teddy bears and tell me what she wants to eat. She can count to five and say all of her colors (usually to the delight of everyone in the supermarket), and even surprises me by picking up one of her foam letters and telling me what it is. While she still has her tantrums and she's still as demanding as ever, we have noticed a significant drop in the screaming and a much higher willingness to take the time to express herself clearly. Every day she will say a new word out of the blue and it blows my mind - she WAS absorbing everything all along, just waiting for the right time.

So yes, I suppose speech is a milestone for a child, but Luna has taught me, in more ways than just speech, that patience is also a milestone to achieve at any age. Communication is not only the ability to speak but also the patience to listen and absorb. Language can often be a tricky thing, and when somebody has a big voice but no words to release it, other ways of expression need to be used. There are other ways of helping a child express themselves; you just need to find out which one, for some it may be sign language, others it may be through pointing or pictures. I realize how much more laid back and "go with the flow" I am now that I have a second child, but at the same time I really hope that she won't find it as difficult as Luna did... There were so many times that we were both in tears out of frustration and it hurts my heart still to think how hard it must have been for her. In the end I shouldn't have worried so much about it, but it was hard not to when having to deal with upwards of 8 tantrums a day!

Middle of the Night Thoughts

It just suddenly hit me, a punch to the stomach, so hard I had to catch my breath. They will never be little again. Not little, little, tiny baby little. Tears well up in my eyes when I think of those sleepless nights holding my little Luna, her brow constantly creased into a frown. I wish I hadn't shouted at her today. She's so fragile but so strong and likes to push every boundary as far as she can. I want to not snap but sometimes it's impossible. She will never be that teeny tiny screaming infant again, the one who only wanted her mother, unless it was 4am and then daddy would do. These days it's all "mama mama mama", a scream, an angered yell and then "mama hold me" or "hug?"

I don't spend enough time staring into Aurora's eyes and telling her I love her. Or maybe I do, but that happens in the middle of the night when we are the only ones awake. Her eyes teach me that patience really is a virtue, because she has so much of it, enough to give away and still be fine. I whisper in her ear how much I love her, kiss her soft little cheek and hope that she doesn't remember all of the times that her sister pushed her over. Or hit her on the head with a toy. There is something remarkable about being the second child... Putting up with all of that and still smiling. Maybe she is just remarkable. She is to me anyway. They both are. My little sunshines and moonlights and my reason for wanting a better life in a better place. My motivation to make sure we pursue our dreams.

I don't want to forget any of these moments. I embrace them, I snap pictures of them, I put them into words, store them away in my mind, in clouds, on paper. I embrace it all, the darker parts, the struggles, the dawns and the rainbows, even the passage of time. But I still shed a tear for those moments that I will never get back again, when everything is new and overwhelming and difficult, but beautiful and hopeful.

Daytime Thoughts

I fully believe that it's important to never make a judgment based on appearances. But we always do, no matter how hard we try. Some of us try and some just don't really give a shit anyway and spend their lives judging others based on their religion, skin color, language, background, clothing, whatever. I always hope that I'm in the first group, and that I have learnt from any mistake I may have made in the past, making sure that I never do it again.

If you don't really know me, then you probably don't know how shy and how anxious I am. I've spent many a year hiding it beneath layers and layers of toughened up skin and bone, but it always finds a way to pop up when I least expect it. I've worked on myself over the years, using alcohol to find a way to hide my shyness, then sobriety to find a way to accept my shyness and to get past it. I've learnt to get over my fear of calling people I don't know and accomplishing tasks over the phone. I've managed to get past my utter fear of putting my writing into the public eye and I've traveled to places and talked to people even though I often felt like I was crippled with anxiety inside. I've even forced myself to speak in public, although I don't really think I want to do that again. I'm actually quite happy working from behind my screen now, with my children playing in the background (or hitting each other or screaming at me, whatever happens to be occurring at that moment).

With motherhood also came a dip in the confidence that I had slowly built up over the years, and then, after the first few months went by, came an actual gain in well-being, confidence and strength. For the first time in my life I felt like I had actually finally become the person I was always supposed to be. So those days when my confidence takes a beating I seem to feel it even more. It is kind of like climbing a mountain and instead of falling a few steps right near the top you tumble a quarter of a mile down again. Even the stupidest of things can make me feel like I've fallen down the mountain, just as the smallest of things can often bring me right back up again immediately afterwards. It's a strange feeling, trying to keep that middle ground of stability while your emotions are pulling you both up and down!

I've always been a good loner. I love my close friends from the bottom of my heart and miss them all terribly now that I have moved away, but I've always been good at creating and fully using my alone time. Books and walks and words and photos, lunches by myself watching the world go by and long trips to places where I didn't know a soul. None of those things ever fazed me. Put me in a room full of people completely sober and ask me to make myself heard, now that would give me anxious shakes and a desire to create a hole for myself to curl up in. I know, being a bartender and working in an extremely busy restaurant don't really seem to be the best jobs for an introvert from the outside, but that is actually wrong. Many of my fellow service industry workers are complete introverts. Many of my musician and actor friends are the same. That face that smiles at you and serves you your drink while chatting about the latest gossip is all an act, part of the job. An act that is pretty easy to sustain, a uniform that you mentally put on every time you walk into work. They are just jobs. Jobs that I absolutely adored before I became a mother, and would do again in a heartbeat if I didn't have two little children. I DO have tons of confidence, but only when I feel in control of my environment and comfortable in my place. It's a bit of a two-pronged sword being both confident and shy at the same time, because sometimes you end up creating a role for yourself which kind of portrays how people want to see you rather than how you actually want to be seen. Sometimes it leads to a lot of bitterness and sadness when you can't make your real self seen or heard when you really need to. And sometimes it makes it harder to explain that you need space and silence once in a while, time away from everyone and everything.

I'm still not confident as a writer, after all these years. I still hesitate every time I submit an article or deliver a job. I'm still always surprised when I receive great feedback and always a little hurt when something gets rejected. I kick myself when I read something similar to what I have written and hidden deep in my laptop's memory and wonder why I don't dare send these things out to others to read and love. Why do I watch others do it and sit back and wish that I had the confidence to put myself out there like that? Why do I hide behind my screen waiting for something that will never happen if I don't "put myself out there" so to speak?

And then I realize that I do. I do it every day. And maybe there are many, many things that I will not publish, just because they may be too personal or involve others or just don't belong here, they still belong somewhere, and some day I will find a proper home for them. I still have trouble with social media, with being more pragmatic and less involved in making friends and actually considering people humans rather than just one more person to read my blog, but I know there are others out there like that, who are trying to promote their work while making friends at the same time, and I'm happy to know these people, sometimes work with them, but mostly because their photos and comments make me smile, their thoughts are similar to mine and because they are all inspiring, funny and most likely have the exact same worries and thoughts and self-confidence dips as I do. I do admire those people who have been able to create a "brand" out of themselves, but I cannot do that, and at the same time I don't know anybody personally who has. Anyone I have actually "met" on social media is like me, just another person using words and thoughts and images to touch others. The whole "brand" thing is really not me at all. And that's fine, I don't need to do that, I just need to work on what I really want in a better way. (Sometimes I regret not being so proactive in my 20's and instead of writing a blog at that time that made no sense to anyone but me I could have actually created something a little more meaningful!). I think this is why I continue to refuse to make my blog into something more "streamlined" – it was always meant to be a platform for me to "publish" my creations, before I became a mother and after, and I don't want to change it. I may possibly set up something else in the future with some friends, I don't know, I would need to be more focused on one thing rather than letting myself be pulled in all types of directions.

Years ago I took all of my "things" that I had left with my mother for safe keeping back, including journals dating back to my first at 9 years old. There was however one missing, quite an important one, from my late teens in the late 90's. This past weekend my mother came back from her storage unit with a box with my name on it, and amidst my Cure 45s, some Ted Hughes and Shelley books was that journal. I'm not ready to go down multiple rabbit holes just yet, but I read a few pages of it and see myself, 20 years ago, so shy but so exuberant, angry and happy, and I'm glad I've lead the life that I have. And while I will always regret a few things, mostly those moments when I couldn't tell people how I felt, those moments when I couldn't explain how uncomfortable I was or even those moments when I didn't dare speak up and voice my opinions. But I can catch up on that now. And one day all of those stories that I have written along the way and all of the essays and the thoughts and the poems that I have jotted down will find their own place too.

I suppose all these words came about over the weekend when I was feeling a little down, seeing photos of my friends at the Rockaways, my favorite beach in the world, or at the Stone Roses concert in NYC and missing them, reading nasty comments posted by ignorant and bigoted people from all over the world on internet articles, and with just the sheer amount of utter shit that is going on in the world all the time, every time I look at my phone or check out my social media feeds. Some days it is very hard to live with having both a hurting heart and an overflowing heart. In the end we all bleed the same; I just wish I could stop the unnecessary loss of blood and life with my own hands.

So maybe, next time we look at someone and start to judge them based on something about them, maybe, maybe we should take a step back and remember that they are people just like us, with hearts and minds and souls and worries and stories and families and feelings. And maybe we all stand up and talk about everything that hurts and destroys us as a community, a nation and a world and bring about real change instead of just looking the other way. And when someone is trying to express themselves stop and listen to what they have to say, because it may be a moment to learn and grow, you never know.

And maybe I will remember to tell myself that despite everything I put in my own way my words will be heard by some, and in the end that is all that matters to a writer.

We Lead By Example

Back in 2011 I came across an article discussing the plight of a woman named Naomi Dunford who was being viciously bullied on the internet. It was on that same day that one of my sister's friends found a photo of herself up on one of those horrid slutshaming sites. Anyway, I wrote a short post on all of that, with a few links to cyberbullying and how to help take a stand against it. At that time, although I had been blogging for years, I was only just starting to actually take it more seriously, and was trying to finally start a real career in freelance writing. I was so disgusted by how easy it was to completely tarnish someone's reputation or even ruin their lives by just a few well-placed malicious words and images. Little did I know at that point that the internet had started to mimic a school playground, but on a much, much higher, larger and more dangerous level, and even more so today, just a few years later.

I don't know about you, but back in the days when I was at school, primary and high school, there was no internet and there were no cell phones. Bullying was probably just as bad on school grounds, or on your way home, but once you were away from the bullies they left you alone. Not that it made bullying any better, so to speak, but nowadays there doesn't seem to be anywhere to hide. At school, at work, at home, in your car, anywhere in the world... And we can still say that old song of "sticks and stones will break my bones but words will never hurt me", but we all know how incorrect that is. Words can hurt more than anything, twisting and turning their way inside, embedding themselves as deep as possible. Words hurt, even when they come from a faceless stranger.

I remember writing an article about internet comments and how terrible people could actually be, hiding behind their computer screens, a while back, before my second child was born. This time I was outraged by the sheer meanness coming from people just because a woman had decided to run a marathon without wearing a tampon. You know, maybe if we all got a little more outraged by how kids have been blown up by bombs in Syria for over five years, instead of over the trivial sight of some period blood, or a breastfeeding mother, then this world wouldn't be so bad. But then again, I suppose it's much more "fun" to bash another person online rather than raise awareness about some real evil that continues to happen. (Insert sarcasm font).

So here we are, five years after I shot off that cyberbulling rant back in 2011, and a lot more aware of what happens nowadays online. I've managed to avoid most of the mean comments myself, but mainly because I am not always comfortable putting myself out there so much, and I also have a great group of online friends who are genuinely wonderful people and who fight against these waves of mean girl gangs and women bashing each other. While I was never a mommy blogger per se, From the Inside has existed since 2002 in some form or other (LiveJournal then Blogger and now on Squarespace), I do write a lot about motherhood and my own personal journey as a mother. This also means that I spend time reading through other parenting and "mommy" blogs, often learning something or other, disagreeing with some things and agreeing with others. I also used to spend time reading through comments too, but I gave up on that a long time ago. It is horribly disheartening when you see a bunch of women just lashing out at each other from behind their computer screen, insulting each other and trying to make everyone else feel like whatever they may be doing is wrong. It feels like high school all over again, except a lot nastier and a lot more vicious. And these comments and these attacks are not reserved just for parenting blogs, they are everywhere, men and women, adults, attacking each other about beliefs, lifestyle choices, guns, whether women should be allowed to choose what they do with their wombs or not, even probably even ridiculous things like the use of soap vs. shower gel.

Granted, people have bitched about each other for ever, people have fought about things forever, but the relative anonymity of the internet, or at least the fact that you can type something into the universe and not really feel the fall-out of your words, makes bullying so much easier. I try to be very careful with my words, I have always been one who prefers not to say something rather than hurt someone's feelings, and the idea of putting a part of myself out there for others to judge still scares me (and part of the reason why I blog because it pushes me to do so). Reading strangers criticize and insult each other's choices makes me feel quite sick to my stomach. Not that my personal opinion is going to change anything, but I will continue to be kind to people unless they attack me.

Because we have to lead by example.

I've never been a model human being, and of course I have my faults, but I want to raise my kids in a world where they don't have to worry about being bullied by both people they know and people they don't know. And I want to also make sure that they don't join cliques that spend their time putting others down in order to feel better about themselves. Yes, it is easier to feel strength in numbers, but how can you be a real leader if you aren't able to see beyond the group? We all want our kids to live in a better world than the one we see around us, so let's try and build a better one for them from the ground up.

So what am I trying to say with all of this? Our kids learn about interacting with others from us. If I am always talking badly about others in front of them, how are they going to learn not to do that? If I am constantly talking about someone's weight or look or face or hairstyle behind their backs, then how will my kids know that that isn't a very nice thing to do? If I spend my time telling others what they should be doing with their lives and why what I think is more important than what they think, how are my kids going to learn about tolerance and diversity? Seriously. We lead by example. I do not want my kids to fall into the hands of bullies, and I don't want them to become bullies either. I want them to stand up for their rights, for equality, for love, for diversity and for all the good in this world. And I want them to stand up for their friends and not fear the mean girl waiting to trip them up. Nothing wrong with falling on your face now and again, but it's important to stand up and stand tall and show everyone around you that you cannot be bullied.

You know, it's OK to sometimes feel a little envious of someone else's life. It's so easy to feel bombarded with perfect stills of perfect lives on social media, but we have to remember that what people show on their feeds is not always their real life day in day out. I love photography and capture moments on my cameras all the time, but for every photo of a smiling child there is a blurry one and probably two tantrums in between. Life is so multi-layered that there is no way to know what lies beneath each photo or each caption, and that is fine. I mean, honestly, I have friends who I have spent many a day or evening with and I only really know one side of them too. So yes, it IS fine to feel a little envious, but that envy should never be translated into bitterness or anger, or just a downright mean attitude towards others. In my own humble opinion we only have one life and we should try to spend it by seeing the beauty, experiencing the world and loving as much as possible.

And that said, I adore the wonderful group of women I have "met" online who, however tired, depressed, happy, grateful, overwhelmed or just downright disappointed they feel, always take a moment to make sure their friends are feeling OK and to encourage and help others. Because in the end we are all in this thing called life together whether we like it or not.

I'm not going to change the world with my words, but I want to lead by example, empower my girls to be strong and good, and stick up for others around me. Nobody should be bullied online or offline and I feel like we should all take a stand to speak out about things that matter rather than spend time talking shit about others. Who has time for that anyway?

20 Years a Vegetarian

As a kid I was one of those people who always ate what I liked the least first, and saved the best until last. I still try to do anything that way even today, although procrastination does tend to get in the way sometimes. In any case, I still remember quite clearly chopping up meat or fish into small pieces and shoveling it down my throat as fast as possible so as not to have to taste it or even chew it. It didn't matter if it were steak, burger, salmon or squid; it was rare that I would actually enjoy anything that had to do with meat or fish. The only things I can actually remember being OK with were mincemeat (ground beef), canned tuna and chicken breast (as long as there were no "black bits" in it). In our house growing up you finished your meal whether you liked it or not (pretty common procedure back then), so I just sucked it up. The idea of eating ribs still conjures up nightmares and the texture of those little octopi in my mouth will never be forgotten. Oh, and we lived above a butcher's shop for a while. I still remember the smells.

I suppose it came as no surprise when I suddenly decided to become a vegetarian at the age of 17. My sister used to laugh at me and talk about "delicious bloody steaks" in a loud voice around me (she was a really annoying 15 at the time so that was to be expected), but my mother seemed to release a huge sigh of relief and most of my friends didn't find it to be very weird. To be honest, I think I just said it out loud one day and decided to stick with it to save face. And I say that not because I didn't want to be a vegetarian, but that becoming a vegetarian at 17 in France in the 1990's wasn't an easy feat. It meant that I actually had to start thinking about what I ate a little more, and making sure that whatever I ate didn't contain any meat or meat by-products in it.

My mother had been vegetarian for a few years in her youth and gave me some recipes to try. She even started to make things separately for me on Sundays when we had a roast dinner or other family meal. Sundays were the only days that we actually made time to eat together as a family at that point, as work, school and friends seemed to get in the way during the rest of the week. It's only now when I make different meals for everyone that I really realize how much of an effort she made to make sure that I always felt included during those meals, especially during special occasions like Christmas and Easter. At restaurants my go-to meals would be "a salad without the bacon, ham or tuna please", or ravioles (still one of my favorite dishes), or an "omelette au fromage", or just a simple baguette with Brie. There were many times when I had to send something back because it still had meat in it, or I had to pick around something because I was too embarrassed to say anything. I went to visit a friend in Blois for a week and we ate lunch at the same restaurant every day... On the final day, after ordering the same salad minus any meat the chef came out and asked me if I was vegetarian and reprimanded me in the nicest way possible for not saying anything. He had so many meal ideas that he would have loved to make me! From that moment onwards I decided to be more confident and while I still had the odd "oh my gosh I thought I was clear about being a vegetarian" moment, I ended up eating some amazing meals. Just because a country appears to have a very meat-heavy menu, it doesn't mean that a vegetarian cannot eat well and healthily. You just have to think outside of the box a little and not be afraid to speak up.

I never actually missed meat. Around the age of 19 I suffered from a bout of severe anemia, most likely due to growing pains, too much running around working and playing and a bad diet of pains au chocolat and ramen noodles. People advised me to go back to eating some steak, but I couldn't stomach it. The anemia disappeared once I settled down into a healthier routine for myself, and never came back. My iron levels have been stable since then, even through two pregnancies and tandem nursing children. For me that is proof enough that we don't NEED to eat meat, our bodies absorb nutrients from a varied diet, and I am pretty sure that it is healthier for us to not have to digest meat or meat products...

It's been over 20 years now and since I became vegetarian I have tasted meat exactly twice. I was drunk both times and thought it would be funny. Once I took a bite of bacon. It was disgusting. Another time, I tried a cecina taco. It was gross. Nothing has changed for me: I still can't stand the taste or texture of any kind of meat, fish or seafood. I'm a real texture AND taste eater, so if anything resembles or tastes like meat or fish I can't eat it. You know how smoked cheese can smell like bacon? It tastes like bacon to me and I can't eat it. Or if a meat replacement product has exactly the same texture as meat I have to push it aside. I like the idea of these products as it's a great way for those who actually like meat to cut down on their meat consumption, but they aren't necessary for me. It's easy enough to replace meat in dishes like chili or shepherd's pie with beans and chunky tomatoes. I've been using a little bit more of these products recently in dishes, just so that my other half doesn't feel like he is missing out, but during most of my vegetarian years I have done without.

I will not handle or touch meat or fish. It honestly makes me want to vomit, the idea of eating it, the texture, the smell, so I refuse to have anything to do with it. This therefore means that as I cook most meals for the girls they also have a vegetarian diet for the most part. I say for the most part as I am a little hesitant on the subject. They have both eaten meat before, from their father's plate, but it's been a rare occurrence, and Luna isn't a fan (but she isn't a fan of much anyway). Aurora seemed to enjoy it, but she enjoys most things, so that wasn't much of a surprise. They do eat the same diet as me, which is a bit of everything outside of meat, fish and seafood, and it's important for me that anyone ask me before giving the kids anything to eat (I had to grit my teeth when a shopkeeper gave an 8 month old Aurora a lollipop once; and realized too late after the fact that my sister had fed Aurora meat without checking with me first, and I ended up not saying anything because it was hours later – please people always ask parents if you can feed their kids something before you do, you never know what kind of allergies or intolerances they may have. I don't blame my sister because she was just having fun feeding things that Aurora obviously wanted to try but I obviously still need to learn to be a better advocate for my beliefs). Long story short, the girls will choose what they want to do when they are old enough to make the choice, but in the meantime we will offer them a variety of what we eat at home, which will rarely include any meat unless Cesar is cooking it for himself.

I've toyed on and off with the idea of becoming vegan. I like the idea of never eating anything "animal" again, but at the same time I love cheese, and appreciate other dairy products and eggs. Then again, eggs have to be fully cooked all the way through, especially the white part, and I can't eat certain types of yogurt due to their texture. But I also can't find anything that actually replaces the amazingness of cheese, and to be honest I don't really want to either. So I have been thinking about reducing my dairy consumption, maybe halving it, and would love to start buying milk and eggs directly from local farms, or even own our own chickens at least. Even the dairy products labeled "organic" and the eggs labeled "free range" aren't as cruelty-free as we imagine them to be. It's hard to navigate through all of the products available, the prices ranging from dirt cheap to outrageously expensive, with labels full of words that make them seem fresh and organic, but don't actually state "how" organic or fresh they are.

Aurora has not yet really been introduced to cow's milk yet, because whenever she has a couple of sips it goes straight through her within minutes. She sometimes has yogurt, and often has cheese because she loves it (and she is my daughter), but I feel like she has an intolerance, and probably has tummy ache at times that I have possibly interpreted as teething pains (although there are a lot of them too). So I have decided to remove all dairy from her diet for a couple of weeks and then doing the Milk Ladder which is one of my allergy mum friends is using. If things aren't any better by her 15 month appointment in November we will see what the doctor says. I suppose this is as good a time as any to cut down on my own dairy consumption then. I shall not be changing anything in Luna's diet as she only ever eats when and what she feels like anyway (and that's a whole other issue).

I do want to add that a vegetarian diet isn't immediately healthier than a meat-eaters diet. Being a vegetarian doesn't just mean removing meat and fish from your diet and continuing along your way. It's important to know what you are putting inside your body and aiming for as varied a diet as possible. In my opinion this isn't just because of nutritional needs, but also because it's easy to get bored when you have no variety. I love an array of colors and always try to create colorful dishes. Green, red and orange always add wonderful pops of color to anything, and as I don't like dark leafy greens (no kale here thank you very much), there are always peas and carrots, red peppers and mixed greens in the fridge. I love lentils, beans, chickpeas, tofu, root vegetables, pasta, fruit, most vegetables, all kinds of food deemed "healthy", and they are naturally a large part of my diet. But I also love chips and fries and candy and if I didn't have to worry about making sure I remain somewhat healthy I could also live off of that for the rest of my life... It takes work to eat any kind of a healthy diet, and vitamin deficiencies can appear with any diet if it is not varied.

Several completely unrelated items spurred the writing of this article. One being several people raising their eyebrows when I state that I would like my kids to be vegetarian (no, I don't think I am depriving them of anything). Another item is the mere idea that killing off huge amounts of beautiful wild horses to create space to build places to kill huge amounts of cattle makes me feel physically ill. And last of all just because I look back at those days in my youth where I wanted to vomit and cry, but forced the food down without showing any of my repulsion, and remind myself to take the time to listen to my kids when they say that they don't like something. It's enough proof to me that we all have different tastes even before we can talk.

High Needs Child - Sleep is a Luxury

I skimmed through Dr Sears' The Baby Book right before I gave birth, looking for last minute tips on how to establish breastfeeding and how to get through labor without needing meds. I loved his writing style and how he promoted all types of attachment parenting logic, and the book actually made me feel all warm and fuzzy inside. Then it was put back into my bookcase to be forgotten about and never really revisited, not until months and months later when I was frantically searching "18 month sleep regressions" on Google that I came across a Dr Sears article on high needs children. For the first time in 18 months I actually felt like I hadn't done anything wrong with Luna, or failed her in some way. She ticked every single box on his list. "High needs child" was finally something that I could use to explain everything without searching through my sleep-deprived brain for an answer to why my child never slept, never wanted to be apart from me and had meltdowns over just about anything.

No one ever expects to have a high needs child (unless you already have one and just assume it's the norm). There are no warning bells that go off during your pregnancy, or right after delivery. I remember getting a cab home from the hospital in Brooklyn to Queens, and getting stuck in horrendous traffic on the BQE, and a two day old Luna screaming and screaming. That basically became our norm for many months.

I had bought an adorable little bassinet for her months beforehand, and her little 18 inch body looked so tiny in it. Swaddled or unswaddled she refused to sleep in it, falling asleep contentedly in my arms and screaming as soon as I put her down. Those first nights I wondered if it was me, was I not nursing her properly? Was she hungry like the nurse had said in the hospital? Was I an absolute failure at breastfeeding and actually starving my child? Dr Google told me to count her diapers and she was peeing and pooping more than enough, so that wasn't the issue. Cesar went back to his 80 hour a week job and needed all the sleep he could get so I just moved to the couch where I could nurse the baby for hours and hours and watch entire seasons of shows with zombie eyes, hoping to be able to place her on her lounger for a few minutes in order to close my eyes for a while.

I followed the advice of creating a routine and sticking to it and it didn't make one ounce of difference. She would never nap according to a schedule unless I popped her in the sling and went out for a walk, not too far mind you because if she woke up suddenly I was in for it. She had her bath at the same time every night, and loved it, followed by baby massage and a story and then I would nurse her to sleep, but about two weeks in she would start crying hysterically at that point, body completely rigid, and nothing would soothe her. I would text Cesar hysterical texts myself, not that he could do anything either seeing as he was at work... Eventually I figured out that maybe she was overtired or gassy or both and moving everything a half an hour earlier and adding a few drops of gripe water and some leg bicycling to the mix seemed to fix the regular 7:30pm on the dot hour of screaming.

It didn't fix the actual sleeping issue. Everyone tells you to sleep when you can, sleep when the baby sleeps. You know that you aren't going to get a full 8 hours of sleep anymore, but what happens when you actually have a baby that never sleeps? How do you actually get by on 20 to 30 minutes of sleep a night (literally) because your child will only sleep in your arms (and yes we tried everything, she even rejected the stroller). I know people probably thought I was exaggerating or doing something wrong, so I just stopped talking about it except to those I knew really understood. I dreamed of just two hours of uninterrupted sleep. There were days when I thought I would actually sell my soul willingly for just an hour of sleep.

We adapted. A friend of mine bought us a baby swing around the two month mark and Luna ended up sleeping in it for two to even three hours at a time at the beginning of the night and it saved my sanity. She even slept in it at night (not proud of that but it was the only place she would actually sleep for more than 20 minutes apart from my arms), but in the end I was so tired and after three months just couldn't face any more sleepless nights, and gave in and took her in the bed with us. I suppose if I had done that from day one I would have saved myself and Luna a lot of tears, but I was just following what everyone said to do. Of course now I know that safe bedsharing is absolutely fine and am not worried about it, but I felt so guilty at the time! That said, at 2.5 years old Luna still sleeps with us and still nurses around the clock so they don't just "grow out of it" like that.

I would see people mention "sleep regressions"... We never had any of that because she never slept anyway. Teething? It was apparent when she became more fussy than usual, but as fussiness was our norm anyway it was never actually too bad (and all of the molars came through without me even really noticing too much of a difference in mood). Going out? Cesar and I went out once together when she was about 6 months old and she cried for a lot of the time that we were out (three hours tops). We didn't revisit that until her sister's birth nearly a year later. Going out altogether? It was a struggle, but I'm one of those people who won't give into my fears easily, so I used to push through them and learnt how to breastfeed just about anywhere in public (without a cover because if I ever tried to cover her, her banshee screams could be heard for miles). I learnt that it was OK to cancel on something if I didn't feel like we could make it through without a meltdown (and we canceled a lot of things the first year). I can't praise ErgoBaby enough for creating a comfortable contraption that not only helped us navigate trips into the city and grocery shopping, but also through simple activities like walking to the park, making dinner and vacuuming. There is no way I would have got anything done without our precious baby carriers. I used to take her into the city by myself, go visit friends, walk around with her strapped to me, always with a little bubble of fear that her mood would suddenly change and we would be stuck on the subway with nowhere to go to. She always refused to have a pacifier, which I'm happy about now, but I was always jealous of those babies who would suck contentedly on their paci in their strollers.

Luna is two and a half years old now, and still very much a high needs child. She's extremely smart; fiercely independent in some ways and still very clingy in others. She nurses as often as her little sister and still wakes up several times during the night and fights naps during the day. She has very nervous tendencies, biting her nails when she feels uncomfortable or crowded, and has to have everything her way or she has a meltdown. She loves to walk everywhere, but if she gets tired she wants to be carried instead of sitting in the stroller, and although I hate to admit it, I use a lot of bribing tactics to just get us to places. A lot of my days are spent trying to avoid a meltdown of some sorts, figuring out in my head how long we can do something, or the best time to do something... Sometimes I am surprised at how flexible she has become over time, and then other times I realize that everything can change in a second. She is an absolute delight, the sweetest little thing, and she will be a strong and determined young woman one day, conquering everything that life throws in front of her. She also tests my own abilities and patience every single day, and although at the end of the day I sometimes want to just curl up, spent, I also know that she chose us as her parents because she knew that we would all be able to figure it out together. And that's what we do, one step at a time. There is no rush for her to be potty trained, to sleep in her own bed or to wean, she will be ready for all of these things when she's ready, and that is fine by me.

I do understand that people don't understand. It's fine, I'm not asking them to. I do however ask that people respect the decisions that we make as parents, because for the most part I know exactly how Luna is going to react in any given situation and also that while she may seem fine at the time, we often all suffer from it for days afterwards. One missed nap can mean two days of tantrums and meltdowns. I have had to ask her pediatrician and cardiologist to make a note on her file that she finds visits very stressful and to be as gentle as possible so that we can work on making her realize that doctors and nurses are there to help and not hurt her. Getting frustrated with her usually just escalates any situation, and that is something that I also need to work on myself every day. It's hard.

Luna can detect my moods and emotions easily and I have to constantly check myself to see that she doesn't notice my own anxiety or sadness.

I think that having a second child really helped me work through a lot of the feelings of parental failure I felt through the first year of Luna's life. As babies, Aurora and Luna were like night and day, even though we proceeded in the same fashion with both of them. It just showed me that no child is the same, and that having one high needs child doesn't mean that you will have another. And that some children actually like to sleep. All kids like to have the odd tantrum though... No one gets out of those!

I bet people wonder why we decided to have another child amidst all of this sleep deprivation... I guess I thought it would pass by the time she could speak?! We were actually more than prepared for years and years of never sleeping again, so you probably can imagine my surprise when Aurora started sleeping through the night two weeks after being born. But don't worry, she doesn't do that anymore, she loves to wake up at least three times, and still sleeps in bed with us too. Teething has been a real long, drawn-out pain for this poor little one and her new trick is to try to nurse for hours during the night. These dark circles won't be leaving my eyes very soon!

I wouldn't have had it any other way to be honest. I've learnt a lot about myself over the past three years, my own strengths and weaknesses, and that in the end we adapt to our environments and to our young. They are only little once, and in my opinion this is the time to help them feel both safe and independent at the same time, even if they don't make it easier for us. I'm glad that I had my high needs child first. Because after those first few months I was ready for anything, and still am. Long-term sleep deprivation and a full day of work at home while making sure the kids aren't killing each other? I got it! (As Luna would say). I still feel like I have failed both kids sometimes, but I also know that that is not correct, and have to cut myself some slack sometimes. No one is perfect, and no one will ever be perfect. All we can thrive to be is the best that we can most of the time.

Is Five the Final Number Then?

I have to laugh at it all sometimes when I think about it. In early 2013 I had decided that having children was not on the cards anymore, and here I am in late 2016, with two beautiful toddlers and another little one on the way. If you had given me a view into the future back then when I was standing behind the bar indulging in a shot or 10 of Powers and chatting with my regulars I would have probably laughed in your face before pouring you a Guinness.

While I may not have a huge extended family, I come from two lines of families where the women tend to have many children. And I think I say that I don't have a huge extended family just because we are so dispersed, having lived in different countries for many years – in reality there are quite a few of us around. I remember many a Christmas as a child in England, and then in The Netherlands and France, where we would fly home to be with our extended family. But once you become an adult you tend to start revisiting those childhood traditions in your own home, nostalgic for the past, hopeful for the future. I've spent many a Christmas alone in NYC, celebrating with close friends, missing my family. And then Christmases with my own growing family, teaching my partner and kids about my childhood traditions. I've written about these times on several occasions, here and here, so I won't rehash them today, but I suppose the main theme of Christmas will always remain family for me. My mother had three kids, and all of us will be together this Christmas for the first time in years. My mother's mother had five children, all girls, and her mother had 10 (!) children. My father's mother also had five children, two boys and three girls, and her mother had 4 kids (all girls too!). And if you go through my family tree, (that my mother has been painstakingly researching for the past few years), you will find that it was very common to see a multitude of sisters and brothers in each family. So I suppose I really had to do my part to continue on this family tradition!

It's funny how things change very rapidly. After a bit of a long pregnancy with Aurora but the exact birth I was hoping for, which helped ease away some of what Luna's more painful birth and recovery had left, I said that I was done. And then slowly but surely, once the weight started to come off and when raising two children didn't seem as difficult as I had expected it be, we started slowly talking about another one. Not so close as the first two, because two under two with a very high needs child is no walk in the park, and not until one had weaned. Let's not even try until 2017 we said. As with anything in my life real planning always seems to take a backburner because events just seem to happen naturally, as if I'm not allowed to feel too comfortable for too long. I'm still nursing both toddlers very frequently and have no willpower to wean anyone, and, well, it's still 2016... But a few days before the presidential election I realized that this carsickness feeling that had started a few days before seemed a little too familiar, especially seeing as I actually hadn't been in a car... That week was a little bittersweet, because we were meant to be bathing in happiness, but at the same time the elections brought on a wave of disbelief, despair and sadness that I have a hard time brushing away. It took me a while to feel "normal" again, and to be honest I don't feel "normal" (have I ever?!), but I do feel very happy, and am completely and madly in love with this little munchkin that is growing in my tummy, just like I was with the other two.

This little one is due on July 3rd, so when he or she comes Luna will be three years and a few months old and Aurora will be just under two. Luna is already excited about "the tiny baby in mummy's tummy", although how much of that she actually really understands is yet to be known. It will be fun to see her actually be able to express her thoughts about my growing belly this time around, as she was so young when I was pregnant with Aurora. It will be fun to see how Aurora reacts too... Once I get past this insane 24/7 nausea that has been plaguing me since I was 5 weeks pregnant and will hopefully start easing up now, I will be able to focus more on the future. In the meantime it's basically been on a day to day basis, make sure the kids eat, get fresh air and are somewhat entertained, get through my work before bedtime, so that I can collapse in bed with the kids and hope that sleep will bring some relief. I definitely had all day nausea with Luna, and had it a lot worse with Aurora, but this has been even worse still. Not that it has stopped me from eating. Just from eating most things apart from bread, Brie, lettuce and pasta. Everything also tastes super salty, which has never happened to me before and has basically put me off most food. Except Brie. Nothing will ever put me off Brie.

And so there we are, 6 more months, give or take a few weeks, and we will have another one in our midst. Girl or boy, it doesn't really matter (of course a boy would be great, just to mix things up a little, but we do have an absolutely beautiful girl's name lined up too, and it would be such a pity not to use it...). The adventure continues and I couldn't be happier to be honest. One day at a time, hoping that the weeks don't fly by too fast and that we will have another happy, healthy baby.

So Much Outdated Information Still Out There

This is my third pregnancy and my second pregnancy while still breastfeeding. I've been breastfeeding for nearly three years, and obviously will be going on for another few after this one is born. Basically, I know what I'm doing and I also know my limits. If I start feeling too tired, overwhelmed or uncomfortable, I will start the weaning process. If not we will just continue onwards as we have been. I don't imagine nursing three children at once, but I also don't imagine my first born all of a sudden deciding to wean. As I always say, we will see. I don't really care what others think either, what works for us, works for us. What works for you, works for you. What bothers me is when people decide to tell me something that is first of all incorrect, and second of all, just silly.

Apparently it is the California process to make sure you see a counselor at least once during your prenatal journey, so I saw the one assigned to me by the clinic this morning. She was lovely, very friendly and engaging, and made me feel completely at ease. Until she asked me about my diet and hydration and I mentioned that it was hard to drink enough water when all I wanted to do was vomit it back up, and that I really forced myself to down 3 liters a day as I was still breastfeeding two kids.

She said: *"you do know that after 6 months there are no more benefits in breastmilk for the child, right? It's only for comfort after that."* I just responded that my doctor and nurse were both perfectly comfortable with me tandem nursing while pregnant, and while she did say that I should at least wean one, she backed down and said *"but in the end you know best as the mother."* My eyes must have begun to flash daggers! I no longer feel like an inexperienced mother when faced with these types of situations, but I know that when I was I would feel upset and confused. So let's get some facts straight here.

1). The American Academy of Pediatrics (AAP) does not recommend the introduction of solids until 6 months, and advocate breastmilk and/or formula to be the main source of nutrition for the first year of life.

2). Solids are introduced little by little over the space of 6 months, so by the time the child reaches the age of one he or she will be enjoying three meals a day as well as snacks – although this is by no means always achievable. Some babies take longer than others. It is still important to remember that breastmilk and/or formula are recommended as main source of nutrition until at least one year of age (see above).The AAP does not recommend the introduction of cow's milk until after one.

3). Breastfeeding AFTER one year of age provides a whole slew of benefits. These benefits are in addition to any nutritional benefits come from eating solid food. The World Health Organization (WHO) recommends breastfeeding until at least two years old (and beyond).

Breastfeeding benefits do not magically disappear once a child starts his or her first spoonful of pureed avocado or smashed banana. Breastmilk DOES magically change its breakdown based on the age and needs of a child, even on a day-to-day basis. It just drives me quite insane that even in today's world people who have a certain influence on what a pregnant woman may or may not do can spout nonsense. Whether you are planning on breastfeeding or not, it's so important to be able to find out proper information from those who are supposed to be professionals. And professionals who talk to you about breastfeeding/formula feeding, introducing solids and weaning should always be aware of the latest recommendations. Granted, these do change quite often, but it's really not too difficult to read the updated AAP website or medical papers once in a while. We now know that introducing solids before 6 months can cause issues down the road, and that rice cereal really isn't the best first food. So even if our mothers or grandmothers or great-grandmothers may say that they did it their way and no one died, I still believe in science and research. (For example, I always put my babies to sleep on their backs even though my mother put us to sleep on our tummies. Research has proven that this is the safest way for babies to sleep). So yes, all I want to say is while Dr Google is not always the best place to go for questions, it is always good to do some research and ask different people about breastfeeding rather than listening to someone who has outdated and incorrect advice to give. Breastfeeding can be really difficult for some at first, and lack of support and/or correct information can lead to women giving up before they are really ready to.

(As a side note I have to say that I chose the prenatal clinic I go to because of how they promote breastfeeding and non-intervention birthing. Both my doctor and my nurse practitioner are 100% behind me and don't have any issues with me breastfeeding while pregnant. I think this counselor just had very outdated views and I probably should have mentioned that to her while I was there. I'm just not as outspoken as I would want to be at times, which often leads to ranty blog posts!).

What Mama Means to Me

I'm a bit of a paradox. I always imagined I would have kids, at least one daughter, but I would roam through my life, picking up and taking off whenever I felt like it, trying not to become too attached to anyone, soaring away any time I felt trapped. When I turned 34 I suddenly realized that I probably would never have children, and actually felt at peace with that. I liked my life in New York City, I loved my crazy lifestyle and the whirlwinds and the ups and downs and the all-around colorful pictures I painted of it all.

A few months after that realization I found out that I was pregnant. Only a few weeks along, but very much pregnant. Fear raced through my heart and images shot through my brain, but after a five minute talk my partner and I knew that no matter what, we were going to be parents. No more alcohol, no more cigarettes, no more running around from bar to bar after work and no more eating here and there, if and when I remembered to be hungry. I went from free-spirited party girl to responsible adult as soon as I saw that pink line appear and haven't really looked back. Nostalgia can be a lovely feeling, but that lifestyle had been getting old anyway, and I will never regret taking a huge step back and focusing on life and love.

Motherhood came easily to me. The aches and pains and sleep deprivation not so much, but the nurturing and that heart-crushing and earth-shattering love did. During those first few months it was impossible for me to see the bigger picture, what mama meant to me then was holding my tiny high-needs infant all day and all night and never wanting to let her go. It was a force that stripped me bare and built me up, my instincts grew sharper, my confidence waxed and waned and my worries deepened. I noticed that my focus on the world in general deepened again, my activist instincts whirred back into place and I felt more focused and possessed by a conviction that I would do anything to make sure my daughter grew up in a better world than the one we currently live in. I wanted my legacy to be one of many who at least tried (and that still stands today).

Despite the fact that I didn't sleep more than an hour a night in three months, that my child continued to nurse around the clock and that it took me ages to heal from a difficult childbirth, for some strange (insane) reason both my partner and I wanted another child. At 4am when he would come home from work and find us both wide awake we would sit and eat ice cream and talk about our next child's name and whether we would have another girl or a boy this time. I wanted to go through pregnancy again, this time with less fear, this time with a birth that I was in control of, not one that was induced. We both wanted two little ones to grow up together, close siblings. Family became everything that I had been looking for in my travels and adventures, a grounding point that could lift off at any minute, but never alone anymore, always together.

So, 7 months into motherhood found me yet again pregnant and still nursing my firstborn, overjoyed and excited about the prospect of having another little child in our arms. The pregnancy was different, slower, easier in some ways but so much harder in others. While I wasn't running up and down managing the restaurant 70 hours a week this time around, I was at home working on different writing projects and trying to be the best mother I could be to my little Luna. By that point motherhood had evolved into something I felt I finally had a handle on, we were all doing OK, but at the same time it started to feel like a bubble waiting to pop. I felt more isolated, stuck in the far end of Queens, unable to actually pick up and run to Coney Island or a show or just brunch with friends due to an always needy baby and what was becoming a bit of a problematic pregnancy. We were all super healthy, but my doctors were concerned about a few issues and didn't want me to do any lifting or extensive exercise. I didn't want to become that person who complains about never seeing her friends anymore or feeling stuck in a rut so I surrounded myself and our family with tasks and activities and everything that I wanted us to accomplish before little sister's arrival. Of course most of those never happened, and those last few weeks of pregnancy involved extra check-ups and gallons and gallons of water and hot, hot summer days where all I wanted to do was nap and scrub floors with bleach.

Aurora came into our lives one bright morning, after I paced the living room, groaning as softly as I could so as not to wake Luna who, for once in her life, was sleeping through the night. Motherhood then became strength and another thunderbolt of that intense love that seems to grow and grow and never stop growing. Motherhood also became messy and disorganized, loud voices and silent screams, toddler tantrums and late night thoughts wondering if we had done the right thing. Two under two makes for a fun hashtag, but a hashtag doesn't give the term enough justice or depth... On the one hand it is a deep pit full of unknowns and sludge, on the other it is a bouncy cloud on a perfect English summer day, rays of sunshine touching rainbows and pots of gold. I still count my blessings that my partner and I come from a long line of adaptable people, and managed to easily adapt to the changes that another child brought with her birth. Her birth also gave us the strength to make a few decisions that were necessary for the well-being of our family life altogether and for our future happiness.

We moved away from the city that we had adopted as our home for so many years, towards the sunshine and the embrace of family members. California is where my toddler started to speak, finally using the words that she had been storing up inside for months and months, where "mama" became a standard word uttered at least every 3 minutes, and where my baby uttered "mama" for the first time. And my heart still melts every time I hear their sweet voices say it. Oh my gosh, they mean me! I am a MAMA! I am THEIR mama! And I know that just like it has over the past few years, that word will evolve in meaning, but it will continue to melt my heart every single time I hear a little voice saying it. Mama means everything to me, my world, my love and my family. I never thought I would feel this way, but I can't ever imagine not feeling this way!

And so there it is, for me motherhood is a constant evolution, discovery and sometimes a struggle, but in the end I see endless strength, love and so much patience in the heart of the word. Mama means unconditional love with a few tears and screams along the way.

Happy, Healthy and Glowing

I used to have a "uniform" of sorts, one that started in my teens and followed me all through my 20's and half of my 30's. Skinny jeans or shorts, tank tops and band tees and biker boots or Doc Martens. Dresses, leggings and boots. My weight didn't fluctuate too much over those decades, maybe up or down a size or two at the very most, and I could tell exactly how something would fit by just looking at it in a shop, no need to try it on. That said, I was never comfortable with my body, some days it was too big, other days too small, some days my hips looked enormous, other days my breasts were non-existent. I never totally accepted that my body was strong, healthy and used to dealing with a less than optimal lifestyle of cigarettes, alcohol, meals when I felt like it, and long, long nights. When I look back at photos now I see this slim woman with long legs and arms and wonder how on earth I didn't appreciate it when I had it!

I know that for some people, pregnancy doesn't really change their body, or they find it easy to get back into the same shape as they were pre-pregnancy pretty easily. Some women barely put any weight on at all, naturally, and breastfeeding actually leaves them lighter post pregnancy than they were before. Neither of those statements worked for me. I put on 50lbs with my first, weight that was in a way much needed as I started off underweight, and it wasn't from overeating. I think that for the first time in my adult life I was healthier than I had ever been before, and my body was soaking it all up. And for the first time in my life I felt 100% comfortable with myself and how my body was changing. I loved that I was all belly, and I loved dressing myself, layering cute band tees over maternity jeans, keeping my personal style and adapting it to my pregnant body. And I felt absolutely amazing, right up until the last few weeks when everything started to feel super uncomfortable and painful. I still look at those pictures and see how I was confident for the first time in my life, proudly displaying my little-big baby bump.

And then I gave birth and had a pretty tough recovery. Baby bump became baby flab and sleepless nights lead to days of fog. I will always remember going to the mall and trying jeans on, bursting into tears when nothing fit like it was supposed to anymore (I was only three weeks postpartum and it was the most stupid thing I could have done at that time for my self esteem). I emptied my closet of all of my skinny jeans, donating them to friends and the thrift store, knowing that I would never fit a hip in those jeans again. I naturally lost half of the weight gained but the rest stuck to me, my body refusing to let go of the extra pounds it needed to breastfeed and stay healthy. So I compromised with myself and bought pretty maxi dresses and skirts and decided to embrace the changes, knowing that at some point my body would drop the excess weight when it was ready.

That "at some point" wasn't meant to happen for a few more years though, as I got pregnant again 7 months after I had my first. I started this pregnancy 25lbs heavier than I had started my first pregnancy, and even though I put on less weight, and I physically felt a lot better during the pregnancy, I also felt absolutely huge. And that belly just grew and grew and grew! Everyone thought that I was going to have a ginormous baby, even my doctor, but no, she was still under 8lbs, like her sister, just very long. I boxed up all of the clothes that I wore during the last few weeks of that pregnancy and will not be using them again – I felt huge, clumsy and just really BIG. I'm glad I forced myself to take pictures, but the idea of being that big again does worry me a little. Not because I don't want to be "fat", I'm not worried about that, but because of the sheer amount of time and effort it took to feeling like myself again. The second time around, I lost 20lbs post birth and then nothing.

Two months later, nothing. I was eating normally, walking with the kids, breastfeeding both of them around the clock and I still remained at the same weight that I was right before I gave birth to my first child. I weighed myself once a week (no more), and just wanted to cry every time I did, not understanding why it was so difficult to lose it. I saw people I knew who had had babies and they looked amazing and I just felt like a frumpy old woman. I realized that I needed to go back to seeing my body in a positive light again and to set myself some attainable goals that I could easily reach, starting with making sure that I got outside every day and walked at least 10,000 steps a day, and started making sure that I was eating three proper meals including snacks a day. Tandem nursing makes you ravenous at all times of the day and night and it's so important to keep the blood sugar levels on an even keel, because otherwise you feel faint and even sick.

I gave myself a first goal of getting to the weight I was when I got pregnant with my second. With my new positive outlook, a few pieces of clothing that I bought that were cute, flattering and in my style, and a little perseverance I managed to get to that goal by the summer, the next goal being to meet my "ideal" weight on my second's first birthday. My "ideal" weight was 15lbs over my pre-pregnancies weight, and I actually made it there, lowering my goal then to my "final" goal of being 5lbs lighter. I very nearly made it, and started my third pregnancy within 2lbs of my final weight goal. I'm really proud of myself for actually persevering, because it helped me learn a lot about my body but also how the way we view our own bodies can be very destructive. It is very important to me to teach my kids to accept and love themselves, physically and mentally, and in order to do that I need to accept my OWN body.

This will be my last pregnancy, and I am determined to love every minute of it as much as I loved my first pregnancy, embracing the weight gain and the changes all over again. My wardrobe is a mismatch of things that are either too big or too small, and after seeing a photo of myself the other day, and wanting the delete it immediately I decided enough was enough, and to spend a little money on some clothes that help me feel like I am beautiful, rather than large and frumpy. And it worked! I will yet again be all belly, but if it means growing a happy, healthy baby again, for the last time, then I will happily display it to the world. Having three kids in three years means that I started showing before the baby was even bigger than a grape, but I'm OK with that. One of my plans for the new year is to make sure I take better care of myself again, and a bit of self love does wonders for the self-esteem. I don't know if there is a message in all of this really, but I think it's important to remember that we are ALL beautiful, whatever our shape or size, and we are the worst when it comes to judging ourselves. Here's to a happy, healthy and wonderful third and last pregnancy!

We Marched and Now We Fight

I don't think that anyone can deny how amazing the marches were this past Saturday, millions of women, and men, and children, coming together in cities all over the US, AND all over the world, to march for equality, for human rights and to make our voices HEARD. And they were heard, but whether they were actually listened to is an entirely other question and one that we need to ask ourselves every day. In my opinion this was only the beginning, now every day we need to take action: call, write, discuss, and never let anyone shut you up.

I found it quite telling that on Friday when my mother posted #notmypresident on social media, a white male told her to shut up and another told her to grow up. And yes, we are all free to say what we want, but it was a little ironic that it had to be a man telling a woman to "shut up" because she dared to voice her opinion. My sister posted the same hashtag and received messages from people she didn't even know to "go back to where she came from". So as women we are meant to "shut up" and as immigrants we are meant to "accept it or fuck off". Or even better "you are OK because you did it the right way". Because, of course, there are "right" immigrants and "wrong" ones... Although, having been "both" I can tell you that you will never know who is what, because funnily enough there are only grey areas in immigration.

I have been reading many articles discussing the marches and their impact on social media, and was a little perplexed by the sheer amount of women discrediting them and telling us that "we all had equal rights anyway and we should just stop crying and work harder if we weren't making enough money". Well, thankfully, millions of us aren't so self-absorbed, and stood up for not only ourselves but for every other woman on this planet. Women in Kenya were marching for their rights to own property and to end genital mutilation and for our rights too, together, as sisters! We stood up together, as one. And if you can't understand that, then I can't understand you either. There have been some really awesome posts in response to all of the backlash already, so I won't add to that, but if you can't see past your own privilege then you live in a very, very small and whitewashed world.

So what are the next steps? It can't stop here. Every day I see a new order being signed, and a new freedom disappearing. Our planet, our rights, our fellow humans are all in danger, and we <u>can</u> stop it. But this means apathy is NOT an option. I want my kids to be able to visit orangutans in their natural habitat, to ride horses along the ocean and to breathe in fresh air. I want my fellow humans and animals to be able to drink water that has not been contaminated. I want to always be able to say what I think out loud without being worried about being shut down. I want my kids to always be proud of their mixed heritage and not live in fear. I want to see everyone treated as equals, no matter who they are and how much money they have. I want many things, but mainly I want us to fight for what is right, and what is right for those around us. I may not have the right to vote in this country but I DO have a voice. This week I will be writing letters to my senators, Dianne Feinstein and Kamala Harris, and every week from now on I will be writing letters to my representatives. I will call, and talk and write and motivate. I will continue to teach my kids to question everything. I sometimes have difficulties finding the right words when I am talking, but writing is my tool and my art, and I will use it in more ways than one to make my voice heard.

Yesterday Dianne Feinstein's office asked for any of us who had participated in the marches in California to send a quick email describing why we marched, so that she could use some of the examples in her opening statement in the Senate today. I feel like what I sent describes exactly what I feel. (I could have added a lot more but they only asked for 2-4 sentences).

"I marched because I am a survivor of sexual assault; an immigrant who spent years and years not being able to join the rest of my family here

because I happened to be 21 when they immigrated together; the partner of a Mexican immigrant, and the mother of two beautiful British-Mexican US citizen girls. I marched because I want them to always be proud of who they are, and to always stand up for others who are not able to use their voices. I marched because I believe we are all equal, no matter where we were born, what the color of our skin is, what our religion is, what our gender is and who we fall in love with is. I marched because my eldest was born with a heart defect and without access to consistent cardiology appointments she may one day fall down and die, appointments that we can only afford with affordable healthcare. And finally I marched for all of my sisters, because together we are stronger."

My eldest daughter, nearly three years old, demanded to walk on Saturday, and ran, skipped, clapped and sang her way to the Capitol. My youngest laughed all the way, comfortable in her stroller seat. Both girls were calm and excited, and enjoyed being part of this huge gathering. I am very glad that they got to experience this with me and with their auntie, friends and millions of other women all over the world. This is only the beginning. Now please, get writing and calling and demanding to be heard.

With Spring Comes Hope

I lie in bed, at some point between midnight and 2am, surrounded by little toddlers sleeping peacefully, a cat curled up at my youngest's feet, other half dreaming about something nice, and I close my eyes and wonder when I will allow myself that deep, uninterrupted sleep again. If I place my hands on my belly, I can feel tiny little baby moving around little kicks and punches here and there, finding a comfortable spot to sleep in. There is ample room in this womb, used to growing little babies now, my belly appearing so much bigger than the baby it is holding.

I'm so hyper aware of cherishing every moment, the last first kick, the last time I will meet the halfway mark, but my days are full of toddlers and words and important moments that I rarely have the time to sit down and remember that I am actually pregnant again. Even during those moments when I am standing under the shower I am usually singing children's songs or talking to the girls through the shower door, hoping that I won't walk out of the bathroom into a mayhem that even Winnie the Pooh cannot curtail for 5 minutes. Sometimes I just stand there under the hot water and talk to tiny little baby in my head, telling him or her little stories, just like I did with Luna and Aurora.

In the morning I wake up before everyone else, cuddling those little beings, one on each side of me, knowing that it won't be long before they wake up demanding to nurse, to play, to eat, and that it won't be too much longer after that that they will prefer their own company to mine. Little radiators, hopefully dreaming of the park, the ocean, the tallest skyscrapers and the widest forests, flying over earth on their broomsticks with their beloved pets in tow. Sometimes I feel so helpless about this world and where we are heading, but they are only thoughts I let myself have when everyone else is asleep. Morningtime is for smiles and stories and cuddles. I will keep the silence of the dark to curtail my own anxious thoughts, and devise plans to continue to create a better world, one step at a time.

Nursing two toddlers while pregnant isn't easy, there are moments when I just want them to stop, to push them away and cry "enough!", but I know deep down that it will all work itself out in the end, that once they are ready they will wean. I don't have the strength to work on that right now, Luna is so anxious and needs her comfort, if that is how she finds it for now, so be it. I'm as healthy as can be, so the tandem nursing isn't affecting the baby or me, but the discomfort can sometimes be too much. And I'm certainly not a martyr, I shout as much as the next person, and feel as much guilt as any mother. In the end all that matters is that we provide health, comfort and love, as well as the right tools to deal with what is ahead. No one is perfect, no matter how hard we try.

I've been inspired by several people and happenings and instances recently, leading to me writing some things that I have never been able to write before. They may or may not appear online at some point, and will be published anonymously because I don't have the courage to see my name next to them, not because I fear people knowing certain things about me, but because I just don't want anyone to feel pain or sadness for me, or even anger. Life is what it is, we learn and we grow and we aim not to perpetuate what we may have been subjected to as children. My objective in life since having children has been to grow and evolve and become a better me, for myself, my partner and my children. And writing about certain things is very cathartic and may even help others.

Spring comes earlier on this side of the country, but all we have had since Christmas is rain, rain and more rain. California needed it, but there is moss growing on the wooden roof tiles and nothing is drying properly, and I miss days and days of sunshine. But tiny little baby will be born during the year that the drought broke in California, and I will tell him or her stories of endless rain and green, green grass that hadn't been seen in years, not naturally in any case. And yes, tiny little baby has a name, actually two names, because we still won't know whether we are having a boy or a girl until next week, and are going to keep that quiet until he or she arrives in early July. I'm excited to finally see him or her move around inside me, to make sure that everything is growing well and that we have nothing to worry about. These next 19 weeks are going to go by quickly, and while I am collecting thoughts and words and pictures in a written journal, I worry that it is not enough. Because there will not be another time like this. As Cesar and I mused yesterday, once tiny little baby arrives it will be time to focus properly on all of our futures, together.

With the world declining again into dark, dark times, we must continue to stand up and bring light to those who cannot reach it, or are being denied it. We must continue to write, to draw, to create, to dream, and to inspire others to do the same. I have to tell myself every single day that there are more of us who want love, rather than those who refuse to believe we can all coexist, through fear, or hatred or ignorance. I have to move past all of those comments that I take too personally, people insulting everything I believe in, the existence of my family, my life, and have to remember that the answer lies in the fight and the way that we continue to resist against the dark. The future IS ours, and it will be a better place, and I must continue to smile in the face of adversity. Spring is nearly here and with spring comes a lot of hope.

Appendix

Over the past few years I have had several articles published in different places on the internet, in blogs, magazines and forums, and here is a hodge-podge selection of those. Many thanks to Mamazou, Motherhood and More (Annie Reneau), Womb n Wellness, The Mother Effin Truth, The Confessions of a NICU Mum, Bad Mum, Life With My Little Duck, and Pabarilife for believing in me and making me feel like I can actually be published. It often takes a lot for me to even submit anything due to my fear of rejection or just not being good enough, but my confidence is growing and I have these wonderful people to thank for a lot of this!

Geriatric Pregnancy, What the Hell?!

I never actually considered myself "old" until I got pregnant for the first time. I spent a lot of my twenties traveling around the world, not really interested in settling down for long, and then the rest of that decade and half of the next pretending I wanted to settle down, and then running around acting like I was 20 again. And to be honest, despite all the drinking and smoking and late nights, I was blessed with genes that helped me look 5 years younger than I actually was (can't vouch for that anymore, even though my lifestyle is a thousand-fold healthier!). So, at the grand old age of 35, I found out I was pregnant and decided that being a mother was something that I wanted to focus on. I walked into my first prenatal appointment, biker boots and skinny jeans, and listened to the midwife tell me that I was on the cusp of being of Advanced Maternal Age, but that all my blood work gave the impression that I was still in my 20's, so they were just going to consider it a normal pregnancy. I didn't give it much thought after that, after all I didn't feel "old" so why should I act any differently?!

I had an absolutely normal textbook pregnancy, a bit less of a textbook birth and recovery, and easily got pregnant again 7 months later (don't listen to the hype people, you can breastfeed exclusively around the clock for months, but it may not stop you getting pregnant!). This time around I was 36 years old, and would give birth at 37. I was determined to not let age factor into any of the choices I wanted to make the second time around (natural, unmedicated birth, breastfeed through pregnancy, as little intervention as possible, no invasive procedures and no "extra" care), and while my main doctor was completely on board, the pregnancy was a little more complicated than expected. I had additional scans and a fetal echo to rule out the possibility of a heart defect as my first was born with an undetected one. Then a tear or cyst was discovered on the placenta, resulting in scans every other week to make sure it wasn't growing or rupturing. Then, at 36 weeks I was diagnosed with dangerously low amniotic fluid, and after a failed induction had to go for NSTs and scans every three days at the hospital, in the middle of the sweltering NYC summer. I did get my wish of a fast, natural birth though, just before I hit the 41 week mark, and had an amazing recovery, all of which helped me move away from the darker memories of my first birth, so I could just keep the good parts with me.

I have always said that age doesn't mean a thing; it's all about how you take care of yourself and have a positive outlook. Pregnancy is NOT an illness, no matter how some doctors may treat it that way. Sometimes interventions are necessary, sometimes they save lives, but sometimes it can be a little too much... I remember an early second trimester appointment where my secondary doctor kept trying to push the importance of an amniocentesis, because of "my age and risk factor"... I had to politely and then forcefully decline THREE times before he offered an alternative, a non-invasive blood test that would check for the most known genetic disorders. I don't understand why this isn't offered immediately as an alternative today, I know that it is still pretty expensive and most insurances balk at the price, but I'm sure it's a lot easier than any invasive testing (and less dangerous). And no judgment on whether you do any invasive testing at all, it's just not my thing.

Anyway, a year or so later, and I'm pregnant again (last one I swear and yet again, you CAN get pregnant when you are tandem nursing around the clock and have a period every 6 months or so, I am the proof of that). I'm now 38 years old and will be 39 when the baby arrives. This time the first thing I saw noted on my patient chart was "diagnosis of Advanced Maternal Age". Diagnosis?! Is it an illness?? Although I'm pretty grateful right now that I don't live in the UK where they still call it "geriatric pregnancy"!! But I still feel like I'm 30!! I have a couple of grey hairs, but I'm far from OLD! My body has carried two babies to term (OK one has a heart defect but she's still healthy), and still nurses both of them. My body has kept me standing after a lot of crap that I have thrown at it over the years, and still barely ever lets me down or gets sick. So, again, I had to do a little research and find a doctor and nurse combo who don't bother me about my age, who I let talk me into a few early tests (1 hour glucose test is much more tolerable at 28 weeks than it is at 10 weeks, especially when you suffer from severe all-day long nausea), but who don't bring up any invasive or unnecessary testing. The clinic I go to has a motto of "pregnancy is not a sickness", which works perfectly well for me. And again, I'm looking forward to an easy, unmedicated birth, where I walk into the hospital, push a baby out, and leave again a couple of days later, healthy baby in arms.

I KNOW that studies show that there are higher risks having children later in life, and I know that I shouldn't disregard these risks either, but at the same time, it can be very disconcerting to be told that you are "old", and at risk, especially if you are a first time mother with no prior experience of pregnancy or any idea what to expect. These days more and more women are having children later in life, and I think it's something that shouldn't be seen as "risky" anymore. Yes, I will be 59 when my youngest is 20, but that's the perfect age to retire! Oh and my partner is 8 years younger, so he will still be happily running around after the grandchildren when I have to grab my zimmerframe! And I will still be dancing around to 80's hits all the way to the grave. So, while I know the risks, I also know my body and my mind, and that it comes from a long line of strong, independent females who also happen to be very stubborn. Age really IS just a number in this family, and there is no need to treat this pregnancy any different from my first one.

Keeping a Tradition Going

I love traditions. I love keeping a childhood tradition going, and creating new traditions with my little family, taking some of my other half's childhood traditions and making them our own. I like to celebrate most of the main holidays, such as Christmas, New Year's Eve, Halloween, Día de los Muertos, and Easter, but never in a religious way, more in a traditional sense. Some may think that in order to celebrate these holidays one must be religious, but I don't agree. These holidays can be a time of warmth, laughter, love and family. You don't have to believe in the birth of Jesus to sit down by a Christmas tree, and exchange presents and laughs with friends and family. You also don't need to believe in a God to celebrate life at Easter. At the same time, just because religion isn't involved it doesn't mean that the holidays need to be all about money, presents and chocolate. On the contrary!

My time living in Israel taught me a lot about the importance of tradition. I lived on a technically non-religious kibbutz for many, many months, where holidays were celebrated in the traditional sense, not the religious one. We would all sit down for a big kibbutz Shabbat meal every Friday which was the time for everybody to get together and catch up on life. Purim and Passover were celebrated altogether, as fun and important traditions, and we learnt the importance of Hanukkah, not only the original story, but also the stories and traditions of people who, or whose family, had come from Europe, the Soviet Union, other Middle Eastern countries... Stories of darkness where the light shone through and stories of love and happiness too. It made me realize that tradition is so much stronger than religion, that it brings people together despite their religion, not because of it. Whether we were Jewish or not, it didn't matter. What mattered was that we understood the importance of traditions, of history and of family.

I have lived very far away from my mother, sister and brother for many years. Both across the world and across the country, meaning that I haven't spent a Christmas with everyone together for well over a decade. This is the first time in all of those years that not only will I be spending Christmas with my mother and siblings, but the first time that my partner and daughters will be spending Christmas with their aunts, uncle and Nana/mother-in-law. You see, for me Christmas has always been a magical time. I believed in Santa Claus until I didn't believe in him anymore, but still pretended I did, just because he's part of the whole magic. Santa comes down the chimney/through the window/sneaks in via the basement and drops off presents for everyone in the middle of the night, and has a good munch on the brandy and cookies left out for him. But that's only a small part of Christmas, the part that is mainly for the kids, because there is also the food, the music, the games and the movies. For me it will always be Scrooge with Albert Finney and Oliver! the musical, all washed down with some Pogues, Wizzard, Slade and Wham! Our Christmas tree will always be a mix of old and new, no color scheme, just a beautiful haphazard beacon of light in the centre of the room, and I'm really looking forward to adding my children's own homemade decorations in Christmases to come.

And the food... The most stressful, but definitely the best part! Last year I spent hours in our tiny kitchen in NYC, cooking one dish after another, using my mother's recipes that she had emailed over just so I could recreate my childhood memories. Oat roast, stuffing, roast potatoes, Yorkshire puddings, steamed veggies and roasted parsnips, some meat for my partner and some good old Bisto gravy. Everyone has a different dish, a different tradition and I love to add a little something here and there every year. My partner has a tradition of eating homemade tamales on the 24th, so we have to start doing that too! In any case, it's all about the food, the leftovers and the food again here. It's not that often that we all get to sit down together around a table, and I love that nowadays we all pitch in and make something rather than watch my poor mother slave away for hours every Christmas Day!

So there you go, a little glimpse into my Christmas, one that changes a little every year, but one that I try to recreate, wherever I am in life. I have spent Christmases in England and in France with family and friends growing up, a Christmas in Israel surrounded by new friends, many Christmases in NYC either with friends or family, one even alone, but nothing will ever match celebrating my favorite holiday with my children. Watching their eyes grow in amazement at lights and songs, seeing their faces light up on Christmas morning when they realize that Santa has been... There really is nothing better.

I feel that personally traditions help me stay grounded, remember where I come from, but also remind me where I have been, and are a great way to pass on some of my culture and background to my kids, so that one day they may also share these traditions with their loved ones.

Stories from the Land of Tandem Nursing

Sometimes I feel like all I am is a human milk-making machine. One after another, day in, night out. I twist and turn at night between the two, on the one side a talking toddler, on the other side a mumbling baby. We've been doing this for over 8 months now, this thing they call tandem nursing. Although technically I'm not really tandem nursing, I'm nursing two children but never at the same time. Always one after the other. I admire the ladies who manage to nurse both baby and toddler together; I've just never managed to acquire the skill of dealing with both squirmy baby and toddler kicks simultaneously.

There are days when I really wonder why I do this. While the World Health Organization (WHO) recommends breastfeeding up to at least two years of age and beyond, I find myself more and more frequently hoping that my toddler will decide all by herself that she doesn't need her mother's milk anymore. Luna was only 7 months when I got pregnant with Aurora and my first concern was that I was going to deprive her of what seemed to be her main comfort in life, breast milk. As weeks turned into months it appeared that I would most likely be nursing all the way until the end, and although the sessions were reduced to 3 or 4 over the space of 24 hours, Luna still didn't give up. Nursing during those last few weeks wasn't comfortable but by that point I wasn't ready to give those moments up. When Aurora arrived, her fast and somewhat easy birth lead to a very fast and easy nursing relationship. None of the pain and latching issues and the hour long, on the hour, nursing sessions that Luna and I went through during her first few months of life. My milk came in within 24 hours after Aurora's birth, and with that Luna's voracious nursing appetite also returned.

All of a sudden I was nursing a hungry newborn and a hungry toddler. A hungry toddler who didn't understand why a squirmy little being was taking her favorite spot in her mother's arms. It took a while, navigating through tantrums and tears, figuring out routines and late night feedings, diaper changes in the dark on tiptoes, hoping Luna would sleep through any sudden noise. Our neighbors must have asked themselves time and time again why our toddler would wake up screaming in the middle of the night, and there were moments when I just felt so overwhelmed and exhausted, lying on the bed between the two, scared to even breathe too deeply in case one of the them would wake. I would look at beautiful photos on Instagram of women nursing two children, looking down on them peacefully and I wondered how they got there. Was I failing at something? Was there some kind of tandem nursing memo that I hadn't read?

Then, after a few weeks, it kind of all clicked into place. I gave up on the idea of nursing them both simultaneously and proceeded to follow their cues, navigating our way into a harmonious routine that worked for us all. Within two months of Aurora's birth bedtime became a well-oiled practice and I began to enjoy a few hours of uninterrupted mummy time every single evening. Having two under two can be a challenge even in the easiest of moments, and those evenings gave me the breathing room to find myself, put pen to paper and keep our home looking slightly livable if not tidy. Oh, and to eat. When you are feeding two children you are constantly hungry. Ravenous in fact. So hungry that you want to eat ALL of the things ALL of the time. For those who lose weight while nursing: lucky you! I don't. Not during the first 6 months anyway, and as I was often running on 2 or 3 hours of interrupted sleep most nights, exercise was the last thing on my mind. So much for nursing myself back to that svelte figure that I maintained before pregnancies!

But those routines were only temporary...

Three months ago, when Aurora was 5 months old and Luna 21 months old, we moved across the country. Luna still wasn't sleeping through the night and Aurora had gone from sleeping in 5-6 hour stints to waking every few hours. Right before we moved Luna would nurse every 3-4 hours during the day, and Aurora every 2-3 hours. Aurora settled back into her routine as soon as we landed in California, but my always sensitive little toddler took things a little harder, and with that, upped her need to nurse. She began to talk around the same time, and the word "dootie" appeared in her vocabulary as her way of expressing her need for breast milk. Dootie, dootie, DOOTIE!!!! And that word keeps coming out of her mouth, some days every 10 minutes, others every hour. The first thing she says when she wakes up is "dootie" (followed by Peppa), and I groan, turn around and nurse her, more often than not hoping that she will get bored within a few minutes and run off to play, or even better, will go back to sleep for another hour. Aurora has been teething like a maniac for the past few months and while she is a little less demanding, she also needs to nurse frequently, sometimes for comfort, mostly because she has been going through a constant growth spurt from birth.

We will never be that picture perfect image of maternal breastfeeding peace, Luna and I. We may have been at some point in time, but nowadays it feels like a bit of a tug of war, a battle of wills, me pulling her hand out of the "free" side of my bra, her shoving it back in again, until one of us gives up and relaxes. Aurora is now a distracted nurser, more often more interested in what her sister is up to than nursing, but still easier to handle. I was told that nursing them together would help create a deeper bond, but I feel that they already have their own sisterly bond and they don't need my breasts for that. Maybe one day we will be able to capture a peaceful moment where sisters nurse and hold hands while I look down on them, but I doubt it. In reality I will sigh when I hear the word "dootie" and then my heart will melt when Luna cocks her head to one side, smiles at me and then climbs into my lap. She still needs me, and she definitely still needs my milk, so we will continue as long as I can. I'm no martyr though, one day it will get to be too much and then we will start a real weaning process. I just hope that she can decide when she is done by herself though. Either way, I doubt we will be nursing past three years of age, and the same goes for Aurora. I think it will always be a mental battle for me as I want to continue but at the same time I do feel a little tapped out at times.

So, here we are, 8 months in and I'm not so hungry all of the time anymore. The weight has finally fallen off and we have created new routines whenever the old ones needed changing. While breastfeeding both children takes a lot of my time and energy, and means that there are times that I cannot just rush off and do something by myself, I also know that as long as they ask to nurse I will let them. Tandem nursing, extended breastfeeding, nursing two, whatever you want to call it, in the end I just say that I am doing what works for us as a family and wouldn't change a thing if we had to do it all over again. But for those who ask us when we are having another, let's just say that there is no way on earth that I will be nursing three children together!!

Not Fat Nor Skinny

It all started the day I tried my old, trusty skinny jeans back on, a month after I had my first child. Not the skin tight ones, the baggier ones I would wear on my "fat" days. I got them on but I couldn't close them. Not in a "oh it's just a little tight" but in an "I need a bigger size because this is not going to work ever again" way. I burst into tears, and my other half decided it was time for some new jeans. I had no idea what size to try on so I grabbed a few pairs of jeans that happened to be 2 or 3 sizes bigger than my pre-pregnancy size. And I burst into tears again in the changing room. What was this body that I didn't recognize?! I used to be able to pull clothes off the rack and know immediately if they would fit or not. Where had these huge breasts and large hips and squishy tummy come from?! Why was I not dropping pounds instantly due to breastfeeding like everybody told me I would?!

I can't believe that I used to moan about being fat just because my tiny jeans felt a little tight around the waist. I look at pictures now and wish I could hammer into that silly brain that there were way more important things going on in the world and my life than worrying about being fat. At the same time I have always liked to eat and never deprived myself of anything, and even before pregnancy was more interested in making sure I was healthy and strong rather than running after some kind of "skinnier than you" pipe dream. Well I used to tell myself that, but I think it was mainly because I didn't have the willpower to diet or cut things out anyway! It was always easier to go out for a run rather than deprive myself of crisps for a month. But pregnancy really threw my body out of whack and it was hard to reconcile the image in the mirror with the one in my head.

After another good cry I decided that was enough. Enough of the self-blame, enough of the fat talk, enough of the putting myself down. Enough of trying to meet standards that were completely unattainable and ridiculous. ENOUGH. I was strong and healthy and happy, what else did I need?

I thought a lot about how my body had changed, how Western society often judges women by weight, and came to the realization that not only had my body grown and carried a healthy child for 41 weeks, it was also feeding her and keeping me going, even on no sleep and hastily put together meals. This body was a machine! For the first time in my life I started to look at my body properly, understanding how it worked and what made it work, wrapping my brain around what it needed and what I needed it to do for me.

Every time I heard my voice whine "I'm so fat" I wanted to kick myself. Do I want my kids to grow up hearing their mother say that? NO. I want my daughters to grow up appreciating and accepting their bodies for what they are, not intent on molding them into something that they are not. I want them to be comfortable in their skin.

So, after my second pregnancy, when I was at my heaviest, we decided to "ban" the use of the words "fat" and "skinny" when it comes to talking about our bodies or anyone else's body. This means that we don't even call ourselves "fat" or "chubby" jokingly. I know that we can't shelter the girls from the picture "perfect" people that appear in the media or mean-spirited comments from other judgmental people, but we can teach them that there are more important things than size. I don't want my daughters growing up judging people by how they look; I want them to accept people of any shape or size. And I think that this starts at home. Our kids are already different in shape and size and skin color, and we are already going to be fighting certain ingrained prejudices in this country, so why add to it?

So we are not using the words "fat" and "skinny" and have asked our friends and family to do the same around the kids. Since we started doing this I have had to check myself so many times! I try on a cute pair of jeans that I think fit and the first words that try to come out of my mouth are "oh gosh I'm so fat!". The kids hang out in the bathroom when I'm showering and instead of frowning at the skin on my stomach when they point at it I just smile and say "tummy", so they will see it as a normal tummy. Instead of telling the girls that I am going for a run or a walk to lose weight I tell them that I'm going to give my heart and brain a good work-out as well as a dose of fresh air. And I've found that with this attitude comes a huge wave of self-confidence and accomplishment – I've finally accepted my body and with that I hope my girls will always accept theirs.

I want my kids to be healthy, to make healthy choices in life and to never feel bad about what they eat and the sports they may want to do (or not). By healthy I mean strong, independent, comfortable and happy. By healthy choices I mean choosing their friends wisely and not doing drugs. I want them to know that there isn't a set weight that anyone "has" to be, but that if they listen to their bodies and treat them right then their bodies will be the vessel that they need to keep them going, through the tough moments and the easy passes. And I never, ever want to hear them judging someone else based on their looks, or put someone down just because they aren't what society deems to be physically perfect. No one is perfect, because in reality perfection doesn't exist. And with that I shall bake us all a cake and buy a pair of "skinny" jeans that make me feel comfortable AND fabulous.

Half of me, Half of you

"When Mexico sends its people, they're not sending their best. They're not sending you. They're not sending you. They're sending people that have lots of problems, and they're bringing those problems with us. They're bringing drugs. They're bringing crime. They're rapists. And some, I assume, are good people, but I speak to border guards and they're telling us what we're getting." – Donald Trump, Republican president candidate, Trump Tower Atrium in Manhattan on June 16, 2015

This quote still makes me shudder. It's not the only quote that has made me shiver through-out this farce of an electoral campaign, but it is one that comes to haunt me in the middle of the night when I can't sleep. As a white woman the only discrimination I have ever faced has been due to my gender, and even then I can't really say that it has been any worse than any woman on any given day. I benefit from this privilege every single day, most of the time without realizing it. I've always been an introvert, but one who has no issues standing up for myself and others. And I really can't stand any type of discrimination, or anyone placing themselves above others. We are all human beings.

The thing is, I can continue to say that until I am blue in the face, and I can teach my children this, but I can't stop the damage that other people's words may cause them at any point in time. It's no secret that racism is completely ingrained in this country, that immigration is always considered to be a huge cause of concern for people who have no idea what they are talking about, and that the color of your skin can open or close doors. So much for a melting pot hey? If one of the two main presidential candidates can get away with publicly saying that most Mexican immigrants are rapists and that he wants to build a wall to keep them out, then we can't be surprised that kids are going to pick up on this and think it's a normal way of thinking. (I'm not going to even touch on what I've heard say about other minorities... The word "minority" actually annoys me terribly, because it's mainly used to describe anyone who isn't white).

To get to the point of the story, and why I am now affected by these types of quotes more than I was during the last election (I was more fired up about women's rights at that time, still am), is that I now have a partner who is one of those rapist, drug dealing immigrants and we have two half Mexican, quarter English, quarter Welsh and fully US citizen daughters. Oh, and I also happen to be an immigrant, but because I'm white I suppose that doesn't really make me a problem. So does this make our kids half drug dealer rapists? Or can we consider my partner to be one of few "good ones"? Oh gosh, I really messed up didn't I, I should have thought about all of this before falling in love and having children! What on earth was I thinking?! Sarcasm aside, I wasn't. Why should I have been thinking about that?

I always said that I would only have kids with someone who I knew would always be there for us. Someone I would spend the rest of my life with. That's how I made my choice of partner. It's about love and longevity for us; we are in it for the long haul, for good and bad, for the lows and the highs, all of that. I never once thought about our different backgrounds. Yes, there have been times that we have had to climb over a language barrier or two, but we are both pretty adept in that. I've always been surrounded by multiple languages anyway, so that didn't change anything. But I never realized how racism and ignorance could affect us all on a daily basis. And it's usually little things that you might not notice at first until they happen all the time.

Apparently it is impossible for people to write my kids' last name properly, even when I spell it out for them. It is really two very common names with a hyphen in between. People write the names properly, but they seem to stick both names together, forget the hyphen or just go by the last name. If you look at doctors' records, hospital records and health insurance cards their last name is written differently on each of them. I don't know how many times I have had to say "their name is not Hughes, it's Castro-Hughes!!". I think Luna literally had three hospital records created by three different people because they didn't input her name in properly.

Whenever I have to fill in some kind of form for anything there is always a space asking for your ethnicity. I know it's supposed to be a way to ensure everyone is treated equally (although I'm not sure how that is supposed to work), but since I don't want to pigeonhole the girls I usually don't put anything. This was after a lengthy discussion with my other half on what we should do, knowing full well that if we checked the "white" box life might be a little easier for them... So you can imagine my surprise when I was reading through a routine child check up paper for Aurora and noticed that someone had marked her as "Hispanic". So I then checked through Luna's and hers said "White". So even though we, as parents, had decided to not put anything, someone else had. And someone had decided, without much thought, to also separate my girls by ethnicity, which is exactly what we didn't want to do.

Yes, the girls look like sisters, but they also look different. Luna is very pale and looks a lot like me as a kid, and Aurora has darker skin and looks just like her dad right now. But it's very, very important to me that people don't treat them differently, or at least don't treat them differently because of their appearance. I already worry about the girls going to school and all of the ethnic jokes and slurs that I see adults throwing around quite happily be passed down to their kids, who will then use them without a second thought. I remember when I was at school in a different country it was bad enough; I don't even want to imagine what it is like here. The American middle and high school system seems to be tough enough as it is, but with all of the hatred and fear that I see surrounding us I can't imagine it getting any better or any easier. You only have to start reading the comments section of any political article to realize that people still segregate in their minds... How often do you hear or read the words "the Hispanics" or "the Blacks"?! But then how often do you ever hear "the Whites"? It's as if people think it's normal to group a bunch of people together because of their skin color or language (even if their backgrounds are extremely diverse), but not so much for others.

If you have ever been treated differently because of your skin color you will understand the fears I have for my daughters. I never have, but I see it happen on a regular basis. My partner is often treated differently. People assume he doesn't speak English without even bothering to try, talking in a loud, slow voice as if he has a hearing problem. The neighborhood we currently live in is predominantly white, with your visible Trump supporters scattered here and there, and I see the strange glances we sometimes get thrown our way. These things were a lot less noticeable when we strolled around the streets of NYC as a family talking in a mix of different languages. Everything fit in a little easier there. Sometimes I feel that we stick out somewhat, in both predominantly white and predominantly Hispanic areas, and we probably do. For example when we go to a Mexican restaurant I speak in English and Cesar speaks in Spanish, because I'm embarrassed that I don't speak Spanish as well as I should. We don't really fit into a neat little case, like all mixed families. I want our kids to embrace and enjoy all of our backgrounds, my upbringing and languages, Cesar's, as well as the traditions of the country they were born in. I don't ever want them to feel embarrassed about anything.

Anyway, I guess my issue is that while I want to protect my children from all of this, at the same time I want them to be aware of the prejudices and judgments that people carry around with them. I don't ever want them to be surprised and I want them to be able to rise above ignorance, intolerance and hatred. I also don't want them to fall prey to the feeling that they may be superior or inferior to others because of skin color, money, gender, sexual orientation or anything else. We will do our best to build a strong foundation of individuality, compassion, love and strength within them, but I can only hope that the current climate in society won't put a wedge in all of this. I know it's a bit of a utopia, that perfect world I dream of where everyone accepts each other as they are, but I would like to think that if all of us like-minded individuals stick together, one day we can maybe hope for a better world for our kids where we celebrate differences rather than outcast them, or make them feel inferior.

"I've learned that people will forget what you said, people will forget what you did, but people will never forget how you made them feel." — Maya Angelou

Moving Cross Country with Two Under Two

People thought we were a little insane when we planned on having two kids under two. Even I thought we were a little crazy after our second was born and I was still nursing our first. A few months after her birth we decided that it was time to actually do that cross country move we had been hinting about for the past two years. At that point I realized we must have really lost our minds… A high needs 21 month old, an EBF 5 month old, a (small) apartment of stuff, a large cat and two adults, NYC to Sacramento? I never did like to do anything the easy way!

I used to love the hustle of NYC, working around the clock, always out and about, changing the world til way after 4am on a regular basis, but that started to change once Cesar and I had our first child. Neither of us was entitled to any paid maternity or paternity leave in our service industry jobs, and daycare costs were not even worth me going back to work, so we figured out a new way to survive. NYC with one child was fun. We tried to make it work with two, but the walls of our one bedroom apartment started to close in on us, our rent was jacked up yet again, and Cesar was always at work. My family had been asking us to move nearer them in California for years and we kept pushing it off. I always responded with "maybe next year" and changed the subject.

Right around the holidays our landlord pulled a typical asshole New York property owner move by finding a semi legal loophole in our lease to get us out while simultaneously offering us an apartment on the top floor (no elevator) for much more money ("oh but it's been renovated!). No matter how popular Manhattan is there will never be any reason why a grotty one bedroom apartment on the far side of Queens will be worth $1600.

We could have fought it and won, but neither of us had the energy for that. And what, have to go through the same a year later?

We had a month until our lease was up so we decided it was then or never: either we cut the cord with our beloved city there and then or we signed ourselves over to another year of constant financial worry and around-the-clock working. Everything I worried about losing by leaving NYC (the ability to walk everywhere, everything at my fingertips, my beloved family of friends) was outweighed by the positives that California would bring (ability to afford to rent a house with a backyard, family close by, more family time together, sunshine). So we decided to just go for it... Sayonara NYC, hola Sacramento!

Making a decision is usually the hardest part, and the rest just flows after it's done. This was just the opposite. Ever had to organize a decade of life in just a few weeks? With two very small and needy kids and a partner who couldn't take a second off of work? Oh and on a tight budget too... I started by making a mile long list of everything that we had to do, and just checking through each item one by one. Even though I have worked in some shape or form of customer service all of my life, I have always had a real hatred of engaging with people on the phone. So you can imagine how overjoyed I was to have to call a million moving companies to get a quote... And call doctors, insurances, landlords, banks, utility companies. Pack! Sell things that we don't want to take with us! Donate things! Book flights for us all, including Joey Ramone the cat. And anyone with kids knows how hard it is to actually talk on the phone with two small kids around - they tend to act up as soon as you are taken off hold and have to actually talk to someone. Every single time. In the end my mother helped to figure out some of the logistics such as flights, and my phone pinged at me non-stop with reminders, appointments and things that I had forgotten. Friends pitched in to keep an eye on the kids while I packed and called and hid in the bathroom for a moment of quiet.

Packing was the worst. Last time we moved (from Brooklyn to Queens) I was heavily pregnant with Luna and Cesar did most of the work. Over the space of two years we had seemed to accumulate tons more STUFF. How on earth we fitted everything into that small apartment I don't know, but in the end our moving truck left with about 45 boxes and some important furniture pieces. We decided that the move should also mean a new beginning for us. Oh and I think I forgot to mention that while Cesar was leaving one job, he actually didn't have another (yet), so we were really just hoping that as his job (an amazing cook) was usually highly sought after he wouldn't have any issues finding another job on the other side. I freelance, so I can work just about anywhere where there is an internet connection, but I haven't been the main breadwinner for a while. Basically we left hoping for the best, secretly thinking about the worst and assuming we would land somewhere in between the two.

Leaving was very bittersweet for me. I had moved to NYC from France in 2005, hoping that it would be a short stop on the way to joining my family in California. I fell in love with the city, it was my perfect blend of Europe and the US, and after a decade I started my own family there. But we needed to start thinking as a family and not as a couple, about quality of life and money. We needed to start creating more stable plateaus to reside on rather than jumping from one flying carpet to another. Both Cesar and I have moved to different countries on the spur of the moment in the past, so across the country didn't faze us too much. We go by the simple motto of "as long as we are together, it doesn't really matter where we are in the world".

Joey went first, then our belongings, and finally us, taking off from JFK on an evening flight, nursing one child after the other on take-off. The kids slept most of the way, while Cesar and I watched them, waiting for them to wake up screaming (which they didn't). The journey itself was the part that I had been the most worried about, not the preparation and not the unknown on the other end, but when it came down to it that was the easiest part. I loved being in the air, knowing that whatever happened from there on out there was no way back. The most difficult part was leaving, and the three weeks of utmost stress that lead up to it. I'm so grateful for my family and friends who pulled together to help us get through it all! I've always been a stubborn so-and-so, convinced I need to do everything alone, but ever since I became a mother I have learnt that asking for and receiving help is just as important as helping someone else.

We settled into our new lives pretty fast, Cesar finding not only one, but four jobs within a couple of weeks (he is only doing one of them though), the girls have been thriving in the sunnier and warmer climate, as well as being around their grandmother and auntie, and I am finding my feet again. The space and the cleaner air help me breathe more easily, and I can see our horizons stretching out further than tomorrow or the day after. Yes, there are days when I have a sudden and deep longing for certain parts of the city, but I am excited to see what the next few months and maybe years here will bring us. And now that we have done it once, who is to say that we won't do it again? There is a whole world out there that I would love my daughters to discover, starting with their parents' homelands. In the end, it is completely possible to lay roots down in more than one place, and I hope that my offspring will be able to experience that in the same way I did. In the meantime though we won't be undertaking any impulsive moves as I'm quite happy to spend a few years in this sunny and beautiful state!

To My Precious Little Girls

I see you standing there, worried look in your eyes, biting your finger nails down again. You are only two and as much as I have tried, I still haven't been able to shield you from carrying the world on your shoulders. So I resign myself to teaching you how to protect yourself from the world, just like I do. But then I see you so free and so happy amongst the farm animals, cuddling and protecting them, and my heart soars. Maybe I don't need to help you build walls around yourself just yet; maybe instead we just need to find a place where you can expand those barriers, feel safe and happy.

One thing I have learnt in the three years since I became pregnant with you is that sometimes it is good to change your mind. And sometimes it's good to give up on something and start again somewhere new. I really, really wanted to make it work for us all in New York City, and maybe one day you will be angry for taking us away from the place both myself and your father had called our homes for over a decade, but it did turn out to be the right choice, for us all. To be honest I don't even know if we will end up staying here, my feet are not good staying on the same ground for too long, and the political climate here scares me. But what I want you to know, both you and your sister, that there is a great big world out there at your finger tips, one that you will most likely get to know yourself one day, together or alone.

And you, little one, I see you taking your first steps at only ten months, your determination to catch up with your sister as soon as possible taking precedence over anything else. Your smile has always come easily, your voice soft and sweet and occasionally loud and angry, and those little shrieks of delight make me so happy (even though they sometimes pierce through my eardrum in a spectacular manner). Your independent spirit is constantly shining through, no barriers will hold you back, even the ones that I put up to keep you safe while I am cooking dinner. If you want to be somewhere you will always make sure you can get there, barriers, steps and walls just mere annoyances along the way. I hope that nothing ever stops you from getting what you want in life, and that if someone or something tries then you will just step right around them, smile, and continue onwards towards your destiny or dreams.

I love watching you both learn to get to know and love each other. Always one following the other, watching each other, screaming at each other and, usually in sleep, cuddling each other. We wanted you both so close together so that you could grow up together, share friends and clothes and stories, just like I did with my sister. I know there will be fights, sometimes even days or weeks when you will refuse to speak to each other because of a silly misunderstanding, but there will be many, many more days where you will appreciate your friendship more than anything in the world. I love how you both look so different, but so alike, how you already show huge differences in personality, but will grow up complimenting each other and introducing each other to different books and clothes and music and art.

I know that you will both probably drive your father and I insane over and over again (you already do a little), and that we will want to protect you from everything terrible in this world, but that we have to remember to not always surround you with blankets and pillows. We ourselves have to be strong to teach you both how to be strong and sensible and able to make your own way without fear and with real conviction. We will teach you that we are all different but all the same and that this world is a beautiful place that needs to be cherished and loved and saved. We will teach you to love your fellow humans and to not always trust everyone, to develop your own instincts and to trust those. We will teach you that to love is important and to hate is detrimental to not only yourself but to mankind in general. We will teach you to treat everybody as a human being, no matter what their skin color, faith, sexual orientation or beliefs are. We will teach you to cherish all of the animals in this world, to treat them with the respect that they deserve, from the smallest ants to the tallest giraffes. I hope that you will always remember to aim high and follow your own paths while respecting those of others. We are meant to all be happy, and you both make your father and I the happiest people on earth.

We may be a little lax sometimes, I let you climb on things that you probably shouldn't climb on and eat things that you probably shouldn't eat, but you always know when to say please and thank you and don't have too many tantrums in public. We may not be the richest parents in the world but in my opinion love and affection are a hell of a lot more important than money anyway. And I might cuddle you way too often, but that's only because I know that there will be one day soon when you won't need my cuddles or my hand anymore and I will have to learn to let go.

Before motherhood I never knew that such a deep love could exist, and now I don't know how I could have lived without it. My little girls, you are the apples of both your daddy and my eyes, and we will always love you, wherever you are and whatever you do. And this is only the beginning.

Unmedicated Childbirth in a Hospital

I've read many stories about women hoping to go through childbirth without any pain medication, but who felt that their willpower and/or control were diminished once they arrived in the hospital. Maybe they had long labors, unsupportive doctors and family members, or just a realization that the pain was too much. With my first I was told I couldn't leave the bed as my waters had broken. I didn't think I could handle hours of Pitocin contractions lying down so I had an epidural. My daughter was born healthy but I just had some niggling regrets, and I felt like I hadn't been in control of what I felt was the most important moment of my life. Like most women, I really, really wanted that magical birthing story. And we all know that birth is never predictable and usually never magical, but I was determined to do things differently the second time around.

For my second I was hoping for a home birth, but for several reasons it wasn't a possibility. The only birthing center within miles was already full for my birth month, so I shopped around for a new OB. I had just a few basic requirements: supportive of unmedicated labor and birth, no issues with nursing my firstborn during the pregnancy and no induction unless necessary. The OB I chose thought that my "requirements" were completely normal, listened to all of my concerns based on my first birthing experience, and promised me she wouldn't even think of inducing me until I hit 42 weeks.

The best advice I received was to trust my body and to wait as long as I could to go into the hospital. Now, I know that advice is easier to follow once you've been through it before, but I really didn't know what a "normal" labor was actually like because I had been induced with my first. I spent most of my third trimester trying to anticipate the pain while hoping that I wouldn't disappoint myself again, listening to my body and procrastinating on practicing natural pain relief methods. During my 41st week I woke up at 1:30am with light contractions. I told my partner to go back to sleep and tried to do the same. At 3:30am I told our babysitter to stay home as it would "be hours yet" (bad move). At 4am I was pacing and dancing around the living room, with intense but bearable contractions every 5 or so minutes. At 5am I was crying in the shower and by 6am I knew I was in transition. I arrived at the hospital just after 7am and Aurora was born at 8:06am.

Did I scream? Yes. The noises that came out of my mouth came from somewhere I had never tapped into before. Was it unbearable? No. It's difficult to explain because it feels primal, natural but completely surreal. You know it's going to be over, so you simply push through it. Did I scream for an epidural? Yes, but my doctor and nurse just looked me in the eye and said "you have come this far, Jade, and there is no way out now!" My body literally took over and did what it needed to do. I didn't even feel alone, even though my partner only made it a few minutes after Aurora was born. I always felt supported and surrounded. This may sound a little silly, but I felt larger than life both before and after Aurora's birth. I had given my trust to my body and in return my body had given me another healthy child. And that pain? Disappeared into thin air the moment I held my daughter in my arms.

If it is what you want, it IS possible to give birth completely naturally in a hospital setting – you just need to make sure that you have the support you need to get through it from everyone around you, and most of all, that you trust both your instincts and your body. Also, if you have a doctor you trust you can be sure that they will do everything they can to safely respect your birthing wishes.

My advice? Choose your doctor, midwife and hospital carefully. Practice using natural pain relief techniques such as breathing, meditation and hypnobirthing. Stay on your feet as much as possible both before and during labor – walking definitely helped advance my labor pretty rapidly. Don't be afraid to speak up and ask for second opinions if you don't think your doctor is listening to you. Make sure your partner is supportive and willing to help you. If you are a first time mom it can be a great idea to hire a doula to help you navigate through all of the different parts of labor and after birth. And always be open to change. As I said before, birth is never predictable, and the ability to go with the flow and relax can only help you face whatever may happen.

Resolutions were meant to be broken, weren't they?!

My gosh, when I found out I was pregnant the first thing I started to do was to make resolutions. *Stop smoking?* Check. *Stop drinking?* Check. *Make sure I drink 8 glasses of water?* Check. It took me a few weeks to realize that 8 glasses did not actually mean 8 pint glasses... No wonder I spent the first 2 months of my pregnancy trying to find the closest restroom! *Only eat organic vegetables and immediately stop eating my favorite-snack-of-all-time chips?* Hmm. Half check allowed on that one?

I was determined to be super, super healthy, follow all protocols and make sure I only ate and drank what was recommended. Most of that (apart from the obvious) kind of went out of the window after a few weeks. Wasn't this supposed to be the time to really, really enjoy eating? I was always on my feet at work, always hungry and my favorite meals was cheese quesadilla with a side of guacamole (handy seeing as I was working in a Mexican restaurant).

I grew up in France, what do you mean I can't eat Brie?! *Ok then, no Brie.* I kept that resolution into my third trimester and then couldn't stop eating Brie sandwiches. I figured if I bought the Brie myself and cut it myself and refrigerated it myself it would be fine, right? The nurse at the prenatal clinic asked me if I was getting someone else to change the cat litter while I was pregnant. *Pregnant women shouldn't go near cat litter!* Hmm... Was wearing a mask OK? (I used it once). *You don't REALLY need to eat for two you know!* Well, you know what? Peanut butter on an everything bagel is a perfectly good snack at any time of the day (or night), full of protein. And I still stand by that statement, pregnant or not pregnant!

I had many resolutions for the future. Pregnancy was only a temporary state of being and I had a (long) 41 weeks to plan out the next 18-20 years of all 3 of our lives. So many resolutions. *I would never drink again and never, ever go anywhere near a cigarette EVER.* Those two were pretty easy to keep – I'm still breastfeeding 8 months later and we want another child pretty close to our first, so I'm not really interested in drinking. I just need to think back to my not-so-distant past of whisky shots and hangovers to still shudder at the idea of that hell cumulated with the needs of a very loving but very demanding infant. And although it's a little hard to avoid walking through clouds of smoke on the streets of NYC, it's a great deterrent to ever wanting to smoke again. Those were the easy, and most important, resolutions.

What about that one resolution that I made to lose the 54 pounds I put on while pregnant in no time at all by eating a very healthy diet full of (only) fruit and veggies and grains? Did I miss the memo that during the first two months after having a baby it's hard enough to remember to eat, let alone nip off down to the farmer's market at the break of dawn to nab all the best veggies and then cook them into delicious meals? Ah no, pasta was my best friend during that time. *I guess that other resolution about having 2 hour brisk walk every day was another silly one.* I didn't really think about the whole 95 degrees of humidity in the summer weather thing, did I? *And then there was that resolution to not try on any new pairs of jeans until next spring because I would just leave the changing room in tears?* I kept forgetting about that one, and I don't understand why as I don't even want to wear a pair of jeans. Leggings are so much easier to wash and dry!

What about all those resolutions I made for my daughter? *I will never let her sleep in the swing at night!* Third sleepless night in a row I gave in. *No pots of pureed foods ever!* She currently will only eat pureed green beans; everything else ends up on the table and down the bib, so there goes that resolution. *Strict early bedtimes so she sleeps all night!* Who was I to think that I would be the one to decide that?! We currently hover between 7pm and 11pm and my daughter is obviously as stubborn as me, but wins the battle every time. *No TV EVER!!* Hmm yes, and how am I supposed to ever watch my series then?! *We will read books EVERY DAY!* Wait, we actually do that one most of the time!! I could go on and on, and I know I am not the only one! There were days at the very beginning where I would be so exhausted but still refuse to give in, because, oh my gosh, I am going to be a disappointment to motherhood if I don't follow all of those rules I set in stone!!

Nowadays I just have to laugh at most of these resolutions and at how serious I was about them all. The important ones I have kept to, but the rest were packed away as fast as my daughter's newborn-sized clothes were. In the end we can make all these promises to ourselves, but the only important ones are that we do our best to keep smiling, be happy and healthy and make sure we keep our children happy and healthy. And with that I shall go and enjoy that delicious bar of chocolate that is waiting patiently for me in the kitchen, and thank myself that we still don't own scales. *Not weighing myself til spring.*

And the Hammer Keeps Falling...

I woke up at 5am this morning, slightly afraid to look at my phone, just in case yet another hammer had crushed one of our freedoms in this country again. I suppose I got a few hours of respite because it wasn't until around 10am on the West Coast that that awful woman was confirmed as the new education secretary. A person who has no intent on actually improving the already terrible education system in this country, but actually wants to actively make it worse. I shouldn't even be surprised anymore, I mean with everything that has happened here in a few short weeks, who would be? But every day I feel the noose tightening around us, corralling us into a pen, forcing us to kick out in anger, with shouts of "resistance" and "stand up" to them.

I am Jade, 38 year old mother to two little girls with another child on the way. I am not married, but in a very happy and loving relationship and we promise each other every day that we will do our best to bring our children up to be happy, healthy, caring and loving individuals. Doesn't every parent, though? We also are not your typical, average US citizens. Actually not at all! I immigrated to the US on a temporary visa in 2005, falling in love with NYC on landing and never leaving again. My other half is an immigrant from Mexico, arriving in NYC in 2006. We are immigrants (please don't ever call me an ex-pat, that word has no meaning to me), and we fell in love with each other, and have created a family together. Living in NYC for all of those years I loved the multi-cultural, multi-ethnic melting pot of people from all over the world, living and working hard together in one small place. I loved riding the subway and seeing newspapers in at least 10 languages at any given time. I loved being able to eat an authentic American-style diner breakfast followed by street tacos for lunch and a spicy curry for dinner. I loved my Yemeni deli friends who would walk me home if I felt unsafe at night, my French diner friends who would whip me up an omelette at any time of the day and night, and my Irish friends and bosses, our little bar full of people just like us. Some people call NYC a "bubble", I just called it the perfect mix of everything that I love, a small part of every part of the world, all in one place. We were all New Yorkers, running around trying to make the best of things.

Becoming a mother and then moving away from the city changed a lot for all of us. Granted, if you can't be in NYC, California is probably the best alternative right now, because it will always be the most progressive state. But we aren't in a big city like LA or San Francisco, and while I have heard that where we are is the most diverse city around here, it still feels very segregated. Or maybe I just feel that way because of the Trump signs that appeared around us once the election process was in full swing last year. I don't know, but I don't feel comfortable here anymore. I mean when a presidential candidate is calling the love of your life a rapist and drug addict, says that he wants to remove birthright citizenship meaning that my kids would effectively lose their right to live here, and calls many of your friends terrorists, while speculating that it's OK to "grab a woman by the pussy" (amongst so many other things), I don't see how anyone who isn't white and male can actually feel safe and comfortable here anymore. But there were enough people who thought he was up for the job, so here we are.

I hear people say "oh but it's OK, you came here the "right" way" (if only they knew), or "but it's OK your partner works hard and contributes to this country not like others" (oh my gosh you have absolutely no idea what it is like to come here as an immigrant do you?), or even "oh but YOU will be OK" (and what about all of the millions who won't be?!), it literally makes me want to vomit. Have we come to a point where nobody else matters anymore? That none of the executive orders that have been passed in the last few weeks matter until they actually hit you directly? Has the population of this country become so apathetic that it is fine with just watching one civil liberty be washed away at a time, thinking that it's OK because the great US of A will never be ruled by a dictator, because "Land of the Free" and all that?

We aren't rich, so we will be counting on the public school system to educate our children, and I can't see us being able to move to the best school areas just like that. We are immigrants so technically we do not have a voice when it comes to electing officials (although that hasn't stopped me writing and calling as often as possible). We come from different places in the world and want to make sure that our children are proud of us and their heritage, not made to feel like they are second-rate citizens because they are not white and male. Racism is so ingrained in this society, sadly even within supposedly progressive movements such as Feminism, but I still can't believe the comments and slurs that I hear people make quite naturally, on the internet or in real life. It's NOT normal and never will be. As long as we are here I will do my utmost to fight it, but we are making steps to go somewhere where we feel safer, and where we feel our children will have better chances. I have settled in new places so many times before that leaving one home for another doesn't faze me anymore. But doing it with a family in tow is a whole other story!

Acknowledgements

Over the years I have lost count of the amount of people who have pushed me to keep writing and creating, who have inspired me, and who have always had a kind word to say about something that I have written. A huge thank you to every single one of you. I would never have had the confidence to continue without you. Writing has always been my dream, but it is also my reality, and every word from you has been a brick in building my confidence as a writer. Thank you.

Of course none of this collection would have been possible without the support of my family, Cesar, Luna, Aurora and our tiny little baby to come, as well as Joey Ramone our slightly silly but very cuddly cat. And the unwavering support from my mother, sister and brother, as well as my Grandmother. My best friend Meg who is the best person and friend anyone could ever ask for (and who sends me pictures of sunrises and sunsets over the ocean every day just because she knows how much that means to me). And my ladies Lynn, Charlie, Stephanie, Henna, Ebedet, Ally and Jenny, consistently supportive and lovely, and just wonderful human beings in general.

We all have a journey, and every journey is as important as the next.

Jade Anna Hughes, Sacramento, March 2017

About the Author

Jade Anna Hughes was born in Rutland, England, grew up in Grenoble, France, spent over a decade pounding the streets of New York City in search of stories, oblivion and hope, and now lives in sunny Northern California with her other half and two toddlers. Jade has been writing since she can remember and blogs on a regular basis on From the Inside, her own creation, as well as several other publications. She also works as a freelance writer, creating content for other people to use to their hearts content.

This is her first collection of essays, but not the last. Look out for more to come in the near future on a whole array of different subjects!

With Spring Comes Hope

CPSIA information can be obtained
at www.ICGtesting.com
Printed in the USA
BVHW04s0012170318
510866BV00010B/176/P